DEMOCRACIES AND INTERNATIONAL RELATIONS:

Can Ours Survive?

DEMOCRACIES AND INTERNATIONAL RELATIONS:
Can Ours Survive?

Compiled and Edited by
URBAN G. WHITAKER, (JR)
San Francisco State College

CHANDLER PUBLISHING COMPANY
SAN FRANCISCO

TO ADELE SIMON

An Expert Laywoman

Preface to the Series

The series of readings of which this volume is one part stems from a prolonged practical experiment in the teaching of international relations. In the time since the origin of the academic field of international relations at the close of World War I, the question of what should be done in the introductory course has never been resolved to the satisfaction of a majority of college teachers and students but, on the other hand, the interest in how the course ought to be organized and what it should include has never flagged. The pluralistic character of American higher education makes certain that no flat uniformity in the college curriculum will prevail. In a truly unique fashion, each American institution arrives at its own choices of how it will meet the two basic responsibilities of the higher learning—the transmission of what is known and the exploration of what remains in mystery.

At San Francisco State College, faculty deliberations between 1946 and 1948 led to the creation of a new core curriculum in the lower division. One of the courses of study that the faculty brought into being was a broadly conceived and basic study of the international environment of the twentieth-century world. Almost a decade of trial and error with this course confirmed two hypotheses: (1) The teaching of the principles and processes of international behavior is a part of liberal education that college students appreciate for its importance to their understanding. (2) It is extremely difficult to construct a coherent and significant course of study that will meet the standards of the academic disciplines of the social sciences.

A generous grant from the Carnegie Corporation of New York made it possible to launch in 1958 a number of studies and experiments concerned with the undergraduate teaching and study of international relations. These studies and experiments are at mid-point at the time of this writing. They include a testing program of the ideas, attitudes, knowledge, and learning progress of undergraduate college students in international relations, a comparison of the effectiveness of two different approaches to the basic course (as the "transformation course" and as the "area course"), an experiment in high-school instruction in world affairs, some trials of gaming and simulation as undergraduate teaching auxiliaries, and a survey of the organization and content of the undergraduate-major patterns in international relations.

The collections of readings that appear in this series were first assembled with little thought of general publication. The staff of the San Francisco International Studies Project found that it needed to put in the hands of students in the experimental sections of the basic course some reading materials of a kind not found in the textbooks or in other collections of readings. Some twelve hundred pages, organized under ten topical headings, were brought together and used for a year in the "transformation course." Revisions were carried through during the summer of 1959.

It should not be supposed that this series reflects the full conception of the experimental course as it is being taught. Only a few of the more successful sets of readings appear in the series. Further, each of the collections was designed to illustrate through cases, problems, and issues some main aspect of drastic change or transformation going on in the international environment of the immediate past and present. Of course, one does not grasp the nature or significance of drastic changes in the conditions of international relations without a knowledge of what has gone before and of the attributes and characteristics of past practice and previous organization. We have supplied this necessary description of the past by means of classroom lectures and assignments in the standard textbooks and other reading. This series of readings carries, however, the main burden of introducing the changeful, novel, uncertain, and controversial elements of the situation.

The full theme of "transformation" might be set forth as follows: "In the system of relationships among nations, including interpersonal, intergroup, interorganizational, and intergovernmental aspects, what are the influences and forces that are impelling rapid and fundamental changes? If the relatively stable arrangements of the international affairs of the nineteenth-century world are taken as reference, what do we find of significance in the emerging international system of the late twentieth century?" Thus, the multiple revolutions in the military technology, in national organization, in communications, and in economic-ecological conditions become of central interest in the setting of how international relationships used to be maintained and how they appear to be taking on new forms and new functions.

It is the experience of the San Francisco International Studies group that the transformation theme can be developed in several different ways and in a number of conceptual perspectives. However the job is done, we have found at first hand that college students, once they have grasped the general idea, become eager to read, learn, and discuss its specific aspects and its broad implications. It is the hope of the compilers of these readings that they will be found useful to other college teachers and students. We venture the further suggestion that, in light of the many overlappings of subject matter and meaning in the social sciences and the humanities, one or several of these volumes may have value for courses that do not bear the formal label of international relations.

Charles A. McClelland
DeVere E. Pentony
Urban Whitaker

May, 1961

Acknowledgments

This book of readings was made possible by funds granted by the Carnegie Corporation of New York. That Corporation is not, however, the author, owner, publisher, or proprietor of this publication and is not to be understood as approving by virtue of its grant any of the statements or views expressed herein.

The editor gratefully acknowledges permission granted by the following publishers, publications and individuals to reprint materials for which they hold copyrights: The Macmillan Company, The University of Chicago Press, The University of Illinois Press, Harper and Brothers, Oxford University Press, Prentice-Hall, *The New York Times, American Political Science Review, Journalism Quarterly, Review of Politics, Yale Review,* Ben H. Bagdikian, Adlai E. Stevenson, Harold Guetzkow, Walter Lippmann, and Archibald MacLeish.

The preparation of this book would not have been possible without the assistance of Miss Merrit Cross of the San Francisco International Studies Project. Jean Whitaker, Willard Johnson, and Langston Bannister assisted in selecting and organizing materials, typing, and proofreading.

Urban Whitaker

Tuckahoe, New York
May 2, 1961

Contents

DEMOCRACIES AND INTERNATIONAL RELATIONS:

Can Ours Survive?

Introduction

Three interconnected questions of contemporary interest form the outline of this study: (1) What is the role of the individual in international affairs? (2) What is the nature of international relations as a type of human activity and as a field for academic study? and (3) Is democracy, as a means of organizing a society, fast enough and efficient enough to survive the twentieth century?

No one of the three questions could be answered without consideration of the other two. To describe the role of the individual we must study the inextricable connections between his objectives in life and the forces and events which take place in the shrinking world around him. To understand the nature of contemporary international relations we have to ask about the place of the individual in his international environment and the kinds of political organization which are effective in helping him to achieve his basic goals. And, whether democracy will work depends on the performances of millions of individual citizens and on the quality of their citizenship, which, in turn, depends on their understanding of the nature of international relations and on the effectiveness of their education in that field.

It is the purpose of this reader to facilitate the student's consideration of these three basic questions, which he will find to be of continuing importance to him as a citizen in a democracy during the last four decades of the twentieth century.

The readings and commentary are organized around a simple actors-ends-means concept and divided into three parts corresponding to the three major questions which form the theme of the book.

First, the role of the individual in world affairs is discussed under the title, "Idealism versus Realism—The Great Debate about

1

Objectives." In this section the desires and goals of individual human beings are studied and their relationship to world affairs is analyzed.

Second, various viewpoints on the nature of international relations are presented and the difficulties of studying the subject are analyzed under the title, "Art versus Science—Difficulties in the Study of International Relations."

Third, the efficacy of democracy as a means of conducting twentieth century international relations is discussed under the title, "Expert or Layman?—Can Democracy Survive in the Twentieth Century?"

The first section discusses the *actors* (both individuals and nation-states) and their *ends*. The second section discusses *means*, to the achievement of those ends. The third section seeks a solution to the problem of organizing the formulation of ends and the search for effective means in a rapidly changing international environment.

I

Idealism versus Realism— The Great Debate about Objectives

The great thread which runs through the whole panorama of human relations and marks them as similar at every level from the individual's affairs to international affairs is the constant striving of entities to achieve their objectives by the most appropriate means available. The academic disciplines of biology, psychology and the various branches of sociology all share this entities-ends-means approach to the analysis of their subject matter. It is a particularly appropriate analytical tool in the study of international relations because those relations comprise the activities of such diverse entities as individuals, business enterprises, fraternal groups, cultural associations, churches, political parties, nation-states, governments, and international organizations. That which these entities share in the international relations process is the constant striving of each to achieve its own objectives. The international process itself is the process of the adjustment of the ends and means of the participating entities as they come into contact with each other.

Several types of behavior are noted in international relations (as in other human relations). When the ends of two or more entities correspond, cooperation *results. When the ends clash,* conflict *results. In the former case there is peace; in the latter there is often war.*

But the great bulk of both individual and international relations results in accommodative behavior patterns which fall somewhere between peaceful cooperation and violent conflict. When ends conflict or when the means to their achievement are not readily available the entities accommodate themselves to the situation by revising their objectives or improvising new means. The study of international relations is largely the study of these accommodations.

Among the entities engaged in the international relations process the individual is central. It is his objectives which become the objectives of the nation-states which formally conduct the most vital and celebrated relations. Indeed all the other entities, including the state itself, can be described as means utilized by the individual toward the attainment of his ends.

The Formulation of Objectives

In the first reading Lord Bryce discusses the relationship of the individual to the state both in the formulation of ends and in the selection of means. Although he wrote more than four decades ago his observations remain pertinent today. In fact he not only anticipates the questions to be discussed in part III of this book but suggests a solution which is receiving serious consideration from contemporary scholars.

SELECTION 1

DEMOCRACY AND FOREIGN POLICY*

JAMES BRYCE

JAMES BRYCE *(1838-1922), British historian, travel writer, and government official, was one of the best known scholar-statesmen of the nine-*

* Reprinted from *Modern Democracies* by James Bryce (Viscount Bryce) (London: Macmillan and Co., 1921), pp. 367-383, used with their permission.

teenth and early twentieth centuries. His most famous book, The American Commonwealth, *first published in 1888, has been a standard work for more than seventy years. In 1904 he published* The Holy Roman Empire *which also became a standard work. In 1880 Bryce was elected to Parliament and held a succession of government positions for more than three decades until he retired in 1913 after six years as Ambassador to the United States. He lectured at Oxford, Cambridge, and many foreign universities but spent so much time traveling and writing that he was unable to accept a permanent professorship anywhere.*

Modern Democracies, from which the selection below is taken, was his last book. The selection is composed of excerpts chosen by the editor from a chapter entitled, "Democracy and Foreign Policy."

Statesmen, political philosophers, and historians have been wont to regard the conduct of foreign relations as the reproach of democratic government. The management of international relations needs—so they insist—knowledge, consistency, and secrecy, whereas democracies are ignorant and inconstant, being moreover obliged, by the law of their being, to discuss in public matters unfit to be disclosed. That this has been perceived by the people themselves appears from the fact that modern legislatures have left this department to officials, because it was felt that in this one department democracies cannot safely be democratic.

Per contra, popular leaders in some countries have, with an increasing volume of support, denounced Foreign Offices as having erred both in aims and in methods. They allege that the diplomacy of European States is condemned by the suspicion which it has constantly engendered and that the brand of failure is stamped upon it by the frequent recurrence of war, the evil which diplomacy was created to prevent.

These views, apparently opposite, are not incompatible. Oligarchies, and the small official class which in many democracies has had the handling of foreign affairs, may have managed them ill, and yet it may be that the whole people will manage them no better. The fault may lie in the conditions of the matter itself and in those tendencies of human nature which no form of government can overcome. What we want to know is not whether oligarchic and secret methods have failed—that may be admitted—but whether democratic and open-air methods will succeed any better. What light does history throw on the question?

Here at starting let a distinction be drawn between Ends and Means in the sphere of foreign policy, a distinction, which, though it exists in all branches of administration, is less significant in the domestic branches, because in them Ends, if not assumed as generally recognized, are and must be determined by the people through their representatives. Justice, the maintenance of public order, economy in expenditure are understood to be aims in every department, while the particular objects for which money is to be spent and the modes of raising it are prescribed by statute. But the relations of States to one another, varying from day to day as the circumstances which govern them vary, cannot be handled by large assemblies in a large country, but must be determined by administrators who are incessantly watching the foreign sky. Modern legislatures accordingly, though they sometimes pass resolutions indicating a course to be followed, or condemning a course which has been followed, by a Ministry, have recognized that in foreign affairs the choice of Means must belong to a small body of experts, and have accordingly left to these persons all details, and the methods which diplomacy must employ in particular cases, allowing them a wide, possibly a too wide, discretion.

But while Foreign Offices and diplomatic envoys may be the proper persons to choose and apply Means, the general principles which should guide and the spirit which should inspire a nation's foreign policy are a different matter, too wide in scope, too grave in consequences, to be determined by any authority lower than that of the people. There may be a divergence of opinion on these principles, i.e. on the Ends to be pursued, between the People of a country and those of their servants to whom the daily conduct of foreign affairs has been left, and it may be that the latter do not obey the real wishes of the people but seek Ends and apply principles which the people, if consulted, would disapprove. To this distinction as affecting conclusions regarding the range of regular action, I shall presently return.

About one aim there can be no divergence. The State must preserve its independence. It must be safe from attack, able to secure fair opportunities for its citizens to trade and to travel abroad unmolested; and these legitimate aims can be pursued in a spirit of justice and friendliness to other States. All States, however, whatever their form of government, have pursued other aims also, and pur-

sued them in a way frequently at variance with justice and honor.
. . . Most States have, in pursuing these objects, been a law unto
themselves. When strong, they have abused their strength, justifying
all means by the plea of State advantage. They have disregarded good
faith from the days when democratic Athens wantonly attacked the
isle of Melos, killing and enslaving its inhabitants, down to the days
of Louis XI and Caesar Borgia, and from the days of Borgia's contemporary Machiavelli down to those of Frederick the Second of Prussia,
who began his literary career with a book designed to refute the
maxims of the Florentine statesman. Though in considering how
popular governments have succeeded in the sphere of foreign policy,
regard must be had to the moral quality of that policy both in Ends
and in Means, moral aspect may be in the first instance reserved,
and the enquiry may go only to the question whether a democracy
is in that sphere more or less efficient than other forms of government. Supposing "success" to mean the maximum of power a State
can attain in the world arena, what kind of government will best
attain it? We can thereafter return to the moral side and enquire
what sort of government will be most likely to observe justice and
good faith, doing its duty by its neighbor States as a good citizen
does his duty by his fellows.

Does Ignorance forbid success to a democracy? Let us hear the
case which professional diplomatists make.

A monarch is free to select his ministers and ambassadors from
among the best informed and most skilful of his subjects and in an
oligarchy the mind of the ruling class busies itself with foreign relations, and knows which of its members understand and are fitted to
handle them. The multitude has not the same advantage. It is ill
qualified to judge this kind of capacity, usually choosing its ministers by their powers of speech. If, instead of leaving foreign affairs to
skilled men it attempts to direct them either by its own votes, as did
the Greek cities, or by instructing those who represent it in the legislature, how is it to acquire the requisite knowledge? Few of the voters
know more than the most elementary facts regarding the conditions
and the policy of foreign countries, and to appreciate the significance of these facts, there is needed some acquaintance with the history of the countries and the characters of the leading men. Not
much of that acquaintance can be expected even from the legislature. One of the strongest arguments for democratic government is

that the masses of the people, whatever else they may not know, do know where the shoe pinches, and are best entitled to specify the reforms they need. In foreign affairs this argument does not apply, for they lie out of the normal citizen's range. All he can do at an election is to convey by his vote his view of general principles, and in the case of a conflict between two foreign nations, to indicate his sympathies.

If the masses of the people have been inconstant in their views of foreign relations, this is due to their ignorance, which disables them from following intelligently the course of events abroad, so that their interest in these is quickened only at intervals, and when that happens the want of knowledge of what has preceded makes a sound judgment unlikely. They are at the mercy of their party leaders or of the press, guides not trustworthy, because the politicians will be influenced by the wish to make political capital out of any successes scored or errors committed by a Ministry, while the newspapers may play up to and exaggerate the prevailing sentiment of the moment, claiming everything for their own country, misrepresenting and disparaging the foreign antagonist. Consistency cannot be expected from a popular government which acts under a succession of impulses, giving no steady attention to that department in which continuity of policy is most needed.

Secrecy in the conduct of diplomacy is vital in a world where each great nation is suspicious of its neighbors, and obliged by its fears to try to discover their plans while concealing its own. Suppose the ministry of a country to have ascertained privately that a foreign Power meditates an attack upon it or is forming a combination against it, or suppose it to be itself negotiating a treaty of alliance for protection against such a combination. How can it proclaim either the intentions of the suspected Power or its own counter-schemes without precipitating a rupture or frustrating its own plans? A minister too honorable to deceive the legislature may feel himself debarred from telling it the facts, some of which may have been communicated under the seal of confidence. It is all very well to say that an open and straightforward policy best befits a free and high-minded people. But if such a people should stand alone in a naughty world, it will have to suffer for its virtues. As a democracy cannot do business secretly, it must therefore leave much, and perhaps much of grave import, to its ministers. Herein the superiority for foreign affairs of a monarchy or an oligarchy is most evident. . . . [Editor's note: Lord Bryce follows this introduction to his subject with a series of case studies illustrating how far democratic governments "have shown wisdom in following sound aims and have succeeded in applying the means needed to attain them." His remarks about France, Britain and Switzerland are omitted. About the United States he says that because the rule of public opinion is "more complete than elsewhere, it furnishes the best index to the tendencies and capacities of a democracy."]

The Republic [U.S.] has been engaged in three wars within the last hundred years. That against Mexico in 1846 was the work of the slave-holding party which then controlled the Executive and the Senate, and whose leaders brought it on for the sake of creating Slave States and strengthening the grip of slavery on the Union. It was widely disapproved by public opinion, especially in the northern States, but the acquisition, by the treaty which closed it, of vast and rich territories on the Pacific Coast did much to silence the voice of criticism.

The war against Spain in 1898 might probably have been avoided, for Spain had been driven to the verge of consenting to withdraw from Cuba when the breach came. But the nation, already wearied by the incessant troubles to which Spanish misgovernment had given rise during many years, had been inflamed by the highly colored accounts which the newspapers published of the severities practiced on the insurgents by Spanish generals, and the President, though inclined to continue negotiations, is believed to have been forced into war by the leaders of his own party who did not wish their opponents to have the credit of compelling a declaration. In obtaining, by the peace which followed a short campaign, the cession to the United States of Puerto Rico and the Philippine Islands, the President believed that he was carrying out the wishes of the people. This may have been so, for they were flushed with victory, and were moved not merely by the feeling that victory ought to bring some tangible gain, but also by a sort of philanthropic sentiment which was unwilling to hand back the conquered territories to Spanish maladministration. This war, therefore, though it shows that a popular government may yield to excitement and gratify its ambition for enlarged territory, cannot be deemed a case of mere aggression for the sake of conquest.

The war of 1917 against Germany and Austria is too fresh in our memories to need comment. There was certainly nothing selfish or aggressive in the spirit that prompted America's entrance into it. The sinking of the *Lusitania* and other passenger vessels supplied a definite *casus belli;* the mind of the nation had been stirred to its depths by the sense that far-reaching moral issues were involved. . . . [Editor's note: After citing several other historical examples the author concludes:] All these cases gave evidence not only of the authority which popular opinion exerts over the main lines of foreign policy, but also of the growth in it of a spirit of good sense and self-restraint such as was not always seen in earlier years. The nation, when it came to full manhood, laid aside the spirit of self-assertion and the desire for conquest, and gave proof of a sincere desire to apply methods of arbitration and show its respect for the rights of other nations. . . . An instance of this was furnished when in 1914 Congress, at the instance of the President and at the bidding of public opinion, repealed an Act by which it had in 1912 hastily asserted a particular power over the use of the Panama Canal, which the people, after the matter had been fully discussed, convinced themselves that they disclaimed by the treaty with Great Britain of 1901. With this higher sense of justice there has also come a stronger aversion to war. No great people in the world is equally pervaded by the wish to see peace maintained everywhere over the world. . . .

In these last few pages Ends rather than Means have been considered, though it is hard to draw a distinction, for most Ends are Means to a larger End; and the facts examined seem to show that in determining Ends the voice of the people must have authority. But what is to be said as to the details of diplomacy in which, assuming the main ends to be determined by the people, a wide choice of means remains open? It has been deemed impossible for the people to know either which means are best suited to the purpose aimed at or, if the people is kept informed of them, to apply those means successfully, for in our days what is told to any people is told to the whole world. So long as each nation strives to secure some gains for itself as against other nations by anticipating its rivals in enterprises, or by forming profitable alliances, or otherwise driving bargains for its own benefit, those who manage the nation's business cannot disclose their action without damaging their chances of success. Hence even the countries that have gone furthest in recognizing popular control have left a wide discretion in the hands of their Ministers or envoys and have set bounds to the curiosity of parliamentary representatives. Must this continue? If it does continue, what security have the people against unwise action or the adoption of dishonorable methods?

One expedient used to overcome this difficulty has been that of a committee of the legislature which can receive confidential communications from a Minister and can bind its members to keep them secret. This is done in the United States, where the Foreign Relations Committee of the Senate, though it cannot dictate to the President (or his Secretary of State), can through its power of inducing the Senate to refuse assent to a treaty exercise a constant and potent influence. . . . So also in France each Chamber has a Commission for foreign affairs. In both countries declarations of war must proceed from the legislature. The committee plan has its defects. No secret known to more than three men remains for long a secret; and a Minister can, if he likes, go a long way towards committing his country before he tells the committee what he is doing, taking of course the chance that he may be disavowed. Sometimes, moreover, action cannot await the approval of a committee, for to be effective it must be immediate.

The voices which in European countries demand the abolition of secret diplomacy and the control by the people of all foreign relations appeal to an incontestable principle, because a nation has every right to deliver its opinion on matters of such supreme importance as the issues of peace and war. The difficulty lies in applying a sound principle to the facts as they have hitherto stood in Europe. If publicity in the conduct of negotiations is to be required, and the mind of the people to be expressed before any commitment is made by its Ministers, there must be a renunciation of such advantages as have been heretofore obtained by international combinations or bargains secretly made with other nations. If, on the other hand, these advantages are to be sought, secrecy must be permitted and discretion granted to Ministers. The risk that secrecy and discretion will be abused will be gradually lessened the more public opinion becomes better instructed on foreign affairs, and the more that legislatures learn to give unremitting attention to foreign policy. In England as well as in America few are the representatives who possess the knowledge needed, or take the trouble to acquire it. It is this, as well as party spirit, which has led Parliamentary majorities to endeavor to support their party chiefs, even when it was beginning to be seen that public opinion was turning against them. If ministries were to become more and more anxious to keep as close a touch with the feeling of the nation in foreign as they seek to do in domestic affairs, the risk that any nation will be irrevocably entangled in a pernicious course would diminish. So too if there should be hereafter less of a desire to get the better of other nations in acquiring territory or concessions abroad, if a less grasping and selfish spirit should rule foreign policy, fewer occasions will arise in which secret agreements will be needed. The thing now most needed by the people and its representatives is more knowledge of the facts of the outside world with a more sympathetic comprehension of the minds of other peoples. The first step to this is a fuller acquaintance with the history, the economic and social conditions, and the characters of other peoples.

The conclusions to which the considerations here set forth point are the following:

In a democracy the People are entitled to determine the Ends or general aims of foreign policy.

History shows that they do this at least as wisely as monarchs or oligarchies, or the small groups to whom, in democratic countries, the conduct of foreign relations has been left, and that they have evinced more respect for moral principles.

The Means to be used for attaining the Ends sought cannot be adequately determined by legislatures so long as international relations continue to be what they have heretofore been, because secrecy is sometimes, and expert knowledge is always required.

Nevertheless some improvement on the present system is needed, and the experiment of a Committee deserves to be tried.

Whatever faults modern democracies may have committed in this field of administration, the faults chargeable on monarchs and oligarchies have been less pardonable and more harmful to the peace and progress of mankind. If the recently created League of Nations is to succeed in averting wars by securing the amicable settlement of international disputes, it must have the constant sympathy and support of the peoples of the states which are its members. That this support should be effectively and easily given, the peoples must give more attention to foreign affairs and come to know more of them. Ignorance is the great obstacle.

Choices of Objectives

We shall return, in part III below, to the major questions posed by Lord Bryce about democracy and foreign policy. The remainder of the readings in this first section are concerned less with how national objectives are formulated than with the nature of the objectives themselves.

In selection 2, Kenneth Thompson describes three different schools of thought concerning the appropriate objectives of a national state. The selections which follow tend to illustrate each of these three schools although the authors all share a healthy respect for realism. Professor Thompson also discusses the nature of the international relations process which will be studied again in part II.

George Kennan (selection 3) attacks the "legalistic-moralistic" philosophy which he thinks dominated American international relations during the first half of the twentieth century. Mr. Kennan's analysis, like Lord Bryce's, anticipates the evaluation of democratic procedures in foreign affairs which will be our concern in part III. It also extends Bryce's explicit consideration of ends and means with its suggestion that "total victory" is an unrealistic national objective which ought to be revised in order to avoid disastrous international conflict.

Adlai Stevenson (selection 4) does not address himself solely to questions of international relations but concentrates on the problem of adjusting private and public interests to each other. His discussion illustrates clearly the applicability of similar ends-means analyses to the problems of individuals, of intranational and of international relations.

Thomas Cook and Malcolm Moos (selection 5) express vigorous dissent to Kennan's (and in some respects to Thompson's) realism. Accepting something of both the realist and idealist schools they go further perhaps than the school of thought which Thompson describes as "eclectic." In selection 5 the two writers deny the legitimacy of identifying separate schools of realism and idealism and present a detailed argument which has found widespread agreement in contemporary academic circles.

Selection 6 is a short selection from the writings of Professor Hans Morgenthau, who has been identified as the founder of the *school of political realism. It is placed last, however, because it rings a note of agreement with the preceding selection which was first written partly in refutation of the Morgenthau philosophy. This final selection also returns the discussion to the individual and recasts the entire international process in terms of individuals seeking to attain their objectives by the most suitable means available.*

SELECTION 2

THE STUDY OF INTERNATIONAL POLITICS: A SURVEY OF TRENDS AND DEVELOPMENTS*

KENNETH W. THOMPSON

KENNETH W. THOMPSON *is an Associate of the Rockefeller Foundation in New York City. He is co-editor (with Hans J. Morgenthau) of* Principles and Problems of International Politics *(1950) and author of* Political Realism and the Crisis of World Politics *(1960). He has presented papers before many professional conferences and has contributed many articles to scholarly journals. The selection below is part two of the Introduction to his article, "The Study of International Politics: A Survey of Trends and Developments." Footnotes are numbered as in the original.*

2. THREE THEORIES OF INTERNATIONAL POLITICAL BEHAVIOR

It is frequently said that one test of the independent character of a discipline or field of study is the presence in the field of theories contending for recognition by those engaged in thinking and writing. It may be significant that underlying the study of contemporary international politics are two general theories of human nature and politics. Moreover, there are already the first signs of the origin of a third way of conceiving the nature of international affairs. At this time, however, political idealism and political realism are the major competitors for recognition as the theory of international behavior.[9] In the past there has been no coherent

---

* Reprinted from *The Review of Politics*, Vol. 14 (1952), pp. 433-467.
[9] George F. Kennan, *American Diplomacy, 1900-50.* (Chicago: University of Chicago Press, 1951.)

political theory evolved from the ancients which deliberately sets forth to explain politics within a system that is not ordered and controlled by an all-powerful central authority.[10] Indeed idealism and realism as conceived and defined in political theory from Greek times to the present have little in common with the assumptions and premises of the two philosophies of contemporary international politics. Each in its sphere has its own tacit or explicit assumptions. In world politics, the philosophy of idealism or utopianism so-called includes most of the thinking which was done in the intervening years between the two World Wars. The philosophy of realism which had prevailed throughout most of the eighteenth and nineteenth centuries has been revived both in theory and practice especially in the years following World War II. The current most useful and original literature has been contributed primarily by those concerned with testing the assumptions of realism. Yet it is fashionable especially in circles of older scholars to proclaim that the distinctions between realism and idealism are unreal and exaggerated. Moreover, there are many who contend that both terms are fraught with emotions and value judgments and thereby are disqualified from use in social studies. In contrast, great diplomats in the West including the most distinguished representatives in 1952 have rarely been seized by such fears and doubts. Our wisest diplomats and statesmen have taken idealism and realism for granted. For example, the most learned and perceptive of American diplomats and the present Ambassador to Moscow, Mr. George F. Kennan, has declared: "I see the most serious fault of our past policy formulations to lie in something that I might call the legalistic-moralistic approach to international problems. This approach runs like a red skein through our foreign policy of the last fifty years. . . . It is the belief that it should be possible to suppress the chaotic and dangerous aspirations of governments in the international field by the acceptance of some system of legal rules and restraints. . . . It is the essence of this belief that instead of taking the awkward conflicts of national interest and dealing with them on their merits with the view to finding the solutions least unsettled to the stability of international life, it would be better to

[10] John H. Herz, *Political Realism and Political Idealism: A Study in Theories and Realities.* (Chicago: University of Chicago Press, 1951).

find some formal criteria of a juridical nature by which the permissible behavior of states could be defined."[11] Mr. Kennan concludes his estimate of the philosophy of utopianism by pointing to the beliefs and attitudes in the United States which have made this viewpoint meaningful and creditable. "Behind all of this, of course, lies the American assumption that the things for which other peoples in this world are apt to contend are for the most part neither creditable nor important and might justly be expected to take second place behind the desirability of an orderly world, untroubled by international violence. To the American mind, it is implausible that people should have positive aspirations, and ones that they regard as legitimate, more important to them than the peacefulness and orderliness of international life."[12]

Another wise statesman, a young Conservative Member of Parliament, Captain Peter Thorneycroft, who in 1951 was to become the youngest member of Prime Minister Churchill's Cabinet, voiced on February 28, 1945, essentially the same beliefs that Mr. Kennan was to express in 1951. In a debate in the House of Commons on the issues arising from the Polish settlement agreed to by Prime Minister Churchill, President Roosevelt and Premier Stalin at the Crimean Conference, Captain Thorneycroft chose the occasion to cast his specific comments in the mold of general principles of international politics.

> I believe the real difficulty in which my hon. Friends find themselves is not so much Poland at all. I believe it is in the apparent conflict between documents like the Atlantic Charter and the facts of the European situation. We talk to two different people in two different languages. In the East we are talking to the Russians. The Russians are nothing if not realists . . . I believe that the Russian Foreign Office is perhaps more in tune with the advice which would be given to the Tsar than to the potentates of the twentieth century. In such circumstances we talk in language not far removed from power politics. In the West we are faced by the Americans. They are nothing if not idealists. To them we talk in the polite language of the Atlantic Charter. Somehow or other we have to marry those two schools of thought. If I could persuade the Americans, particularly in the Middle West, to have something of the Russian realism in international

---

[11] Kennan, *op. cit.*, pp. 95-6.
[12] *Ibid.*, p. 96.

relations, and persuade the Russians to have the idealism that exists
on the East coast of America, we might get somewhere, but let us face
the fact that the process will be a long and painful one. You do not
move suddenly from a world in which there are international rivalries
into a world where there is international cooperation. It is the world
that we are in that the Prime Minister has to deal with. We could
not come back from Yalta with a blueprint for a new Utopia. . . .
The rights of small nations are safeguarded by a mixture of diplomacy and military power . . .[13]

These two expressions of an American and British conception
of the nature of international politics are significant because of the
strong clear light they throw on the two opposing theories. They
indicate that professional diplomats and statesmen are unable to
indulge themselves the luxury of shying away from the facts of international life. The assumptions underlying the two points of view
may be enumerated in relatively simple terms. For the political realist, rivalry and some form of strife among nation-states is the rule
and not a mere accident of backwardness in the past. There are
harmonies as well as disharmonies to be sure but the failure of
every scheme for world peace in the past must be sought in the conditions which have created the disharmonies and not through com-
parisons with a blueprint of a commonwealth of absolute world
harmonies. In all social groups, whether in states or in smaller more
intimate communities, a contest for influence and power goes on
unceasingly. On the international scene, however, rivalries among
states are uncontrolled by effective law or government. The business of statesmanship and diplomacy under the conditions of present-day international society is to limit the struggles and restrict
their extent and scope. The means available in the absence of government are the unceasing pursuit of new balances of power and
rough equilibriums among contending parties. The aims include adjustment and accommodation on the basis of mutual recognition
that an equilibrium does exist. The realist strives to mitigate the
rivalries among nations, through checks and balances and by compromise and bargaining. Abstract moral principles may be the ultimate object and purpose of the bargain or agreement but an abstract principle is not an essential part of the bargain itself. Real-

[13] *Parliamentary Debates* (Hansard). *House of Commons.* Vol. 408, February
28, 1945, pp. 1458-1459.

ism would prepare the student of international politics for the tragic and stubborn discrepancy of means and ends in international politics. It accepts for the guide and premise of its thought the permanence and ubiquity of the struggle for power. But it strives unceasingly through every means at its disposal to contain and limit concentrations of power and to compose and relieve tensions which could lead to a situation of war.

The utopian philosophy has little in common with political realism nor has it shown much patience or understanding for this brand of thinking. It chooses to abjure the toils of power politics since at most they are considered an abnormal and passing historic phase. In fact, with the creation of one universal society, so primitive and barbaric a form of international politics, if not indeed politics itself, will be eliminated. Political realism, it is claimed, is a distortion and cynical corruption of the true meaning of history. It is claimed by the spokesmen of political idealism that if there have been group controversies throughout history, these struggles have centered not in political rivalries for influence and power but in the clash between incompatible ideals and principles. A concrete example which is offered is the aggression of fascism against democracy. At such time, therefore, as fascism and the other philosophies whose aims have made conflict inevitable have been permanently smashed and destroyed, power politics and war will disappear. Historically, utopianism has offered three alternatives for moral nations confronting the practical problems of survival in a world of archaic power politics. Ultimately, power politics must be eliminated through instituting a universal world government. Practically, power politics will be abolished when their main exemplars, the totalitarian states have been erased from the face of the earth. Provisionally, their evil influence will be progressively and decisively undermined by the example of moral and upright nations foreswearing relations with corrupted, power-seeking nations, pursuing neutrality policies and abstaining from all forms of traditional power politics.

In practice, moreover, the nations of good will who have accepted the philosophy of utopianism have pursued foreign policies reflecting precisely these three alternatives. It is not by accident that the United States as the nation over recent decades that has yielded most readily to utopianism has pursued a foreign policy that has vacillated between these three possibilities. For in these terms we can account for the neutrality policy of the United States before both World Wars. In each pre-war period, we tried to abstain and withdrew from the impure and corrupted power politics of the European continent. Any concession in terms of territorial guarantees against German expansion would have been unworthy of the philosophy we espoused. Any intervention in the affairs of Europe for the purpose of bolstering and strengthening the Weimar Republic would have weakened our moral position. When at length we were driven by the inherent logic of utopianism to justify our role in World War II, we turned from neutrality to a holy crusade against the evil incarnate in fascism. When through no fault of our own war became unavoidable—for had we not meticulously avoided any political action that could have invited the conflict— we gave unstintingly of our resources and our principles. We engaged in the world struggle not selfishly or for political advantage but in order to end conflict in the west and destroy and eliminate those evil men and ideals who had been responsible. These wars were not ordinary struggles for more territorial adjustments, new balances of power or specified political gain but were crusades for advancing the spread of democracy. They were holy wars of "unconditional surrender" against solitary infidels and troublemakers. For these men and ideas had caused the catastrophies; therefore, with their elimination, aggrandizement and rivalry would disappear.

The third stage in the utopian journey, however, has been for us the most basic, fateful and far-reaching. After the war, it was clearly essential that what had been undertaken and achieved in war be sealed and perfected in peace. The agents of power politics lay mortally wounded; now the climate in which their nefarious politics had thrived must be cleansed and transformed and international organization substituted for politics. In this new commonwealth, the problem of power would disappear. What this meant in concrete terms was that the *status quo* with its prevailing lawfulness based on the relative satisfaction of the victorious powers must be made permanent through the regularized procedures of new international organizations. Thus through our policies of neutrality, moralistic crusades and the substitution of organization for anarchic world politics, we have consistently pursued in recent times the aims of political idealism.

Hence the crucial difference and the real point at which political idealism and political realism diverge is with respect to the positions they take regarding the problem of power. Power is an attribute of an archaic and transitory international situation for idealists who have chosen not to recognize it as enduring. Power for the realist is the single most stubborn social psychological factor by which international behavior is influenced. Only through understanding this phenomenon can man hope to improve the melancholy status of his present situation. There is a third general approach or theory, however, which departs explicitly from both of these theories of politics. A viewpoint which is perhaps best designated *eclectic* has been asserted to represent a new synthesis. Thus in the second revised edition of George Schwarzenberger's voluminous *Power Politics,* the author rejects both idealism and realism as unscientific.[14] Neither, he claims, has seen fit to state its major premise which he finds on the one hand in the case of realism to be that of pessimism and on the other hand with idealism that of optimism. Mr. Schwarzenberger concludes: "What is actually required is a primarily empirical approach to international affairs."[15] Eclecticism in these terms asks the student to start without any *a priori* assumptions in making his inquiries in the field. The eclectic point of view has shown a preference for a sociological approach to the problems of world politics. There would appear to be three reasons alleged for this practicality. First, only present-day sociology with its separation of facts and values and its resistance to *a priori* judgements is equipped with a tradition of having pursued truly empirical studies. Also, the sole catholic and inclusive approach to the study of international politics is that of sociology. For example, in the case of tariff legislation, the international lawyer can discuss the legal and normative implications of treaties and treaty observance; the economist can assess the purely economic aspects of the problem; and the political scientist will contribute to an understanding of the political conflicts going on within a certain nation. Yet the only discipline which will cover all these separate facets under the enveloping umbrella of a single conceptual framework is sociology. Thirdly, sociology alone is capable of providing tests or clues by

[14] George Schwarzenberger, *Power Politics*. Second Revised Edition. (New York: Frederick A. Praeger, Inc., 1951), pp. 5-6.

[15] *Ibid.,* p. 5.

which to separate subject matter that is clearly international in character from what is essentially domestic in nature. It finds this test in the general principle of whether or not a given issue or episode affects the growth or the disintegration of international society. In American foreign policy, for example, the scientific way in which to think about the Truman Doctrine or the Marshall Plan would be to estimate their effects on the integration or disintegration of international society.

Of the three approaches or theories of international politics, eclecticism has come on to the scene most recently. Its claim that it foreswears the espousal of one viewpoint or another regarding human nature and politics is hardly substantiated in concrete studies by scholars like Professor Schwarzenberger. For that author, after disclaiming the assumption of realism that man is competitive and possesses a lust for power as well as the belief of idealism that he is rational and good, actually proceeds throughout most of his analysis to employ the working concepts of political realism. Indeed the illusion of much of contemporary social science that the student can in fact approach his inquiry with a *tabula rasa* is hardly supported by the undertakings of Schwarzenberger or any of his colleagues. Yet this view is central to eclecticism as a theory of international politics. If this assumption is false, then much of the work of this approach will in all likelihood be seriously undermined. At this stage, however, the presence of three separate theories each avowing qualitatively distinct assumptions tends to give to the study of world politics the character of something approaching a discipline.

SELECTION 3

DIPLOMACY IN THE
MODERN WORLD*

GEORGE F. KENNAN

GEORGE F. KENNAN *was Permanent Professor at the Institute for Advanced Study, Princeton University, 1954-61. A career foreign service officer, he became a prominent public figure in 1947 as a member of the*

* Reprinted from *American Diplomacy (1900-1950)* by George F. Kennan by permission of the University of Chicago Press. Copyright 1951 by the University of Chicago.

Policy Planning Staff of the State Department and author of the "Mister X" article in Foreign Affairs *which set forth what became the "containment" policy of the United States. He was subsequently Ambassador to the Soviet Union from 1952 until his retirement from the Foreign Service in 1953. He has received several literary awards for his two volume work,* Soviet-American Relations, 1917-20. *In 1961 he was appointed U. S. Ambassador to Yugoslavia.*

The selection reprinted below was one of the Charles R. Walgreen Foundation Lectures entitled "Diplomacy in the Modern World." These lectures, delivered in 1950 at the University of Chicago, and the "Mister X" article were printed together in 1951 under the title American Diplomacy 1900-1950.

. . . I should be most unhappy if anything said in these lectures should seem a mark of disrespect for such men as John Hay, Elihu Root, Charles Evans Hughes, or Henry Stimson. These men embodied that pattern of integrity of mind and spirit, moderation and delicacy of character, irreproachable loyalty in personal relations, modesty of person combined with dignity of office, and kindliness and generosity in the approach to all who are weaker and more dependent, which constitutes, it seems to me, our finest contribution to the variety of the human species in this world and comes closest to embodying our national ideal and genius. They were men so measured and prudent in their judgment of others, so careful to reserve that judgment until they felt they had the facts, so well aware of the danger of inadequate evidence and hasty conclusion, that we would be making ourselves ridiculous if we were to attend their memories and the evidences of their handiwork in any other spirit.

We are another generation, and we cannot be fully the judges either of the demands which faced our elders or of the adequacy of their responses. For the performance of these men in public office I can feel only the sort of sympathy and admiration which one felt for the struggles and works of one's own father, coupled with the invariable conviction of children everywhere that there were features of the modern world which Father understood very poorly and we children understood much better. And if, today, we think we see blind spots or weak spots in their approaches to foreign policy, we would do well to remember what Gibbon said of the great Byzantine general, Belisarius: "His imperfections flowed from the contagion of the times: his virtues were his own."

But, notwithstanding all this, it is clear that there has been in the past a very significant gap between challenge and response in our conduct of foreign policy; that this gap still exists; and that, whereas fifty years ago it was not very dangerous to us, today it puts us in grave peril. We can afford no complacency about these things in the year 1951, and we have no choice but to face up unsparingly to our weaknesses.

I think you have seen quite clearly from the earlier lectures what I hold these weaknesses to be. I do not need to recapitulate them in any great detail. They are ones which relate both to machinery and to concept—both to means and to objectives.

On the question of the machinery of government, we have seen that a good deal of our trouble seems to have stemmed from the extent to which the executive has felt itself beholden to short-term trends of public opinion in the country and from what we might call the erratic and subjective nature of public reaction to foreign-policy questions. I would like to emphasize that I do not consider public reaction to foreign-policy questions to be erratic and undependable over the long term; but I think the record indicates that in the short term our public opinion, what passes for our public opinion in the thinking of official Washington, can be easily led astray into areas of emotionalism and subjectivity which make it a poor and inadequate guide for national action.

What can we do about this?

As one who has occupied himself professionally with foreign affairs for a quarter of a century, I cannot refrain from saying that I firmly believe that we could make much more effective use of the principle of professionalism in the conduct of foreign policy; that we could, if we wished, develop a corps of professional officers superior to anything that exists or ever has existed in this field; and that, by treating these men with respect and drawing on their insight and experience, we could help ourselves considerably. However, I am quite prepared to recognize that this runs counter to strong prejudices and preconceptions in sections of our public mind, particularly in Congress and the press, and that for this reason we are probably condemned to continue relying almost exclusively on what we might call "diplomacy by dilettantism."

That being the case, we still have with us, in what is obviously a very acute form, the problem of the machinery for decision-making and for the implementation of policy in our government. Whatever else may be said about these facilities to date, it can hardly be said that they are distinguished by such things as privacy, deliberateness, or the long-term approach. The difficulties we encounter here are so plain to all of you at this moment that I shall not attempt to adumbrate them. The subject of their correction is an extremely complex one, involving many facets of governmental organization and method. There are those who feel that these difficulties can be satisfactorily disposed of within our present constitutional framework and that they are simply a question of proper personal leadership in government. There are others who doubt that the problem is soluble without constitutional reform—reform which would give us a parliamentary system more nearly like that which exists in England and most other parliamentary countries, a system in which a government falls if it loses the confidence of its parliament, and in which there is opportunity to consult the people on the great issues and at the crucial moments and to adjust governmental responsibilities in accordance with the people's decision.

I must say that if I had any doubts before as to whether it is this that our country requires, those doubts have been pretty well resolved in my mind by the events of the past weeks and months. I find it hard to see how we can live up to our responsibilities as a great power unless we are able to resolve, in a manner better than we have done recently, the great challenges to the soundness of government policy and to the claim of an administration to speak for the mass of the people in foreign affairs.

Here again, I am afraid, the chances of change in the direction I have indicated are so slight that we must dismiss the possibility as one that might have any particular relevance to our present problems.

This leaves us substantially with the question of concept. This is the field in which the scholar's voice can be most useful, and for which it seems to me that this examination of the past yields the most instructive results.

As you have no doubt surmised, I see the most serious fault of our past policy formulation to lie in something that I might call the legalistic-moralistic approach to international problems. This approach runs like a red skein throughout foreign policy of the last fifty years. It has in it something of the old emphasis on arbitration treaties, something of the Hague Conferences and schemes for universal disarmament, something of the more ambitious American concepts of the role of international law, something of the League of Nations and the United Nations, something of the Kellogg Pact, something of the idea of a universal "Article 51" past, something of the belief in World Law and World Government. But it is none of these entirely. Let me try to describe it.

It is the belief that it should be possible to suppress the chaotic and dangerous aspirations of governments in the international field by the acceptance of some system of legal rules and restraints. This belief undoubtedly represents in part an attempt to transpose the Anglo-Saxon concept of individual law into the international field and to make it applicable to governments as it is applicable here at home to individuals. It must also stem in part from the memory of the origin of our own political system—from the recollection that we were able, through acceptance of a common institutional and juridical framework, to reduce to harmless dimensions the conflicts of interest and aspiration among the original thirteen colonies and to bring them all into an ordered and peaceful relationship with one another. Remembering this, people are unable to understand that what might have been possible for the thirteen colonies in a given set of circumstances might not be possible in the wider international field.

It is the essence of this belief that, instead of taking the awkward conflicts of national interest and dealing with them on their merits with a view to finding the solutions least unsettling to the stability of international life, it would be better to find some formal criteria of a juridical nature by which the permissible behavior of states could be defined. There would then be judicial entities competent to measure the actions of governments against these criteria and to decide when their behavior was acceptable and when unacceptable. Behind all this, of course, lies the American assumption that the things for which other peoples in this world are apt to contend are for the most part neither creditable nor important and might justly be expected to take second place behind the desirability of an orderly world, untroubled by international violence. To the American mind, it is implausible that people should have positive aspirations, and ones that they regard as legitimate, more important to them than the peacefulness and orderliness of international life. From this standpoint, it is not apparent why other people should not join us in accepting the rules of the game in international politics, just as we accept such rules in the competition of sport in order that the game may not become too cruel and too destructive and may not assume an importance we did not mean it to have.

If they were to do this, the reasoning runs, then the troublesome and chaotic manifestations of the national ego could be contained and rendered either unsubstantial or subject to easy disposal by some method familiar and comprehensible to our American usage. Departing from this background, the mind of American statesmanship, stemming as it does in so large a part from the legal profession in our country, gropes with unfailing persistence for some institutional framework which would be capable of fulfilling this function.

I cannot undertake in this short lecture to deal exhaustively with this thesis or to point out all the elements of unsoundness which I feel it contains. But some of its more outstanding weaknesses are worthy of mention.

In the first place, the idea of the subordination of a large number of states to an international juridical regime, limiting their possibilities for aggression and injury to other states, implies that these are all states like our own, reasonably content with their international borders and status, at least to the extent that they would be willing to refrain from pressing for changes without international agreement. Actually, this has generally been true only of a portion of international society. We tend to underestimate the violence of national maladjustments and discontents elsewhere in the world if we think that they would always appear to other people as less important than the preservation of the juridical tidiness of international life.

Second, while this concept is often associated with a revolt against nationalism, it is a curious thing that it actually tends to confer upon the concept of nationality and national sovereignty an absolute value it did not have before. The very principle of "one government, one vote," regardless of physical or political differences between states, glorifies the concept of national sovereignty and makes it the exclusive form of participation in international life. It envisages a world composed exclusively of sovereign national states with a full equality of status. In doing this, it ignores the tremendous variations in the firmness and soundness of national divisions: the fact that the origins of state borders and national personalities were in many instances fortuitous or at least poorly related to realities. It also ignores the law of change. The national state pattern is not, should not be, and cannot be a fixed and static thing. By nature, it is an unstable phenomenon in a constant state of change and flux. History has shown that the will and the capacity of individual peoples to contribute to their world environment is constantly changing. It is only logical that the organizational forms (and what else are such things as borders and governments?) should change with them. The function of a system of international relationships is not to inhibit this process of change by imposing a legal strait jacket upon it but rather to facilitate it; to ease its transitions, to temper the asperities to which it often leads, to isolate and moderate the conflicts to which it gives rise, and to see that these conflicts do not assume forms too unsettling for international life in general. But this is a task for diplomacy, in the most old-fashioned sense of the term. For this, law is too abstract, too inflexible, too hard to adjust to the demands of the unpredictable and the unexpected.

By the same token, the American concept of world law ignores those means of international offense—those means of the projection of power and coercion over other peoples—which by-pass institutional forms entirely or even exploit them against themselves: such things as ideological attack, intimidation, penetration, and disguised seizure of the institutional paraphernalia of national sovereignty. It ignores, in other words, the device of the puppet state and the set of techniques by which states can be converted into puppets with no formal violation of, or challenge to, the outward attributes of their sovereignty and their independence.

This is one of the things that have caused the peoples of the satellite countries of eastern Europe to look with a certain tinge of bitterness on the United Nations. The organization failed so completely to save them from domination by a great neighboring country, a domination no less invidious by virtue of the fact that it came into being by processes we could not call "aggression." And there is indeed some justification for their feeling, because the legalistic approach to international affairs ignores in general the international significance of political problems and the deeper sources of international instability. It assumes that civil wars will remain civil and not grow into international wars. It assumes the ability of each people to solve its own internal political problems in a manner not provocative of its international environment. It assumes that each nation will always be able to construct a government qualified to speak for it and cast its vote in the international arena and that this government will be acceptable to the rest of the international community in this capacity. It assumes, in other words, that domestic issues will not become international issues and the world community will not be put in the position of having to make choices between rival claimants for power within the confines of the individual state.

Finally, this legalistic approach to international relations is faulty in its assumptions concerning the possibility of sanctions against offenses and violations. In general, it looks to collective action to provide such sanction against the bad behavior of states. In doing so, it forgets the limitations on the effectiveness of military coalition. It forgets that, as a circle of military associates widens in any conceivable political-military venture, the theoretical total of available military strength may increase, but only at the cost of compactness and ease of control. And the wider a coalition becomes, the more difficult it becomes to retain political unity and general agreement on the purposes and effects of what is being done. As we are seeing in the case of Korea, joint military operations against an aggressor have a different meaning for each participant and raise specific political issues for each one which are extraneous to the action in question and affect many other facets of international life. The wider the circle of military associates, the more cumbersome the problem of political control over their actions, the more circumscribed the least common denominator of agreement. This law of diminishing returns lies so heavily on the possibilities for multilateral military action that it makes it doubtful whether the participation of smaller states can really add very much to the ability of the great powers to assure stability of international life. And this is tremendously important, for it brings us back to the realization that even under a system of world law the sanction against destructive international behavior might continue to rest basically, as it has in the past, on the alliances and relationships among the great powers themselves. There might be a state, or perhaps more than one state, which all the rest of the world community together could not successfully coerce into following a line of action to which it was violently averse. And if this is true, where are we? It seems to me that we are right back in the realm of the forgotten art of diplomacy from which we have spent fifty years trying to escape.

These, then, are some of the theoretical deficiencies that appear to me to be inherent in the legalistic approach to international affairs. But there is a greater deficiency still that I should like to mention before I close. That is the inevitable association of legalistic ideas with moralistic ones: the carrying-over into the affairs of states of the concepts of right and wrong, the assumption that state behavior is a fit subject for moral judgment. Whoever says there is a law must of course be indignant against the law-breaker and feel a moral superiority to him. And when such indignation spills over into military contest, it knows no bounds short of the reduction of the law-breaker to the point of complete submissiveness—namely, unconditional surrender. It is a curious thing, but it is true, that the legalistic approach to world affairs, rooted as it unquestionably is in a desire to do away with war and violence, makes violence more enduring, more terrible, and more destructive to political stability than did the older motives of national interest. A war fought in the name of a high moral principle finds no early end short of some form of total domination.

In this way, we see that the legalistic approach to international problems is closely identified with the concept of total war and total victory, and the manifestations of the one spill over only too easily into the manifestations of the other. And the concept of total war is something we would all do well to think about a little in these troubled times. This is a relatively new concept, in Western civilization at any rate. It did not really appear on the scene until World War I. It characterized both of these great world wars, and both of them—as I have pointed out—were followed by great instability and disillusionment. But it is not only a question now of the desirability of this concept; it is a question of its feasibility. Actually, I wonder whether even in the past total victory was not really an illusion from the standpoint of the victors. In a sense, there is no total victory short of genocide, unless it be a victory over the minds of men. But the total military victories are rarely victories over the minds of men. And we now face the fact that it is very questionable whether in a new global conflict there could ever be any such thing as total *military* victory. I personally do not believe that there could. There might be a great weakening of the armed forces of one side or another, but I think it out of the question that there should be such a thing as a general and formal submission of the national will on either side. The attempt to achieve this unattainable goal, however, could wreak upon civilization another set of injuries fully as serious as those caused by World War I or World War II, and I leave it to you to answer the question as to how civilization could survive them.

It was asserted not long ago by a prominent American that "war's very object is victory" and that "in war there can be no substitute for victory." Perhaps the confusion here lies in what is meant by the term "victory." Perhaps the term is actually misplaced. Perhaps there can be such a thing as "victory" in a battle, whereas in war there can be only the achievement or nonachievement of your objectives. In the old days, wartime objectives were generally limited and practical ones, and it was common to measure the success of your military operations by the extent to which they brought you closer to your objectives. But where your objectives are moral and ideological ones and run to changing the attitudes and traditions of an entire people or the personality of a regime, then victory is probably something not to be achieved entirely by military means or indeed in any short space of time at all; and perhaps that is the source of our confusion.

In any case, I am frank to say that I think there is no more dangerous delusion, none that has done us a greater disservice in the past or that threatens to do us a greater disservice in the future, than the concept of total victory. And I fear that it springs in large measure from the basic faults in the approach to international affairs which I have been discussing here. If we are to get away from it, this will not mean that we shall have to abandon our respect for international law, or our hopes for its future usefulness as the gentle civilizer of events which I mentioned in one of the earlier lectures. Nor will it mean that we have to go in for anything that can properly be termed "appeasement"—if one may use a word so cheapened and deflated by the abuse to which it has been recently subjected. But it will mean the emergence of a new attitude among us toward many things outside our borders that are irritating and unpleasant today —an attitude more like that of the doctor toward those physical phenomena in the human body that are neither pleasing nor fortunate—an attitude of detachment and soberness and readiness to reserve judgment. It will mean that we will have the modesty to admit that our own national interest is all that we are really capable of knowing and understanding—and the courage to recognize that if our purposes and undertakings here at home are decent ones, unsullied by arrogance or hostility toward other people or delusions of superiority, then the pursuit of our national interest can never fail to be conducive to a better world. This concept is less ambitious and less inviting in its immediate prospects than those to which we have so often inclined, and less pleasing to our image of ourselves. To many it may seem to smack of cynicism and reaction. I cannot share these doubts. Whatever is realistic in concept, and founded in an endeavor to see both ourselves and others as we really are, cannot be illiberal.

SELECTION 4

OUR NATIONAL PURPOSE*

ADLAI E. STEVENSON

ADLAI E. STEVENSON *is the Permanent Representative of the United States to the United Nations. He held several posts in the U.S. Government during the 1940's and was Governor of Illinois, 1949-1953. He was Democratic Presidential candidate in 1952 and 1956. He is the author of* Call To Greatness *(1954) and* The New America *(1957). The article reprinted below was one of a series authored by prominent Americans for* Life *in 1960.*

It is not too difficult, I think, to state the classic goals and purposes of American society. We probably cannot improve on the definition offered by our Founding Fathers: "to form a more perfect Union, establish Justice, insure domestic Tranquility, provide for the common defence, promote the general Welfare, and secure the Blessings of Liberty." Add Tom Paine's words—"My country is the world" —to give our goals universal application, and we have distilled the essence out of all the rhetoric about the freedom and the democratic self-government for which we proudly stand.

But the difficulty is that aims in the abstract mean little. A society is measured by what it does, and no Fourth of July oratory will make its purposes great if in fact they are small, or change them into a moving element in the world's passionate dialogue of destiny if they are meager and private and unconcerned.

We have therefore to look at our noble purpose of freedom— and surely no one would deny that it is the organizing principle of American life—in terms of the concrete, practical content which Americans give to the concept. As one might expect in a free so-

* From *Life* Magazine, Vol. 48 (May, 1960), pp. 87-102. Copr. 1960 Time Inc.

ciety, we find at once that freedom itself has many meanings and has implied different things to different people at different times in our national life. In fact one can observe something of a rhythm in the nation's mood, a swing from one definition of freedom almost to its opposite, recurring regularly throughout the almost 200 years of our independent history.

The first mood reflects the *private* aspect of freedom—the right of men to choose their own ideas and pursuits, to be free from the arbitrary interventions of government, to "do what they like with their own." Many early immigrants escaped the arbitrary restraints of governments in Europe and came to set their money and their wits to work in the new climate of freedom. This sense of the link between "freedom" and private business has indeed been so strong that at some periods they have been virtually equated, as when Calvin Coolidge thus defined the American purpose: "The business of America is business."

But equally freedom has had its *public* aspect as the organizing principle of a new kind of society. In the Declaration of Independence, the basic charter of the modern world, the picture is of a great civic order in which governments, deriving their authority from the consent of the governed, help to secure the inalienable preconditions of the good life: equality before the law and in human respect, life, liberty and, most precious yet intangible of rights, the pursuit of happiness. This positive vision of society in which public authority plays its essential part in bettering the lot of all citizens was as inherent as freedom itself in the vision of our founders.

There is no inevitable contradiction between these public and private aspects of American society. Indeed, they are the essential poles of energy in a vigorous social order. Without individual decision and inventiveness, without widely dispersed centers of authority and responsibility, the social order grows rigid and centralized. Spontaneity withers before the killing frost of public conformity. Individual citizens with all their varied relationships—as parents, neighbors, churchgoers, workers, businessmen—are reduced to the single loyalties of party and state. In this century we are not likely to underestimate that danger. We have seen free societies destroyed in this way by totalitarians of both the right and the left.

Yet the pursuit of private interest and well-being does not, as the 18th Century sometimes naively believed, automatically add up to the well-being of all. The strong pursuit of *my* interest can override the vital interests of others, if nature, health, energy and property have weighted the odds in my favor. Social evils pile up when little more than unchecked private interest determines the pattern of society.

At best, the result is a "pressure group" state in which each organized group jostles for its own interests at the expense of the weak, the isolated or the unorganized. At worst, the power and influence of the few can violate the fundamental rights and decencies of the many, as they did in the long survival of human slavery and in the long resistance of industry to child labor laws and minimum wages. In our own prosperous days a new possibility has arisen: that the many can smugly overlook the squalor and misery of the few and tolerate, in the midst of unparalleled plenty, ugly slums, rural destitution and second-class citizenship.

It is the often mediocre and sometimes intolerable consequences of unchecked private interest that have led to the reassertion, at regular intervals in American history, of the primacy of public good. Sometimes the swing occurs because evil has become so obtrusive that only vigorous public action can check it in time. The conviction that the spread of slavery endangered the Union itself helped precipitate the Civil War. The demoralization of the entire economy after 1929 led to the experiments and reforms of Roosevelt's New Deal.

Sometimes the swing seems to occur in response to subtler promptings. Early in this century, for instance, under Theodore Roosevelt and Woodrow Wilson, it was not imminent social collapse but disgust at the materialism which was devouring America that aroused people once more to demand the restatement of America's public purposes and a new vision of the common good.

Whatever the reasons for America's recurrent swing in emphasis from private interest to public responsibility, it has always had a significant *external* consequence. It has aroused both in America and in the world at large the sense that the American experiment has significance far beyond its own frontiers and is in some measure a portent for all mankind.

Today I don't suppose anyone will deny that mankind is in acute need of a convincing working model of a free society. Never in human history has there been an epoch of such profound and sudden social upheaval on so universal a scale. Never has the working model of tyranny made such claims for its own effectiveness;

never has monolithic discipline attacked so savagely what it calls the pretentions of the free way of life. The whole of human society has become plastic and malleable in the flames of social revolution. Thus there has never been a time when the public aspect of American liberty as the organizing principle of a great social order has needed to be more studied and stressed.

But what do we find? Never before in my lifetime—not even in the days of Harding and Coolidge—has the mystique of privacy seemed to me so pervasive. The face which we present to the world—especially through our mass circulation media—is the face of the individual or the family as a high consumption unit with minimal social responsibilities—father happily drinking his favorite beer, mother dreamily fondling soft garments newly rinsed in a wonderful new detergent, the children gaily calling from the barbecue pit for a famous sauce for their steak.

No doubt many of the world's peoples want and mean to get more of this. But it is not *all* they want, and they have to look hard to find the balancing picture of America's wider purposes and to learn that high private consumption is not our ultimate aim of life, nor our answer to all man's evils and disorders in a time of breath-taking social change. For all these good "things" do not solve the problems of urban decay and congestion. Behind the shining child in the advertisement lurks the juvenile delinquent in the slum. Nor does high consumption guarantee to America's children the teachers or the schools that should be their birthright. It does nothing to end the shame of racial discrimination. It does not counter the exorbitant cost of maintaining health, nor conserve the nation's precious reserves of land and water and wilderness.

The contrast between private opulence and public squalor on most of our panorama is now too obvious to be denied. Yet we still spend per capita almost as much on advertising to multiply the private wants of our people as we do on education to enable them to seek a fuller, wiser and more satisfying civic existence. Nor is this imbalance simply a matter of drift and the unmeant consequence of our fabulous new opportunities for wealth creation. It is in real measure the result of deliberate government policy. Except for defense, American public expenditure today is proportionately lower than it was in 1939. And while we raise a cheer at the fact that we are spending less, let us also remember that this means a relative decline in support for such basic needs as schooling, research, health, small-income housing, urban renewal, and all forms of public services—local, state and federal—at a time when there has been steadily more income to spend on every private want, or unwant.

With the supermarket as our temple and the singing commercial as our litany, are we likely to fire the world with an irresistible vision of America's exalted purposes and inspiring way of life?

Even where public spending has been high—for defense and economic aid—our performance has been more defensive than indicative of freedom's positive purposes. We have stressed so much our aim of stopping Communism for our own security that self-interest has often contaminated our generous aid programs. And even in the vital field of military security, the Administration's concern for the citizen as a private consumer, rather than as a mature responsible American who will accept the unpleasant facts about his country's safety, leaves one with the lurking suspicion that budgetary considerations, rather than the stark needs of strategy, are determining our defense effort.

In short, at a time of universal social upheaval and challenge, our vision of our own society seems to be of limited social significance. An air of disengagement and disinterest hangs over the most powerful and affluent society the world has ever known. Neither the turbulence of the world abroad nor the fatness and flatness of the world at home is moving us to more vital effort. We seem becalmed in a season of storm, drifting through a century of mighty dreams and great achievements. As an American I am disturbed.

It is arguable that after the shocks and rigors of the 1930s and '40s, we as a nation needed a period of relaxation—though I would note that the Russians and the Chinese after far greater shocks have had no opportunity for a cozy nap. Now, however, we have had our rest, and I sense the stirring of a new vitality, possibly the beginning of that traditional swing of the political pendulum away from private pursuits to a concern for the nation's broader purposes.

I am persuaded that he who speaks clearly to the Americans of their social responsibilities, as well as their private wants, will now command a more attentive hearing. I believe the old idea of America and its government as a positive instrument for the common weal is being restored once again after all the cheap sarcasm about "bureaucracy" and "creeping socialism." And if a change of mood and attitude toward our public needs and institutions is in fact on the way, I do not think there can be much question about the fields in which the new sense of responsibility must quickly go to work.

At home we must ask ourselves again what *quality* of life we want, both public and private, as citizens of this great republic. Education and the arts are the starting point, for it is only here that the citizens of tomorrow can learn to demand and live a fuller life. A respect for excellence and a sense of discipline in the attainment of knowledge are virtues not just because the Russians pioneered the space age and photographed the other side of the moon, but because the new society that technology is building demands a grasp and competence among the mass of citizens undreamed of in earlier civilizations.

By education and the arts we mean something more than better school buildings, higher teachers' salaries, and more scholarships for the intelligent. We mean a reorientation of our ideals and tastes, the strenuous stretching of mental and artistic talent, the exaltation of excellence above social approval, and of mental achievement above quick material success. We mean, in short, new standards of respect and reward for intellect and culture. And we mean more stable financing for basic research, more concern for advancing knowledge for its own sake. We mean cooperation with other communities of scholars and creative thinkers, as in the International Geophysical Year, in order that our pursuit of truth may be an adventure we share with all mankind. And we mean that the pursuit of truth in itself is the highest activity of man.

Here, then in all its ramifications of expense, of standards, content and opportunity, is a top priority for a great new America and a national purpose few would dispute.

I would include not far below a reconsideration of our urban life. We are adding a city the size of Philadelphia to our population every year. From every large urban center the suburbs spread out and out, without shape or grace or any centered form of civic life. Many are so built that they are the slums of tomorrow. Meanwhile town centers decay, racial divisions destroy harmony, commuters jam the city approaches and a strange, half life of divided families and Sunday fathers is growing up. If we accept both the fact of our rapid growth in population and the fact that most people will live in cities, we can begin a serious attack upon our congested, ugly, inconvenient metropolitan sprawl. We can create the preconditions of a good urban life that could become a new model for an urbanizing world.

Restoration of compassion is a clumsy way to describe another great embracing national purpose. In the past, evils and miseries have been the driving force of majority discontent. But now, for the first time in history, the engine of social progress has run out of the fuel of discontent. We have therefore to mobilize our imagination, our personal sense of indignation, if we are to act on the conviction that gross poverty, curable illness, racial indignity, mental disease and suffering in old age are a disgrace amidst the surrounding luxuries, privileges and indulgence of such a wealthy society as ours.

And here our top priorities must reach beyond our shores. For it is not chiefly in America or in the fortunate North Atlantic basin that the world's miseries are to be found. On the contrary, we confidently predict a doubling and tripling of our high living standards. But in Asia, Africa and Latin America live scores of millions who, on present forecasts, may have no such expectations. This disparity in living standards between the rich and the poor is as great a threat to peace as the arms race, and narrowing the gap is as imperative as arms control.

Our aid programs should therefore be designed not primarily to counter Communism—though they will do this too—but to create conditions of self-respect and self-sustaining growth in economies still behind the threshold of modernization. The needs are so staggering that to achieve this will demand not only the greatest intelligence, perseverence and financial enterprise, private and public, but also a much broader cooperation and joint effort with other advanced nations. If we accept this as fundamental American foreign policy, not on a year-to-year basis but for the next critical generation, we shall develop the perspective and staying power to reach real solutions, not doles, hand-outs, bad debts—and dislike.

And in doing so, we shall do more than set the processes of modernization in healthy motion. I believe that this is the chief way open to us to extend our vision of "a more perfect Union" to all mankind. It is a commonplace that in a world made one by science and the atom the old national boundaries are dissolving, the old landmarks vanishing. We can't have privacy and the hydrogen bomb too. A workable human society has to be fashioned and we must start where we can—by setting up the institutions of a

common economic life, by using our wealth and wisdom to spark
the growth of production in poorer lands, by working together with
like-minded powers to establish the permanent patterns of a workable world economy. In this way we can hope to establish one of
the two main preconditions of peaceful human society—economic
solidarity and mutual help.

The other precondition of peace—and this, of all priorities, is
our highest—is our unwavering search for peace under law which,
in our present context, means controlled and supervised disarmament. Only a disarmed world offers us security worth the name any
longer.

I do not believe, even now, that the world accepts the idea
that genuine disarmament is America's primary, public purpose.
We talk of peace and our devotion to it. But there is far more hard,
unremitting effort in the task than speeches or protestations or
journeys—however distant. What seems to be lacking is sincere and
sustained dedication to this goal and unwearying pursuit by our
highest officers, both military and civilian. There is a widespread
impression that the United States has been "dragging its feet."

I believe that the American people are prepared to face the
cost, the rigors, the efforts and the challenge which are involved in
recovering the public image of a great America. The cost in physical terms—in hard work, in discipline, in more taxes if need be—
is hard to estimate precisely. Any arms control would release resources. Our growing gross national product will certainly provide
wider margins out of which vital public expenditures could be met.
But if the cost is higher than our present level of public spending,
I frankly believe that education and health for our children, dignity and beauty in our civic lives, and security and well-being in
the world at large are more important than the "things" which
might otherwise have priority.

But still more important is America's need to face squarely the
facts about its situation. If freedom is really the organizing principle of our society, then we cannot forget that it is not illusion,
propaganda and sedatives, but truth and truth alone, that makes us
free. Under the influence of the politics of sedation and the techniques of salesmanship I believe that in recent years self-deceit has
slackened our grip on reality. We have tended to skirt the difficult
truth and accept the easy half-truth. Perhaps it is always that way. As
the old humorist Josh Billings used to say: "As scarce as truth is, the

supply has always been in excess of the demand."

But we know from our own lives that reality entails hard choices and disappointments: that it measures real achievement not in terms of luck but in terms of difficulties overcome. I don't believe our national life can follow any other pattern.

No preordained destiny decrees that America shall have all the breaks and soft options. Neither greatness nor even freedom lies that way. So we must surely return to the reality principle, to the bracing, invigorating, upland climate of truth itself. I think we are ready now to move forward into the rigors and glories of the new decade with open eyes, eager step and firm purposes worthy of our great past.

SELECTION 5

FOREIGN POLICY: THE REALISM OF IDEALISM*

THOMAS I. COOK and MALCOLM MOOS

THOMAS I. COOK *is Professor of Political Science at Johns Hopkins University. He has taught at Columbia University, the University of California (Los Angeles), the University of Washington, and the University of California (Berkeley), and has lectured in many other colleges and universities. His best known book is* Power through Purpose *(1954).*

MACOLM MOOS *taught political science at the University of Wyoming and at Johns Hopkins University (1942-1957). He became a White House Consultant in 1957 and was Administrative Assistant to President Eisenhower, 1958-1960. He is the author of* Politics, Presidents and Coattails *(1952) and numerous other books and articles.*

World politics today is admittedly bipolar, and it seems destined to remain so within the foreseeable future. Beset by its sustained tension, Americans have been led to debate, sometimes acrimoniously, the proper foundations, scope, and content of an effective foreign policy. Since presumably the central theme and central purpose of this debate is the definition of what constitutes the American national interest, the first objective is to define the idea of national interest. Thereafter it is necessary to draw proper de-

* Reprinted from *American Political Science Review,* Vol. 46 (1952), pp. 343-356.

ductions relevant to the total world situation, and in turn to apply these deductions as policy to the forces there at work. These forces —political, economic, ideological, and military—in their interconnectedness collectively constitute the raw materials for assessment, judgment, planning, and action in our policy-making.

Resultant differences of opinion therefore can take place at different levels. Initially there are vastly divergent concepts of the characteristics of a nation, of the role of nations in the world, and of the nature of interests proper to a nation. The scope of these divergencies is often hidden by our tendency to find in the term "national interest" connotations of particularism, of exclusiveness, of the nation as against, or superior to, the rest of the world. Yet, save for a few extremists, even the advocates of world government base their position on a theory which takes account of, although it does not give primacy to, the interests of the American nation itself.

Even if agreement on the meaning of national interest is reached, views as to what constitute suitable means for its furtherance can differ greatly. The issues here, manifestly, turn on the logical consonance of means and ends, and on the suitability, both practical and ethical, of means and ends. A concept of national interest may be agreed upon as sound and adequate; but two questions still remain: will suggested means prove efficacious, and will they, even if efficacious, clearly or subtly corrupt professed ideals? Indeed, in a world of fundamental conflict, these questions together may raise in acute form the further question whether it is possible to be at once effective and uncorrupted. The answering of such queries necessitates an analysis of the objectives and instruments of opposing interests. It necessitates an examination of the aspirations and the possible developments of peoples to be influenced and won. It necessitates exploration of the grounds on which and the means by which they may be influenced and won. It necessitates careful consideration of the consonance of those grounds and means with possible and actual concepts of American interests.

At all points in any reexamination of national interest, however, it is essential to avoid a tendency to be bewitched by neatly compacted arguments that either laud altruism and moral abstractions uncritically or defile the idea of national interest as the motivating basis of foreign policy.

I. PERSONS AND NATIONS

Foreign policies are not built upon abstractions, remarked Charles Evans Hughes, "but are the result of practical conceptions of national interest arising out of some immediate exigency or standing out vividly in historical perspective." That nations, like persons, ought to pursue their several real self-interests, and that they will pursue their supposed self-interests, may be taken for granted. As with persons, so with nations, disagreements arise when the attempt is made to define the nature of the self and to deduce consequent interests. Definition of the nation is especially difficult since, unlike the individual self, it is not immediately experienced. Indeed, one major source of disagreement arises from the very concept of a national self. Some persons may and do treat the nation as a real and ultimate being rather than as a continuing organization of the institutions of life. But quite apart from the resultant violence done to individuals, including those who hold this misconception, there results a great oversimplification of the problem. For the major difficulty of properly discovering national interest arises from the fact that it is at once a product and a directional molding of particular interests, of persons and of groups.

For the person, the concept of the self is both immediate and ultimate. The concept of the nation, on the other hand, is derivative and instrumental, even though any individual's concept of his nation and of his relation to it may mold him and constitute part of the framework of his own self. Through inner inconsistencies and conflicts, and even more by reason of unexamined habit, the individual may pursue his interests inadequately. He may even act without regard to, or in conflict with, consciously held ideals of his self, just as he may, through ignorance or misinformation, reasonably pursue sound interests of the self in a manner which is inappropriate from the viewpoint of actual success. But in the case of the nation, with its everlasting interplay of particular interests, of groups and persons ever-changing both in their activities and objectives and in their importance and power within the whole, the very formulation of a coherent view of national purpose and interest becomes inordinately difficult. The never-fixed pattern of these cross-cutting interests makes extraordinarily complicated the sustained pursuit of any national interest that is formulated, especially when the nation is vast, democratic, and pluralistic. The changing weight of interests and the interplay through them of changing concepts of interest, some at one moment dominant and at another recessive, manifestly make a hazardous task of reconciling prevalent views of what constitutes national interest with any reasoned theory of that interest. Similarly, even if the prevalent concept of any moment seems also to be a rational one, there is no guarantee that it will remain central over any significant time span. Thus the measure of national self-interest, as Ortega y Gasset observed of the true meaning of any word or phrase, lies not in the dictionary: "It is in the instant."

It is, indeed these difficulties, reflected in fluid and changing policy, in an absence of neatly coherent continuity and of the possibility of easily relating tendencies of the moment to a systematic pattern, that have led so many commentators to deplore the seeming incoherence of American foreign policy, and even to deny that the United States has possessed anything worthy of the name of policy. Yet such elasticity and variability may well be a reflection of the vitality of our democratic society, and of the effectiveness of government in reflecting the living forces at work therein. The twin drawbacks of our unpredictability to others, who may in time find us even more perfidious than Albion of yore, and of our own lack of a clear sense of where we stand and what we stand for, are inescapable. Yet the gains may well outweigh the losses. In any event, the situation would appear to be a necessary corollary of the democratic way of life.

Certainly it is worth noting that one of the main appeals of modern dictatorships has been their claim to eliminate conflicting concepts of interest by defining one alone as the compelling interest of the nation and attempting to give a permanent ascendancy to it. Dictators have invariably argued that the interest so defined is the full embodiment of, or the nearest practical approach to, what the national interest genuinely is. But their definition has rarely been based on reasoned analysis or on the assumption that human beings are rational, nor has it reflected the view that men ought to endeavor to achieve rationality in their collective behaviors. Observation of the life, and in certain cases the death, of dictatorships makes clear that such attempted singleness of definition of interests has not led to a root consistency in practice, even when it has created useful myths for the genesis and maintenance of an illusion of consistency. Moreover, insofar as the singleness of interest has been consistently pursued, it has rarely led to the predicted results, to the actual achievement of the stated national interest. Indeed, there is reason to question whether such definition, however great the predictability it allows to others, really makes the lasting conduct of foreign policy more successful, although it may simplify diplomacy. When adaptations are actually made while the nature of the controlling interest is professed to remain unchanged, the consequence may well be outrage to others. Their reaction can then prove deleterious from the point of view of the actual pursuit and attainment of the nation's own professed objectives.

In any event, the theory and practice of a democratic society and culture are incompatible with an interpretation of the nation which pursues a super-interest according to which the interests of groups and persons are defined and determined, rather than an interest which is molded and shaped by the more finite interests. The national interest is at most a continuous and quasi-organic outcome and synthesis of an interplay of forces, in which varied concepts of national role and function and of the relationship of particular interests to the nation are an inherent part. The nation is an instrument for persons who, amidst their vast diversity, share some common heritage and some general aspirations which can be pursued by collective action. A national interest, it is true, is not merely a sum of individual interests, which, in part by very reason of their divergencies, cannot be added or averaged. Rather, it is in large measure a set of some conditions which have to be furthered and of which some must be preserved by appropriate action. The reason for compacting the national interest to a meaningful definition is to insure as far as possible that there may be some predictability in change within an order so oriented as to give large degrees of satisfaction to major elements in the society. Thus, the concept of a national interest must commemorate and clarify the continuity of a people at the same time that it identifies for persons generally a promise and an effective program for their continued pursuit of betterment.

Since the political order of the nation, unlike the entity of a person, is an instrument, the national interest is also derivative. So to state is the reverse of denying that the maintenance and functioning of the nation is a fundamental condition for the pursuit of more ultimate personal interests, as it is a limiting or guiding factor in their pursuit. But its derivative character does suggest one limitation on a concept of national interest which is not a part of the loosely analogous concept of a personal interest. No nation could exist without persons, since society is composed of persons; nevertheless, any particular person may properly decide, by reason of the ethical principles which give his life meaning and purpose, to sacrifice his life in the service of others. He may do so especially when specific conditions he confronts present the alternative of death or corruption. The nation, on the other hand, just because it is instrumental, and despite the fact that a society not composed of nations is conceivable, has to maintain itself at least as long as, and insofar as, its structure, organization, and functioning are conditions of the development and fulfillment of the persons, or of the greater part of the persons, composing it. The nation cannot with propriety seek its own elimination. Certainly it cannot pursue a policy calculated to bring about the elimination of all persons, or of the great majority of persons, embraced within it; its interest can never be collective suicide or martyrdom in the name of service to an ideal principle. Because it serves shared interests and properly aims to promote conditions for the better realization of personal interest beyond its own direct creation, purview, or control, its continued maintenance and function is by definition needful.

This reasoning is no argument against all risk-taking by the nation. The collectivity which is the nation may well find that a willingness to risk, though not to court, destruction, is a necessary condition for the fulfillment of persons and groups within it, or at the very least for the prevention of frustration of their purposes, under world conditions not of its own exclusive creation. But the nation, as a political institution with a particular set of functional obligations, has to be operated on the presumption of collective permanence. There is a real interest, on the part both of the nation's own people and of humanity generally, in the development of the social and cultural order which the nation serves. Particular national policies may diminish the interest of other nations in its welfare, and may even lead them to desire the destruction of the existing nation-state. Nevertheless, the enrichment of human culture and the development of humanity make preservation of its component peoples lastingly desirable. Indeed, one criterion of national policy and one basis for evaluating concepts of national interest is the degree to which they do or do not give justification of a rational kind to a desire on the part of others to destroy the existing nation-state. A concept of national interest in any way incompatible with the peaceful existence of the nation which holds it, certainly confronts an initial presumption against its adequacy and correctness. Similarly, and *a fortiori,* a concept of national interest which denies the right of other nations to exist naturally promotes hostility to the particular nation espousing it, to a point where others are prepared to seek and pursue not only the destruction of the existing government, but even the elimination of the nation's people. Such a concept is, on its very face, untenable.

The argument that national self-interest cannot properly lead to a deliberate search for collective suicide must not, therefore, be taken to imply that the nation's interest is the sole and exclusive welfare of its own people regardless of, or in opposition to, that of others. Nor does it imply either the nation's duty to maintain an exclusive juristic sovereignty as traditionally conceived or, yet again, its refusal to accept limitations, by agreement or law, which prohibit purely unilateral action. The nation's acceptance of limitations depends on the relation of prevalent conditions to the furtherance of present and anticipated purposes of its own people as at once involved in humanity, yet distinct, or distinguishable by attitude and interest, from other organized parts thereof. In this context practical decision involves assessment of the current state of the arts and sciences, of technology and intercommunications, and of realizable potentials for a broadened order, capable of satisfying both the people of the particular nation and others simultaneously.

The nation is, in short, a lasting, yet ever-changing thing—"the cup of the community," as Madariaga aptly identifies it. It is not a static bundle of exclusive interests. It is not a real being. It does not exist in a vacuum. Its role and function, its powers and its limitations, are not permanent and unchanging, but adaptive and purposive. It is not to be sacrified in the service of supposed moral ends which, when so defined as to exclude consideration of its own special interests and conditions, are clearly false. Yet it is no insular, narrowing order whose members can fulfill their purposes by an exclusive selfishness. Until a world state which embraces all persons is achieved—when the problem disappears—the nation cannot be unconcerned with the aspirations and the welfare of other peoples. If, however, under existing conditions it is thus unconcerned, it is ultimately unconcerned with its own well-being also.

II. UTILIZING POWER

Much of the difficulty both in defining and in implementing the idea of the national self-interest has arisen from ambiguities in the concept of power. Since today power is usually, though not uniformly, accepted as the very substance, the key idea and concern, of politics, the difficulty tends to grow rather than decrease. In discussions of the international or world order, confusion has been particularly great. For there "power politics," a facile but largely meaningless phrase with overtones of healthy realism or sinister immoralism, has rather generally been taken to denote the essence of the matter, as well as in some mysterious way to provide a key to the analysis and solution of all problems.

The generation, the husbanding, and the application of power are indeed central to politics. They are, what is more, vital to the furthering of most social interests and to the achievement of most human purposes, provided that power be defined in a sufficiently broad way. Because of the instrumental and external nature of political action, however, the creation, preservation, and application of power to achieve the optimum of human political purposes, necessitate a degree of force and constraint over persons. Such force and constraint are not equally necessary to other forms of human influence, where the type of accomplishment desired and the relevant means do not involve the same externality and impersonality. In some institutions, such as the family, appeal is to more tender emotions not characteristic of, or appropriate to, the public order. These emotions may constitute an effective leverage which, though broadly definable as power, is certainly not, either initially or ultimately, force. In other situations appeal can be made to reason and argument; in yet others to common religious belief and consequent duty. In all of them force is rarely successful. It is certainly not identical with power. Indeed, its use or attempted use, as for instance in love, often perverts, corrupts, and ultimately destroys the motivating emotion itself. Force rarely creates, in the sense of evoking willing positive action. But it can prevent action, as it can destroy actors. As a deterrent from undesired action, force may, especially when suitably supplemented by more positive elements of power such as consent, create a base for the effective use and direction of power.

Politics, then, does mean power generated and used, with force and constraint as techniques to channelize and limit activities, although consent is needed to make the power effective by leading to the positive fruition of policy and eliminating friction. Certainly it would be idiotic in internal or international affairs to talk of power-less politics. The issues are always how to generate and to use power; what is the interest which power is to serve; what conception of interest, duly accepted, will be most effective as a generator of power;

and, especially in the international field, what is the relation of force and persuasion to the diminution of conflict and the creation of harmony.

The international order is composed of many powers which differ in their particular interests, yet whose members all share common humanity. Although particular national policies are in competition here, the competition is not simply a struggle between the particular powers at the moment involved in a specific issue. It is also directed toward getting the allegiance or support of third parties, singly or in groups. Since these also have their interests and aspirations which are supported by various degrees of will and strength, power has a limited, though not precisely defined, force at its command. In the resultant competition, the relative effectiveness of any two opposed parties in winning the support of a third, prior to war and short of conquest, is the outcome of a parallelogram of force and principle.

The probable rationale of the otherwise misleading and confusing term "power politics" arises from an essential difference between internal and international politics. In the internal sphere the political institution known as the state is accepted at once as the locus of contention between interest groups and persons and as the necessary order for their better fulfillment. Struggles can normally be solved by essentially diplomatic means, with an accepted enforcement agency endowed with force as a reserve in the background. Such solutions are possible just because of acknowledged common purpose and shared interest. In the world order, however, common purpose is often unrecognized and is rarely dominant, despite acknowledgements of an ultimate common humanity. Similarly, organs of settlement and enforcement of the rules of a common order, when adjustment by politic compromise fails, are rudimentary or nonexistent.

III. NATIONAL SELF-INTEREST OR SHANGRI-LA ISOLATIONISM?

In the world order, more or less coherent systems of national interests and strategies of interest-promotion come into contact and conflict. Under modern conditions of industrialism and intercommunciation, such contact and conflict are the inescapable consequences of nationhood and the possession of national interests. The resultant competitive sharing renders isolation and isolationism meaningless. It would be impossible for the professed isolationist to maintain his stand consistently with the preservation of the totality of his interest, even if other nations should be willing to allow any one nation to enjoy and remain in a position of isolation, which they surely are not. It is also true that divergent concepts of national interests, based on particular traditions and locations, possess a generative power, of which force is indeed one instrument. But for the effective and continued pursuit of interests, including above all lasting material and spiritual satisfactions at home, force alone is, as political thinkers have known for centuries, an instrument both inadequate and inappropriate. It is necessary in the national interest of any nation, to generate power as influence on, and persuasion of, other nations. Such power may be generated bilaterally, and even multilaterally to a certain point, by appeal to common or complementing selfishness. But ultimately it has to rest on a larger common appeal, directed to universal interests, even though these are distorted by the particular immediacies of the power making the appeal and of the power or powers to whom it is made. Such distortion unfortunately gives aid and comfort to proponents of power politics, as it does more generally to those who argue that in the conduct of international relations it is sufficient to rely on the immediate and narrowed interests of neighbors and temporary allies, supported by military preparedness. Perhaps, to put it more fundamentally, this distortion tends to disguise, if not to hide completely, the deeper common principles which nations in truth share and which give meaning to their very immediate self-interests. Undoubtedly, the essential moral weakness of the international order is the absence of an impartial judge and interpreter of claims to rights, presenting a situation analogous to Locke's state of nature. Such a lack is doubly evil: it prevents genuine adjudication of disputes, and it hides the reality of those common rights which are in truth shared interests to be interpreted.

In their policy-making, individual nations may recognize the impossibility, or at the very least the painful inadequacy, of an escapist isolationism as the means to pursue their own concepts of national well-being. As an alternative they may elect, in both the formulation and implementation of policy, to deny the very right to exist of some or of all other nations. They may avowedly or by implication deny the right to treatment as human beings of persons composing other nations. So to do is, of course, to rely on force alone, in the sense of martial might. It is to reject any possible common principle of appeal based on sharing, as it is to forego any freely won allegiance and support. The immediate objective may be the subordination of others as slaves, rather than their total extermination. Yet the probable consequence of any such unreal, "pure" policy is either the elimination of all other nations or, as we have shown above, the destruction as a power of the nation which relies upon it. As C. J. Friedrich has shown in another context, consent and constraint are functionally related in the creation and use of power. The logic of force only is no consent. Its consequence, because it cannot create power based on the sympathy or cooperation of others, is the need to eliminate. The particular nation which takes such a view necessarily proclaims itself, by prideful ambition, the sole state in the world. It rejects international politics; it rejects the possibility of creating and using power in an international order to pursue its real, but limited interests.

IV. THE HARMONIZATION OF NATIONAL SELF-INTERESTS

The actual course of international politics is necessarily mixed. Where one party possesses force and is able to apply it effectively, and the second party is aware of such possession and willingness, the latter, assuming it to be the weaker, will normally redefine its own interest in the light of the actual alternatives confronting it. Such redefinition will relate concepts of ideal national interests, including potentials for their realization, with a view of what constitutes a minimally tolerable collective life. The last of these in turn defines with some precision the limits of policy for the superior power. For, especially under modern conditions, the collective resistance of war, as well as resistance movements to an occupying conqueror, will to a greater or lesser extent frustrate the latter's objectives insofar as they involved the exploitation through oppression, rather than the extermination, of the conquered. Even passive resistance and sabotage may seriously limit the effectiveness of exploitation by a conqueror. This is a consideration which, at the appropriate point in time, must be taken into account when the dominant power defines its own national interest and determines the techniques appropriate to its furtherance.

The preceding analysis, based on the postulate of two unequal powers, involves a great and misleading oversimplification. For a weaker power, calculations of national interests usually present alternatives of alliance with or submission to different major powers. To these may be added opportunities for collective alliances of many minor powers, in resistance to, and to maintain independence from, both or all major powers. Here decision involves calculation of the potential realization of ideals of national interest, or at least of the avoidance of extreme frustration of such ideals. The search is for the optimum way of national life in relation to the force generated, or capable of generation, in the relevant time span.

It is, of course, still possible that a major power might conceive of total conquest over other peoples as a worthwhile and possible undertaking. However, at the least such a totally exclusive viewpoint diminishes potential power. Given the nature of modern weapons and any conceivable balance of available forces under present circumstances, such a policy would probably be self-defeating. It would lead, not to the exclusive domination and population by one people or race of the whole habitable globe, but to the destruction in large part of both aggressor and victim. It might even render major areas of the civilized world uninhabitable for a considerable period.

In any event, the present-day bipolar world does not present this issue; nor, whatever the possible indictments of Soviet totalitarianism, does it warrant the conclusion that Russia maintains this view of national interest. The two major parties in the conflict do indeed have national interests in the short term incompatible with one another. No doubt, too, the Soviet Union desires both to expand and, in the present circumstances, to dominate. Yet each side professes, and uses as a major implement of power, a philosophy which claims universality. Each professes to serve not only its own peculiar interests but the interests of all people, of humanity generally.

A nation's possession of armed might may help persuade other nations to accept a particular and biased interpretation of more universal insights. It may be a means to prevent dissent or backsliding once the viewpoint is accepted. Similarly, it may be a tool to prevent rejection of or escape from domination, by reason of disappointment, once control is achieved, whether by consent or by conquest. But it is a more vital point that the sponsorship by a major power of a moral appeal based on universalism, though addressed to specific national interests and needs, today is urgently required for the very generation of power. The furtherance of particular national interests necessitates their identification with the interests of other peoples, as the latter does in fact conceive them, or can be persuaded to conceive and formulate them. The first and chief weapon of national interest, in time as in effect, is then ideas, which are essentially moral doctrines. Effectively to pursue its own interests, the nation has to profess to be universal in interest, and to accept the equality of persons and peoples. Indeed, the utilization of a national interest concept based upon a moral appeal as the firmament of our foreign policy, holds out the greatest promise for meeting the challenge of events that lie ahead.

One testimony to truth of this thesis is the common use by East and West of the term "democracy." The significance of its use is not lessened by differences in interpretation. Nor is it diminished by possible insincerity in its actual utilization or, where influence or control would permit, in implementation, by one of the parties. In a world where isolation seems impractical and extermination of all peoples save one improbable, even were it desired, the process of furthering national interests necessitates limited identification, appeals to shared purposes, and the generation of power primarily through ideas essentially moral in character. Force, which is but a portion of power, not its prime creator, is indeed relevant as pressure, the utilization of which reflects a lack of an impartial judge under an established law; yet force corrupts the purity and perverts the use of moral ideas. It is finally these ideas—of equality, of sharing, and of liberty, common to the great world religions and philosophies, including Marxism itself—which play a vital role in international politics.

Idealism, far from being utopian and destructive of realistic foreign policy, is basic to such policy. It is likewise basic to the idea that force itself, in the form of warfare, is but a means to creative peace. The purpose of force is to redress evils which, as Grotius first clearly stated and the whole Catholic school of international law has continuously affirmed, stand in the way of man's self-realization through a just social order. The corruption and perversion of moral ideals by simplified propaganda may indeed lead at times to a very unrealistic representation of other peoples or nations collectively as devils, to the detriment both of national and of general human interests. Such falsification can create the belief that, once the devils are destroyed, no further effort is needed: men may then live happily ever after. The error here, however, should not be attributed to idealism; instead, it indicates the necessity for the integrity of factual reality as the basis for moral judgment, just as, on a different level, it is an argument for the proper maintenance and use of force. A moral use of force always necessitates the subordination and service of that force to ethical aspiration. Force is not properly set in balance against idealism itself. Rather, its right application is always subject to moral judgment, even as sound morality necessitates its availability. That curious professed realism which insists that moral ideas are a protective coloration for exclusive and antagonistic interests, is in truth at once immoral and unrealistic. Moreover, to profess it deceives its exponent far more than it deceives those to whom the "realism" is professedly addressed. As a consequence, its potency as a creator of effective power is doubly diminished.

A genuine foreign policy necessitates absence of hypocrisy. Under present conditions it necessitates proceeding beyond the self-delusion that the road to the promotion of political self-interests is military and economic aid to others for selfish reasons only. Effective promotion of American national interests, for instance, requires concern for the real well-being of our NATO allies. It requires, more profoundly, the pursuit of commonly shared ideas and interests beyond the chance parallelism of the moment. It necessitates abandonment of the attempt to create, or, when needed, to recreate, an always precarious favorable balance of power against some other major power, at the present moment Russia. It must be based on a long-term parallelism of interests. It must possess an awareness that universalist moral insight is requisite also from the point of view of technology and communication and must envisage the ultimate creation of corresponding world political institutions. Such institutions, not possible at present, must yet be held desiderata which can be achieved in a foreseeable future.

At the present moment it is vital to pursue and effectuate ideas and policies compatible with the recognized and shared universal interests of those devoted to the ideals of free society and questing man. Certainly these interests necessitate the nurturing and development of the rich diversities of peoples, whose elimination would be impoverishing even were it practicable. Realistic policy is the proof in action of the reality of sharing, despite cultural differences, and beyond any desire to destroy them. It necessitates, above all, the combatting of a hard-boiled, niggardly realism at home. Such realism not only harms our own moral stature, but also gives genuine warrant for realistic insight abroad into the nature of our realism within the confines of its own concepts. The net result is the destruction of the effectiveness of our attempted appeal to moral ideas. Yet we have seen that such ideas are the fundamental generators of power. The essence of the thesis here propounded is that our national power, the organized social creativity of our people, does not diminish, but increases where it works to supplement and to reinforce the generically similar, though in specific content different, creativity in other peoples. The so-called realistic theory of national interest and the balance of power doctrine, insofar as it rests on that theory, constitute in truth a belated translation and preservation of the old economic wage-fund doctrine as a power-fund theory.

V. IDEALISM IN A BIPOLAR WORLD

In the bipolar world as it is today, a major power has to be global in interest and commitment. For one thing, it must recruit support from all lesser and uncommitted powers. It must do so by persuasive demonstration that its doctrines of personality and of democracy and its concept of the compatibility of diverse cultures embraced within a world community, are more sincere and more promising to others, from the point of view of their own national interests, than the alternatives offered. Nonetheless, impurities and biases are inescapable in this imperfect world, not at present capable of world government. The United States must therefore also possess, or rapidly create, the force necessary to reassure others that allegiance to a common cause will not involve the risk of their own rapid destruction or conquest through our failure to support them at all, or by reason of the complete inadequacy of the forces we can make available to the actual task and need. Such force, combined with superior promise and performance in the material realm, can stimulate others to effort and to allegiance freely given because of a conviction of sharing. The sense of sharing can in turn evoke a creative and resistant energy and, if fear is removed, a sense of sufficient strength first to choose our way and then to stand upright in it, in resistance alike to pressure and to force from the U.S.S.R.

The present lack of adequate force on the part of this country, despite a will and a program for its correction, may lead to our espousal of limited commitments on the ground of operational realism. That realism in turn may well result in an indifference to the fate of peoples who are hard to attach to the Western and American program and ideology, and who would be hard to defend in the absence of the necessary force. Yet the very allegiance and energy created by our acceptance of the obligations of an ally possessed of superior power and by our willingness to take risks not narrowly delimited in advance, can themselves create collective power. For they can persuade other peoples that genuine alliance with us offers greater fulfillment of their over-all national interests, defined from the point of view of their ideal objectives, than the alternatives of submersion in the Soviet bloc or of a dubiously secure independence. It is manifestly necessary on our part to indicate the limitations and the difficulties of our own present position of semi-preparedness. It is likewise vital to urge the need for positive action and cooperation by real allies. It is necessary finally to warn them of the possibilities of short-term sacrifices, and even Dunkirks, on their part. In essence, the implications of NATO must be made explicit, while the NATO system must be expanded wherever surviving free powers may, by appropriate effort on our part, be made into allies for peace and prepared for war.

The cost of creating the needed force on our part, plus the cost of aid in the development, both for peace and war, of other peoples, will indeed be great, as the expense of present more limited commitments indicates. It will therefore necessitate short-run sacrifice of standards of living and of leisure on our own part, beyond those at present planned or anticipated. Yet a calculation of immediate national interests based on a narrow calculation of present income and comfort will, in the long run, prove self-defeating. At the very least the following of such a policy risks insufficient power and inadequate force at now unpredictable points where they may be needed. The doctrine of precise and contained commitment, whatever its appeal to the military strategist, is inadequate political strategy, and in truth betokens failure to follow through the concepts of global struggle and possible global war.

In the long run, a more immediately painful policy is more conducive to the national interest. In it lies, not solely the possibility of victory, but the opportunity for the prevention of war and for creative peace. Such policy is our insurance against defeat, in peace or war, by a country which also professes to be the defender and standard-bearer of a universal ethics of social justice. Today that state is more prepared than we, by teaching, and to some extent by actual attitude and behavior, for adequate sacrifices in order to acquire effective power. That its discipline to this end may destroy the very values it professes is here an irrelevance, as it is certainly not an appropriate example. It is our job to achieve an equivalent in morale and effectiveness by a voluntary material sacrifice which avoids the U.S.S.R.'s sacrifice of the values of free men. Similarly, the fact that the Soviet Union, once its power is secure, may prove unwilling to implement its ideals, and may, in lands which accept its promise, in time replace consent and enthusiasm by force, is not relevant to our own case except insofar as the demonstration of disparity between its promise and performance may help create a power friendly to our own cause. Indeed, the combination of the demonstrated unwillingness of the U.S.S.R. to implement its professed ideals immediately or within a specific future with convincing proof of our own will to promote and lastingly to maintain behaviors and institutions expressive of our proclaimed democratic ideals, is the most powerful force on our side by which to evoke the sustaining power emanating from other people, who in the process of generating it and under its impact become more powerful. The long-run implications of this thesis are greater equality of power, as of living standards. They are also, however, security in the creation and enjoyment of higher standards of living, both economic and cultural, than can otherwise be made available. They are, somewhat paradoxically, the preservation of our initial leadership, as of our differential advantages, through a demonstrated will at once to share and to diminish the latter.

Total commitment and a total idealism which is yet self-interest are our appropriate answers to Soviet totalitarianism. They are the means to success in total war, should it come They are also the most probable grounds for a lasting peace based on positive policies. These policies must be conceived and geared to the preservation of continuity in ever-changing situations, just as they must be directed finally toward the creation of more effective international institutions.

An effective, because long-term, concept of national interest cannot, of course, rest solely on the grim alternative "we or they." It must accept a commonly shared universe of aspiration, at the same time that it necessarily condemns the forceful imposing of unity. It must aim to create a situation in which effective power at once discourages aggression by, and stimulates transformation in, Russia. American ideological power is in this context a leverage. Such power must be backed by a collective force, with the will to use it, which is organized though not created by itself. Possible transformation in Russia, long hoped for from without and implicitly promised from within, has been prevented first by fear and then by national pride. The shared aspirations of humanity have been hidden by the short-sightedness of some putative American interests, promoted and defended by actually irrelevant dogmas. In Russia they have been corrupted by a yet narrower dogma, progressively perverted and misused. Yet these aspirations may still be realized, provided that American policy generates power through sincerity.

This last proviso necessitates a refusal to appease, which is not synonymous with a refusal to comprehend or, consistently with principle, to conciliate. Apart from direct appeasement, which compounds injustice and sacrifices others after the manner of Munich, it is also possible indirectly to appease by our own refusal to commit ourselves to risks and dangers, a refusal supported by narrowly defined and ungenerous interests at home. Nonetheless, it is vital for America to abandon the position of an infallible and absolutely just deity sitting in judgment, a position even more dangerous when sincere than when hypocritical. It is necessary to reject the dogma that diversity of political and social philosophy is incompatible with fundamental universality. It is essential to probe behind the evils of the present regime of Russia and to perceive the justified realities of its economic and cultural national interests and aspirations. It is vital to understand the genuine relevance of Marxism to the organization of Russia as a would-be industrial country, even as it is necessary to condemn the perversion of Marxist teaching and the misuse of it. This means that it is necessary to understand the ethical side of Marxist philosophy, with its broad appeal in countries which would avoid Soviet domination as they would avoid dictatorship. It is, finally, necessary to clarify our own theory and practice of a classless society, which is not incompatible with the essential insights of Marx. This society we have been slowly achieving, during a century and more of peaceful change, by an effective wedding of constitutional democracy, here federal and anti-statist, with a highly productive industrial technology, the fruits and blessing of which have been distributed

ever more widely and equally. It is necessary to show that this concept is now closer to realization; that our own national interest
and purpose is to help its realization; that it promotes social economic welfare without the necessity of sacrificing individual freedom or the creative method of constitutional democracy. The preservation and the extension of these last, which can only come
through voluntary acceptance, are surely the essence of our national interest.

Our interest is the fulfillment compatibly of diverse persons
and, by analogy, of diverse peoples. Based on Christian ethics, it
is a doctrine of method in coping pragmatically with the realities
of differences among men and of imperfections in men. Foreign
policy consistently conceived in the light of this tradition and insight at once proclaims, and persuades others of, the realism of
idealism.

SELECTION 6

THE MAINSPRINGS OF AMERICAN FOREIGN POLICY: THE NATIONAL INTEREST VS. MORAL ABSTRACTIONS*

HANS J. MORGENTHAU

HANS J. MORGENTHAU *has enjoyed a brilliant public career as a lawyer
and political scientist. He is currently Professor of Political Science at the
University of Chicago and Director of the Center for the Study of American
Foreign Policy. His book* Politics Among Nations *has been a standard college text since it first appeared in 1948.*

*The excerpt printed below is taken from the conclusion to his article
"The Mainsprings of American Foreign Policy: The National Interest Vs.
Moral Abstractions."*

. . . . The history of American foreign policy since the end of the
Second World War is the story of the encounter of the American
mind with a new political world. That mind was weakened in its
understanding of foreign policy by half a century of ever more
complete intoxication with moral abstractions. Even a mind less

* Reprinted from *American Political Science Review*, Vol. 44, No. 4 (December 1950), pp. 833-+.

weakened would have found it hard to face with adequate understanding and successful action the unprecedented novelty and magnitude of the new political world. American foreign policy in that
period presents itself as a slow, painful, and incomplete process of
emancipation from deeply ingrained error and of rediscovery of
long-forgotten truths.

The fundamental error which has thwarted American foreign
policy in thought and action is the antithesis of national interest
and moral principles. The equation of political moralism with
morality and of political realism with immorality is itself untenable.
The choice is not between moral principles and the national interest, devoid of moral dignity, but between one set of moral principles, divorced from political reality, and another set of moral prin-
cipals, derived from political reality. The basic fact of international politics is the absence of a society able to protect the existence, and to promote the interests, of the individual nations. For
the individual nations to take care of their own national interests
is, then, a political necessity. There can be no moral duty to neglect
them; for as the international society is at present constituted, the
consistent neglect of the national interest can only lead to national
suicide. Yet it can be shown that there exists even a positive moral
duty for the individual nation to take care of its national interests.

Self-preservation for the individual as well as for societies is
not only a biological and psychological necessity, but in the absence
of an overriding moral obligation a moral duty as well. In the
absence of an integrated international society, in particular, the
attainment of a modicum of order and the realization of a minimum
of moral values are predicated upon the existence of national communities capable of preserving order and realizing moral values
within the limits of their power. It is obvious that such a state of
affairs falls far short of that order and realized morality to which
we are accustomed in national societies. The only relevant question
is, however, what the practical alternative is to these imperfections
of an international society based upon the national interests of its
component parts. The attainable alternative is not a higher morality
realized through the application of universal moral principles, but
moral deterioration through either political failure or the fanaticism of political crusades. The juxtaposition of the morality of
political moralism and the immorality of the national interest is
mistaken. It operates with a false concept of morality, developed by

national societies but unsuited to the conditions of international society. In the process of its realization, it is bound to destroy the very moral values which it is its purpose to promote. Hence, the antithesis between moral principles and the national interest is not only intellectually mistaken but also morally pernicious. A foreign policy derived from the national interest is in fact morally superior to a foreign policy inspired by universal moral principles. Albert Sorel, the Anglophobe historian of the French Revolution, well summarized the real antithesis when he said in grudging admiration of Castlereagh:

> He piqued himself on principles to which he held with an unshakable constancy, which in actual affairs could not be distinquished from obstinacy; but these principles were in no degree abstract or speculative, but were all embraced in one alone, the supremacy of English interests; they all proceeded from this high reason of state.

May as much be said by a future historian of the American foreign policy of our time!

American Objectives for the 1960's

No one person or group of persons determines the national goals of the American people. President Eisenhower acknowledged this fact in 1960 when, responding to widely expressed concern over the lack of a coherent set of American objectives, he appointed a Commission on National Goals and specified his desire that it "have no connection with the government." The Commission itself re-emphasized the unstructured nature of the formulation of American goals in its Report of November 16, 1960 which it presented as a set of recommendations designed to stimulate "active discussion" as "the path to a national consensus."

The excerpts reprinted below as Selection 7 include: (a) the Commission's Letter of Transmittal to the President; (b) the introduction to its Report; (c) brief statements of the fifteen American goals which it identified; and (d) the conclusion of the Report.

The President's Commission was composed of eleven members under the Chairmanship of Henry M. Wriston, Chairman of the American Assembly. It sought the services of many other prominent citizens and published essays by sixteen of these consultants as appendices to its report. Not only were there differences of opinion between the Commission and its consultants but, as could be expected in a group including prominent leaders from labor, industry, education, and journalism, the commission itself was not unanimous in its conclusions. The complete report should be consulted for dissenting statements by various members with respect to specific sections of the documents which was transmitted to the President.

The excerpts below are reprinted at this point in this book for two reasons. First, they offer an illustration of many of the difficulties described by the writers of the preceding selections. Second, they serve as a convenient bridge between the discussion of ends to which Part I of this book is devoted and the discussion of means which is the central theme of Part II. In trying to formulate goals for a whole nation the President's Commission found that domestic and foreign goals are interdependent, that lesser goals must be subordinated to greater goals and that the individual is the key to the successful achievement of the national purpose. The conclusions of the Commission's Report lucidly underscore its relevance to the central theme of this book:

"Our goals will be attained and our way of life preserved if enough Americans take the national interest sufficiently into account in day by day decisions. . . . Man has never been an island unto himself. The shores of his concern have expanded from his neighborhood to his nation, and from his nation to his world. . . ."

SELECTION 7

THE REPORT OF THE PRESIDENT'S COMMISSION ON NATIONAL GOALS*

ADMINISTERED BY THE AMERICAN ASSEMBLY, COLUMBIA UNIVERSITY

The Chairman of the President's Commission on National Goals was HENRY M. WRISTON, *President of the American Assembly, Columbia University, and former President of Brown University (1937-1955). Frank Pace, Jr., Chairman of the Board of General Dynamics Corporation and formerly Secretary of the Army (1950-1953) was the Vice-chairman. Members included: Erwin D. Canham, Editor-in-Chief of the* Christian Science Monitor *and President of the United States Chamber of Commerce, 1959-1960; James B. Conant, Ambassador to the Federal Republic of Germany, 1955-1957, and President of Harvard University, 1933-1953; Colgate W. Darden, Jr., Governor of Virginia, 1942-1946, and President of the University of Virginia, 1947-1959; Crawford H. Greenewalt, President, E. I. du Pont de Nemours and Company; Alfred M. Gruenther, General, U.S.A. (ret.) and President of the American Red Cross; Learned Hand, Retired Judge, U.S. Court of Appeals for the Second Circuit; Clark Kerr, President of the University of California; James R. Killian, Jr., Chairman of the Corporation, Massachusetts Institute of Technology; and George Meany, President of the AFL-CIO.*

THE LETTER OF TRANSMITTAL

November 16, 1960

Dear Mr. President:

We transmit herewith the Report of the President's Commission on National Goals. It is in compliance with your request to "develop a broad outline of coordinated national policies and pro-

---

grams" and to "set up a series of goals in various areas of national activity."

We have respected your desire that our efforts be non-partisan, and have no connection with the government. All financial support has come from private sources, with the sole exception of unfurnished offices temporarily available for our small staff. The only participation of government officials has been to supply requested data.

We asked the counsel of approximately 100 people expert in various topics, and invited 14 men and women of acknowledged competence to write essays for our consideration. The response was generous, many accepting the assignment at considerable personal sacrifice. We desire to record our deep gratitude to them. We have also drawn upon excellent work and reports in relevant fields, by many groups and institutions.

However, the Report expresses views that reflect solely our own judgment, sometimes in accord with and other times at variance from those of the several authors. This judgment was arrived at during long hours at the conference table, and members of the Commission participated actively in drafting the Report.

We do not expect our recommendations to command unanimous acceptance. Rather it is our hope that they will evoke active discussion. Under the democratic process this is the path to a national consensus. The Report and the accompanying chapters will be published in cloth and paper-bound editions. We hope the volume will have wide circulation. . . .

THE COMMISSION REPORT: INTRODUCTION

The paramount goal of the United States was set long ago. It is to guard the rights of the individual, to ensure his development, and to enlarge his opportunity. It is set forth in the Declaration of Independence drafted by Thomas Jefferson and adopted by the Continental Congress on July 4, 1776. The goals we here identify are within the framework of the original plan and are calculated to bring to fruition the dreams of the men who laid the foundation of this country.

They stated their convictions quite simply:

"We hold these truths to be self-evident, that all men are created equal, that they are endowed by their Creator with certain unalienable Rights, that among these are Life, Liberty, and the pursuit of Happiness. That to secure these rights, Governments are instituted among Men, deriving their just powers from the consent of the governed."

It was a mighty vision. In the echo of those fateful words can be heard the onrolling thunder of a new age. It was an even broader and bolder declaration than those who made it knew. Its soaring vision enabled our society to meet the trials of emerging nationhood. It placed the young republic securely behind the principle that every human being is of infinite worth. In time it led the nation out of the morass of human slavery. It inspires us still in the struggle against injustice.

To make this vision a reality, a framework of self-government was established nationally and in each state. It rested upon two fundamental principles—the election of representatives from among competing candidates, and the constitutional limitation of power of those elected.

The way to preserve freedom is to live it. Our enduring aim is to build a nation and help build a world in which every human being shall be free to develop his capacities to the fullest. We must rededicate ourselves to this principle and thereby strengthen its appeal to a world in political, social, economic, and technological revolution.

In the 1960's every American is summoned to extraordinary personal responsibility, sustained effort, and sacrifice. For the nation is in grave danger, threatened by the rulers of one-third of mankind, for whom the state is everything, the individual significant only as he serves the state. These rulers seek the "peace" of a Communist-oriented world, in which freedom is suppressed and the individual permanently subordinated. Supporting their aim are the Soviet Union's great and swiftly growing strength, the industrial and military progress and potential of Red China, a great capacity for political organization and propaganda, and the specious appeal of Communist doctrine to peoples eager for rapid escape from poverty.

Meanwhile, weapons of cataclysmic power have come into existence. A major nuclear conflict would be a world catastrophe; violence even in or between small nations could involve the great powers and spark the holocaust.

The Sino-Soviet threat and modern weapons present great

dangers; we have equally great opportunities. With the increase of knowledge and material resources, we have achieved a standard of individual realization new to history. We can continue to improve our own way of life, and at the same time help in the progress of vast numbers in the world whose lives are blighted by chronic sickness, hunger, and illiteracy.

Since 1946, foreign rule has ended for more than one billion people in Asia and Africa. Much of their yearning for independence, for respect, and for abundance has been inspired by Western and especially American example. Nevertheless, historic resentments, inadequate economies, inexperience in self-government, and excessive expectations offer fertile ground for Communist persuasion and conquest. This restless tide of events defines the magnitude of our problems and the scope of our opportunity.

*   *   *   *   *

To preserve and enlarge our own liberties, to meet a deadly menace, and to extend the area of freedom throughout the world: these are high and difficult goals. Yet our past performance justifies confidence that they can be achieved. . . .

This Report identifies goals and sets forth programs. It is directed to the citizens of this country, each of whom sets his own goals and seeks to realize them in his life, through private groups, and through various levels of government. Choices are hard, and costs heavy. They demand subordination of lesser goals to the greater. But the rewards are beyond calculation, for the future of our nation depends on the result.

At the same time, the United States cannot attain its goals alone, nor by offering the free world grudging alms or condescending leadership. We must lead, but in a spirit of genuine partnership. Together, the free peoples of the world can develop unmatched strength and vindicate the mighty vision of the Declaration.

THE COMMISSION REPORT: PART I, GOALS AT HOME

1. THE INDIVIDUAL. The status of the individual must remain our primary concern. All our institutions—political, social, and economic—must further enhance the dignity of the citizen, promote the maximum development of his capabilities, stimulate their re-

sponsible exercise, and widen the range and effectiveness of opportunities for individual choice. . . .

2. EQUALITY. Vestiges of religious prejudice, handicaps to women, and, most important, discrimination on the basis of race must be recognized as morally wrong, economically wasteful, and in many respects dangerous. In this decade we must sharply lower these last stubborn barriers. . . .

Respect for the individual means respect for every individual. Every man and woman must have equal rights before the law, and an equal opportunity to vote and hold office, to be educated, to get a job and to be promoted when qualified, to buy a home, to participate fully in community affairs. These goals, which are at the core of our system, must be achieved by action at all levels. . . .

3. THE DEMOCRATIC PROCESS. The degree of effective liberty available to its people should be the ultimate test for any nation. Democracy is the only means so far devised by which a nation can meet this test. To preserve and perfect the democratic process in the United States is therefore a primary goal in this as in every decade. . . .

The vastly increased demands upon the federal government require at the higher levels more public servants equal in competence and imagination to those in private business and the professions. This involves a drastic increase in their compensation. The President should be given unequivocal authority and responsibility to develop a true senior civil service. . . . The executive branch must also place greater emphasis on the recruiting, training, and stimulation of career employees. . . .

4. EDUCATION. The development of the individual and the nation demand that education at every level and in every discipline be strengthened and its effectiveness enhanced. New teaching techniques must continue to be developed. The increase in population and the growing complexity of the world add urgency.

Greater resources—private, corporate, municipal, state, and federal—must be mobilized. A higher proportion of the gross national product must be devoted to educational purposes. This is at once an investment in the individual, in the democratic process, in the growth of the economy, and in the stature of the United States. . . .

5. THE ARTS AND SCIENCES. Knowledge and innovation must be advanced on every front. In science we should allot a greater proportion of our total effort to basic research, first, to realize fully the

rapidly unfolding opportunities to extend still further our understanding of the world, and second, to enrich applied science and technology so essential to the improvement of health, to economic growth, and to military power.

Today we must give high priority to those aspects of science and technology which will increase our military strength, but for the longer term we should recognize that our creative activities in science and all other fields will be more productive and meaningful if undertaken, not merely to be ahead of some other nation, but to be worthy of ourselves. . . .

6. THE DEMOCRATIC ECONOMY. The economic system must be compatible with the political system. The centers of economic power should be as diffused and as balanced as possible. Too great concentrations of economic power in corporations, unions, or other organizations can lead to abuses and loss of the productive results of fair competition. Individuals should have maximum freedom in their choice of jobs, goods, and services. . . .

7. ECONOMIC GROWTH. The economy should grow at the maximum rate consistent with primary dependence upon free enterprise and the avoidance of marked inflation. . . . Increased investment in the public sector is compatible with this goal.

Such growth is essential to move toward our goal of full employment, to provide jobs for the approximately 13,500,000 net new additions to the work force during the next ten years; to improve the standard of living; and to assure United States competitive strength.

Public policies, particularly an overhaul of the tax system, including depreciation allowances, should seek to improve the climate for new investment and the balancing of investment with consumption. We should give attention to policies favoring completely new ventures which involve a high degree of risk and growth potential. . . .

8. TECHNOLOGICAL CHANGE. Technological change should be promoted and encouraged as a powerful force for advancing our economy. It should be planned for and introduced with sensitive regard for any adverse impact upon individuals. . . .

9. AGRICULTURE. The relative financial return to agriculture in the economy has deteriorated. The ultimate goal must be a supply-demand equilibrium to permit the market, with a fair return to farmers, to determine the manpower and capital committed to this

sector of the economy. To avoid shock to the economy, this goal should be approached by gradual stages. . . .

10. LIVING CONDITIONS. We must remedy slum conditions, reverse the process of decay in the larger cities, and relieve the necessity for low-income and minority groups to concentrate there.

We should also seek solutions for haphazard suburban growth, and provide an equitable sharing of the cost of public services between central cities and suburbs. . . .

11. HEALTH AND WELFARE. The demand for medical care has enormously increased. To meet it we must have more doctors, nurses, and other medical personnel. There should be more hospitals, clinics and nursing homes. Greater effectiveness in the use of such institutions will reduce over-all requirements. There is a heavy responsibility on the medical and public health professions to contribute better solutions. . . .

THE COMMISSION REPORT: PART II, GOALS ABROAD

The basic foreign policy of the United States should be the preservation of its own independence and free institutions. Our position before the world should be neither defensive nor belligerent. We should cooperate with nations whose ideals and interests are in harmony with ours. We should seek to mitigate tensions, and search for acceptable areas of accommodation with opponents. The safeguarded reduction of armaments is an essential goal. . . .

Our goals abroad are inseparable from our goals at home. We must strive toward an open and peaceful world by making democracy ever more effective and individual life freer and more rewarding. . . .

12. HELPING TO BUILD AN OPEN AND PEACEFUL WORLD. *Foreign Trade Policy.* The healthiest world economy is attained when trade is at its freest. This should be our goal. The United States should join with other free world industrial nations in seeking a gradual reduction of tariffs and quota restrictions. We should seek this goal while safeguarding the national economy against market disruption, against destructive competition as a result of grossly lower unit labor costs, and to preserve national defense. . . .

Aid to Less Developed Nations. Our principles and ideals impel us to aid the new nations. The preservation and strengthening of the free institutions of underdeveloped countries, and the defense of the free world, require a substantial increase in the amount of foreign aid, to be equitably shared by the major free nations.

International economic organizations, such as the World Bank, deserve our support. We must devise new forms of cooperation, in which developing countries have opportunities for participation. . . . We must encourage far larger numbers of qualified Americans to live and work abroad.

Half a million American civilians live abroad, as a result of private and government employment. Their number and their ability to represent the United States creditably must rise rapidly in the next decade if we are to attain an adequate level of exports and foreign investment and carry out programs for training and technical assistance. Universities, businesses, and the federal government should each in appropriate fields greatly increase language and other specialized training for such work.

13. THE DEFENSE OF THE FREE WORLD. *The Soviet Threat.* Communist aggression and subversion . . . threaten all that we seek to do both at home and abroad. Consequently, the maintenance of our independence and way of life, as well as our concern for the freedom of other nations, require the most effective countermeasures.

The power and opportunities of the Sino-Soviet nations are such that it will be a major task to prevent their expansion in the coming decade. Nevertheless we must never lose sight of our ultimate goal: to extend the opportunities for free choice and self-determination throughout the world. . . .

Communist China. Communist China's blatant hostility to the United States makes it especially urgent to strengthen our Pacific defenses and our ties with our Pacific allies. . . .

Military Alliances. For the common defense we must maintain and strengthen our military alliances. Our commitment to NATO in particular must remain firm. We should encourage the trend to greater military integration among the European members and the assumption by them of greater responsibilities. Our other military alliances and relationships in the Middle East and Asia must likewise be reaffirmed and strengthened. The Organization of American States must continue to have our unstinting support.

Communist-dominated Areas. In nations subject to Communist domination or influence, our hope must be that the right of self-determination will ultimately be achieved. Trade, cultural exchanges, and occasionally technical or financial aid may be useful policies toward Communist-dominated peoples who are not hostile to us.

14. DISARMAMENT. Since a major nuclear war would be a world catastrophe, the limitation and control of nuclear armament is imperative. Disarmament should be our ultimate goal. It cannot be attained without eliminating the sources of distrust and fear among nations. Hence, our immediate task must be the step-by-step advance toward control of nuclear weapons and their means of delivery, with effective international inspection. A safeguarded agreement to suspend nuclear testing may well be the first step, and would tend to limit the number of nuclear powers. . . .

15. THE UNITED NATIONS. A key goal in the pursuit of a vigorous and effective United States foreign policy is the preservation and strengthening of the United Nations. Over the next decade, it will be under tremendous strain. However, it remains the chief instrument available for building a genuine community of nations.

This requires constant strengthening of world law, through the discovery and adoption of legal principles common to all or at least to many cultures, through improved methods for making existing international law accessible, and through the further development of the International Court of Justice. . . .

It must be recognized that the United Nations provides a forum for Soviet propaganda and tactics of dissension, and an opportunity for Soviet vetoes to block or delay free world advances. On occasion, the growing block of votes from the new and uncommitted nations may turn a decision in the United Nations against our interests. Nevertheless, we should give the world community, as represented by the United Nations, our steadfast support. . . .

THE COMMISSION REPORT: A CONCLUDING WORD

The very deepest goals for Americans relate to the spiritual health of our people. The right of every individual to seek God and the wellsprings of truth, each in his own way, is infinitely precious. We must guarantee it, and we must exercise it, for ours is a spiritually-based society. Our material achievements in fact represent a triumph of the spirit of man in the mastery of his material environment.

The family is at the heart of society. The educational process begins and is served most deeply in the home.

From the first days of our history, every American has been responsible for his own life and livelihood, and for his family's, and has shared responsibility for his neighbor's. In our early years, the perils which threatened were close at hand, and the responsibility was inescapable. Now dangers, and opportunities as well, come from greater distance, and more subtly. But they are just as real. And it is as true as in the days of the frontier that the goals for Americans cannot be won without the efforts of all.

The major domestic goals of equality and education depend overwhelmingly on individual attitudes and actions.

It is the responsibility of men and women in every walk of life to maintain the highest standards of integrity.

American citizens will in this decade have countless opportunities to take the national interest into account in deciding their course of action. Negotiators for labor and management affect the growth of the economy and its ability to compete with industry abroad when they reach a decision on compensation and working conditions, and thus influence the rate of technological change. Young men and women will help shape the course the United States will take by deciding in what occupation they will spend their lives. Americans who live or travel abroad can persuade countless people of the sincerity of American ideals and the values of democracy, or they can tarnish the nation's reputation. Voters will determine whether schools will be built, teachers' salaries raised, foreign assistance enlarged, defense needs fulfilled. Our goals will be attained and our way of life preserved if enough Americans take the national interest sufficiently into account in day by day decisions.

The American citizen in the years ahead ought to devote a larger portion of his time and energy directly to the solution of the nation's problems. There has been repeated occasion in this Report to emphasize the over-riding importance of contributions by private groups and individuals. Many ways are open for citizens to participate in the attainment of national goals. To mention but a few: they may help to control delinquency by organizing a boys' club, serve on a school board, accept a tour of duty with government, participate actively in politics through parties or interest groups.

Above all, Americans must demonstrate in every aspect of their lives the fallacy of a purely selfish attitude—the materialistic ethic. Indifference to poverty and disease is inexcusable in a society dedicated to the dignity of the individual; so also is indifference to values other than material comfort and national power. Our faith is that man lives, not by bread alone, but by self-respect, by regard for other men, by convictions of right and wrong, by strong religious faith.

Man has never been an island unto himself. The shores of his concern have expanded from his neighborhood to his nation, and from his nation to his world. Free men have always known the necessity for responsibility. A basic goal for each American is to achieve a sense of responsibility as broad as his world-wide concerns and as compelling as the dangers and opportunities he confronts.

II

Art versus Science—
Difficulties in the Study of
International Relations

When (see selection 1) he completes his discussion of the Ends sought by individuals and their national states, Lord Bryce asks what Means they might use in order to achieve their objectives. He concludes that:

The thing now most needed by the people and its representatives is more knowledge of the facts of the outside world with a more sympathetic comprehension of the minds of other peoples. The first step to this is a fuller acquaintance with the history, the economic and social conditions, and the characters of other peoples.

Part II of this book is devoted to a discussion of these means. How does an individual go about acquiring "more knowledge of the facts of the outside world" or developing a "more sympathetic comprehension of the minds of other peoples"? Can one gain a "full" acquaintance with the "characters of other peoples"? Are such "facts" available and is such "sympathetic comprehension" and "fuller acquaintance" possible for all citizens or for only a few who have unusual intellectual capacity and unique opportunity for study and travel?

Discussion of these questions is a necessary prerequisite to informed consideration of the vital questions around which part III of this book is organized: Whether experts or laymen should handle vital international affairs in the twentieth century? In order to lay an adequate groundwork for that discussion the readings in this section have been selected to illustrate the nature of international relations as a subject of study. They are presented in three groups. The first group concentrates on problems of acquiring information. The second group focuses on problems of evaluating information. The third group discusses problems of organizing and using information. Taken together they pose the question whether international relations as a subject of study is an art or a science—whether the difficulties of acquiring and organizing facts, developing sympathetic comprehension of the minds of other peoples, and gaining acquaintance with the characters of other peoples are so great that they can never be satisfactorily surmounted (and the subject must remain an art) or whether the techniques of modern social science research are effective enough to make international relations a science.

Problems of Acquiring Information

First among the problems which the student of international relations faces is that of acquiring the information relevant to selecting the most suitable means for achieving his objectives. It is a problem for individuals and for groups of all sizes and functions, including the nation-state. Part of the problem is almost mechanical. There is so much that is relevant when, for example, an individual citizen wonders whether to vote for one candidate or another, or when an agency of the national government wonders whether to propose foreign aid in the form of loans or of grants.

The amount of information which is readily available is staggering. It would be a full time job for anyone to even browse through all the "must" reading which the bookstores, libraries, newspapers and journals have to offer. Yet a cursory inspection of most international problems will indicate that there is, alongside the problem of "too much" information, a problem of "too little" of the right information. The desires of governments for secrecy and the desires of individuals for privacy combine to put many locked doors in the way of the diligent international relations researcher. There are, also, language barriers and problems of interpreting the information which the various academic disciplines often provide in their own technical language and symbols. Added together, these difficulties in the acquisition of factual information form a sizeable barrier even for governments with their many bureaus of experts.

Two of the following readings are taken from a UNESCO world press survey. The first (selection 8) is from the concluding chapter of the survey and describes the development of news agencies during the past century and comments on some of the problems which have arisen in keeping all the people of the world informed about international relations.

The second (selection 9) comments briefly on the characteristics of each of the world news agencies and then goes on to give a detailed description of two of the most important ones, the Associated Press and TASS. Since this UNESCO survey was compiled, two of the world agencies, United Press and International News Service, have merged to form a new agency, United Press International (UPI).

The third item (selection 10) is a table taken from another UNESCO survey. It shows the number of daily newspapers serving various populations around the world.

The fourth and fifth readings (selections 11 and 12) bear on the problems that grow out of the usefulness—to governments—of secrecy. The dilemma of a democratic society trying to compete in the international relations of the jet age was clearly illustrated during the Cuban crisis of April 1961, the month when the anti-Castro forces attempted landings on Cuba's coast. In view of the reactions of world public opinion, it was clear that news reports before, during and after the event were of major significance. It is possible that the United States suffered an unnecessarily severe propaganda defeat because of news reports emanating from Miami which incorrectly reflected the objectives of the "invasion."

In any case, President Kennedy was sufficiently disturbed by the reporting of the Cuban crisis to make a major address on the subject of "freedom and the press" on April 27, 1961. His address (selection 11) and an editorial comment the following morning in the New York Times *(selection 12) are reprinted below. The problem with which these readings are concerned is not confined to the acquiring of information. For individuals it is a problem of acquiring and of evaluating information. For the press it is a problem both of evaluating and of using information. For the government it is the difficult problem of maximizing the freedom of information without which a democratic society cannot survive, while preserving the freedom from excessive publicity without which a modern government cannot successfully compete with foreign adversaries.*

SELECTION 8

NEWS AGENCIES: THEIR STRUCTURE AND OPERATION*

The following selection is from the conclusion to a study of news agencies conducted by UNESCO in 1952. Chapter One of that study contains an outline of the origins, development, and interrelationships of the principal agencies.

Side by side with the spread of education in the early nineteenth century went a growing thirst for news; in the twentieth century, news has become a necessity for millions of people. To meet

* Reprinted from *News Agencies: Their Structure and Operation*, UNESCO (Paris: Georges Lang, 1953), pp. 199-201.

this need organizations which are today known as telegraphic news agencies began to be set up around the middle of last century, through the enterprise of a single person or of a group of newspaper owners. They collected news and sold it, at first to private individuals, then to newspapers, and more recently to broadcasting stations. These news agencies were set up either as profit-making commercial enterprises or as cooperatives.

The first agencies, Havas, Wolff and Reuters, aimed together at becoming world agencies, that is, at collecting and distributing news throughout the world. In order to lower their operating costs they concluded alliances. . . . They divided up the world into zones of influence in each of which one agency enjoyed the monopoly of collecting and distributing news. This system remained in force until the first world war. It provoked serious criticisms, principally from the directors of newspapers and agencies in the United States, but it was not until 1934 that the system of alliances was completely abandoned and all agencies obtained full freedom of action.

In the course of the last 100 years the press, which made up by far the greater part of the agencies' clientele and which provided them with their chief source of income, has acquired considerable power and an ever-increasing circulation; many countries where newspapers were practically non-existent have now a large and vigorous press. Moreover, in the last 30 years, broadcasting stations have become new clients for the agencies, bringing them important supplementary sources of revenue.

Telecommunication facilities have also improved immensely in the course of the last century. Thanks to the work of the International Telecommunication Union there is no longer any technical barrier to stop or even to slow down the exchange of information. From the technical point of view, news can be transmitted rapidly and without difficulty all over the world.

But the number of world news agencies has not increased since 1918, and although it is true that the number of national agencies has gone up considerably, especially in the last 30 years, there are still whole great regions, particularly in South America, in Africa and in the Near East, where none is operating. Moreover, a comparison of the status, operation, scope and equipment of the different agencies brings out not only the diversity of their activities but the inequality of their means. News distribution over the world is thus unequal, and world coverage is ensured only by a small number of organizations which are themselves national in character.

The problem is a double one:

With regard to domestic news it would obviously be desirable that there should be in each country at least one independent national agency to collect domestic news of interest to the general public for the local press and broadcasting companies, and also to furnish the big world agencies with a local news service, which would provide them with a far fuller flow of copy than they could collect themselves. The chief obstacle to the establishment everywhere of such independent national agencies is the absence in so many countries of a local press and broadcasting services able to finance their operation. It has been suggested that a first step towards their foundation might be taken by the setting up of regional agencies, which would not at all tend to become world agencies but which would limit themselves to meeting the needs in domestic news of a group of neighbouring countries. Such regional agencies could for example be set up for Western Europe, Central America, South America, the Arab States, the Far East, Africa, etc. They could conclude agreements between themselves for the exchange of regional news, until such time as a truly international world agency came into existence.

With regard to the world news the point to emphasize is that no truly international news agency has yet come into existence. Until 1934 world information was not free, since a small number of big agencies had shared out among themselves the monopoly of news collection and distribution in the principal regions of the world. Today there is nothing to prevent the agencies from extending their activities to any country they please (except the Soviet Union and the "popular republics"), but though news distribution has improved through the resulting competition it has still not become international. The six world agencies are themselves in reality national in character. They have set up organizations which cover the entire globe because the press and radio of the countries in which they have their headquarters are very highly developed and demand a world-wide news service. They have also undertaken distribution in a great number of countries, either direct or through national agencies, but their capital, their directors and chief executives, the majority of the staff they employ, are from the United States, Britain, France or Russia as the case may be. The news they collect and distribute is chosen, written up and presented almost entirely by United States, British, French or Russian journalists. No newspaper, no broadcasting station anywhere in the world, can obtain news on world events except as seen, selected and edited by these men and women. And however impartial they may be, however strictly they may comply with the professional code of ethics, they will inevitably judge and present news from the viewpoint of the country of which they are citizens.

At a time when the development of international relations, not only political but military, economic, financial, scientific, educational and cultural, is leading more and more to the creation of international organizations (towards the first step is often the establishment of pools or regional groups) it seems paradoxical that the tendency in the field of information should be the exact reverse. Yet over the last century the whole trend has been from a system of close alliances and wide-spread agreements between the news-gathering organizations to a theoretically free-for-all struggle for the sale of news. The present policy of the world agencies seems to stem from a survival of the nationalistic principles current in the years between the two world wars, of which the most outstanding manifestations were the proliferation of State-operated news agencies and the growth in strength and independence of the United States agencies. The world agencies are not truly international. They maintain their national characteristics, since they are either cooperative organizations whose membership is made up of the press and the broadcasting stations of a single country, or the property of a national commercial company, or again an official government department.

All the same, one feels bound to ask whether the news agencies may not one day find it necessary to follow the policy of international cooperation which is gaining ground in so many other domains. Whatever the answer may be, it is important to stress the fact that the agencies, which represent one of the most powerful factors in promoting that cooperation, remain purely national organizations.

Is it possible to put the spreading of news on an international basis?

Two solutions have at various times been envisaged. The first would consist in the creation of a telegraphic news agency attached to an appropriate body of the United Nations. It would be an international agency whose directing, administrative and journalistic staff would be recruited among specialists from all member countries.

But this solution would meet with the immediate and implacable opposition of the majority of the profession, who would refuse to use the services of an agency organized, even indirectly, under governmental control.

The second solution would lie in the creation of a world cooperative agency. The newspapers and broadcasting stations of all countries would be shareholders in such an agency, which would in effect be their property. The contribution of the newspapers would be assessed in proportion to their circulation; that of the broadcasting stations in proportion to their national audience. The capital would thus be international, as would be the directors, the editorial staff, the correspondents and the operators, and the agency would be able to collect and distribute a news service as free as possible from any national influence. The greater the number of national agencies (not to speak of the possible emergence of regional agencies) the easier would the work of such an international agency be, for it would have at its disposal abundant sources of news which its own staff could complete and edit. Competition, indispensable to the speed and quality of a news service, would still be forthcoming from the major world agencies at present in existence.

Professional press circles might be willing to study the possibility of setting up such an organization, but it is to be anticipated that certain agencies would oppose it. . . .

SELECTION 9

WORLD NEWS AGENCIES:
ASSOCIATED PRESS AND TASS*

The following selection from UNESCO's publication World News Agencies *describes the history and operations of two of the major agencies, Associated Press and TASS. Similar studies of the other world agencies are also included in the UNESCO study.*

Six telegraphic news agencies: AFP, AP, INS, Reuters, TASS and UP can be classified as world agencies.[1] This term is used to

* Reprinted from *News Agencies: Their Structure and Operation*, UNESCO (Paris: Georges Lang, 1953), pp. 35-36, 43, 56.

[1] INS and UP combined in 1958 to form one agency, United Press International (UPI)—Editor.

denote an agency which maintains a network of correspondents to collect news in a great number of countries and a headquarters staff which edits these news items, as well as domestic news, and despatches them as quickly as possible: (a) to the agency's bureaux abroad for local distribution to newspapers and broadcasting stations; (b) to national agencies with which it has an agreement; and (c) directly to subscribing newspapers and broadcasting stations abroad. Such agencies use extensive telecommunications facilities for the reception and transmission of their services.

None of the world agencies in fact distributes news in every country of the world, though technically they could supply their services, made up of items collected in the great majority of those countries, to all newspapers and broadcasting stations which wished to subscribe to them.

Three important points must be stressed:

First, the world agencies, which came into existence between 1935 and 1918, were set up in countries where the press was particularly developed. It is because the readers of the numerous newspapers there wanted news from all parts of the world that the agencies were created to collect news on a world-wide basis. Subsequently, they extended their distribution activities to other countries.

Secondly, the world agencies also play the role of national agencies. That is to say, they collect and distribute to newspapers and broadcasting stations in the country in which they have their headquarters an abundant service of domestic news. Only the British agency, Reuters, does not collect and distribute domestic news, but it distributes abroad news of Britain collected by a national agency, the Press Association. The Press Association is in fact one of the principal share-holders of Reuters, and both agencies are owned by the British Press.

The scope and length of the services distributed by world agencies, the number of clients and extent of their communication facilities, sharply distinguish them from national agencies which operate exclusively or almost exclusively within individual countries, and cannot be compared to the world services of the six major agencies.

Thirdly, the six world agencies differ from each other, with regard to their juridical status, their internal organization, the number of their subscribers and of their correspondents, and the extent of their technical facilities. But AFP, AP, INS, Reuters and UP are alike in that they all distribute a service of world news on a paying basis to subscribing newspapers and broadcasting stations in a very great number of countries. All important national agencies and many newspapers and broadcasting stations subscribe to the services of one or several of these world agencies.

The TASS agency, though its juridical status as the official agency of the Government of the Soviet Union is quite different, though it forms a part of the Soviet administration and though its services reflect official policy, is nevertheless classified as a world agency. For it maintains a network of correspondents abroad, has a staff at headquarters to deal with foreign copy, uses technical facilities which enable it to distribute abroad an extensive service of world news, and because national agencies, newspapers and broadcasting stations in different parts of the world regularly receive its services, though these are usually given free.

ASSOCIATED PRESS

HISTORICAL REVIEW. Founded in 1848 under the name of Harbour News Association. Address: 50 Rockefeller Plaza, New York City, USA.

The foundation upon which the Associated Press (AP) was to be built, was laid in 1848, when six New York City newspapers formed the Harbour News Association in order to share the cost of collecting news by means of "news boats" which met incoming ships from Europe. This association, which in 1857 became the New York Associated Press, never had more than seven members, all of them New York City newspapers, but they began to share their news service with newspapers in other parts of the country. In order to cut the telegraphic cost, wherever possible, they dealt with groups of papers, some of which in time, formed themselves into regional associations, such as the Western Associated Press, the Southern Associated Press and the New England Associated Press. These groups felt, however, that the news was being restricted in the interests of the New York papers and, in 1885, Western Associated Press withdrew from the cooperative. In 1892, a group of middle-western publishers reorganized the former Western Associated Press as the Associated Press, incorporated in Illinois. The New York association had fought this reorganization, but lost and went out of existence because the idea of a true news cooperative, in which all members should be equal, was too strong. The new Associated Press then signed an exclusive exchange contract with Reuters (and through Reuters with Havas and Wolff), thereby securing, for a few years, a distinct advantage on European news coming into the United States. Dependence on exchange arrangements with other agencies for foreign news was relatively shortlived; the members of AP soon demanded direct representation in foreign capitals.

By the middle 1890's the Associated Press was serving 700 papers and was expanding rapidly, both in services and in members. In 1900 the agency was forced to reorganize and re-incorporate in New York to maintain its cooperative basis. Its headquarters have been there ever since.

In 1902 AP established some bureaux in Europe but was slow to develop its system of news distribution abroad. In 1920 certain Latin American newspapers were admitted to membership, but the agency was handicapped by its agreements with Reuters, Havas and Wolff, as AP and other agencies had agreed to respect each other's territory. In 1934 AP declared itself released from all cartel agreements with other organizations and set about building up its service to newspapers in other countries.

Two changes have taken place in AP organization since 1945. In that year the United States Supreme Court condemned the clause of the AP constitution under which the members could block the effort of a competitor in the same city to obtain the association's news service through election to membership. In 1947 radio stations were, for the first time, accepted as members of the association; they had previously subscribed to a subsidiary service which served radio exclusively.

SERVICES DISTRIBUTED AND SUBSCRIBERS. AP started by collecting news and it was only later that it began to provide its service to newspapers all over the world. The number of countries in which AP provides news to subscribers has steadily increased within the last six years. In 1944 AP had subscribers in 38 countries while today the figure is more than 70. . . .

A number of new countries have appeared on the list since April 1949. These include Portugal, the Anglo-Egyptian Sudan, Cyprus, Kuwait, Morocco and Pakistan. Newspapers in Iran and Thailand have also recently become subscribers to the AP services.

Reception of the AP news service . . . may be affected in one of three ways. Firstly, the news may be received by an AP bureau, which is then responsible for the distribution, and, in most cases, the translation of the news. Secondly, in a few cases, AP news may be distributed by a domestic agency; for example, in the UK, the Press Association distributes the AP service to subscribers outside London; and in Canada, distribution is through the Canadian Press. Thirdly, in countries where no AP bureau exists and there is only a correspondent for the collection of news, subscribers may receive the service directly by means of receivers which are generally located in the newspaper offices concerned.

From New York a cable runs directly to the AP world desk in London. The amount of news transmitted runs into several thousand words each day and principally deals with events in the Western Hemisphere and Pacific areas including Korea (Southern region). In London, the news is edited and distributed by leased teleprinter circuit to a large number of subscribers in Europe.

The teleprinter network links London with the following points in Europe: Amsterdam, Berlin, Brussels, Copenhagen, Frankfurt, Hamburg, Luxembourg, Milan, Oslo, Paris, Rome, Stockholm, Vienna. Connecting circuits exist for subscribers in France, Germany, the Netherlands, Scandinavia, Italy and Belgium, who are not in the cities mentioned above. A telex relay from Stockholm provides subscribers in Finland with the AP service. The Hell report transmitted from Frankfurt, goes to such countries as Hungary and Greece in Europe, Turkey, Egypt and Israel in the Middle East, and the Federation of Malaya, Burma and Iran further east.

Subscribers in Latin America are chiefly served by radio newscast from New York transmitted for 19 hours every day and consisting of approximately 16,000 words. This transmission will soon be converted to radioteleprinter, greatly increasing the volume. The news deals with events all over the world. There are leased wire connections to Mexico, and Havana, which function for part of the day, and direct teleprinter communication from Dallas, Texas, to Mexico during the remaining hours.

From San Francisco radioteleprinter is used to serve the Hawaiian Islands and the entire Pacific area. AP transmits some 40,000 words daily through leased channels over a period of 24 hours, reception being effected in such places as Manila, Tokyo, Singapore and Hong Kong where there is a regional morsecast of Far Eastern events between such points as Manila, Hong Kong and Tokyo, the latter being also picked up in San Francisco. Alaska is served by a direct circuit from Seattle; and Toronto, the headquarters of the Canadian Press, has a direct connexion by wire with New York City.

AP provides all its foreign subscribers with the same type of service as that given to newspapers and radio stations in the U.S. For example, a twice-weekly supplementary service by post is sent to all foreign bureaux and a number of special subscribers in London. The San Francisco office provides a smaller service to points in the Pacific area, consisting of background material to the news. Among other items are articles from all sources and a business news service specially prepared in New York. The larger foreign bureaux have a third function in addition to collecting and distributing the news. The London office not only covers news from the United Kingdom and Ireland but it is a focal point for relaying news from a large part of the world to the Americas and is also concerned with the preparation and transmission of the AP foreign news service on the European leased wire.

TASS

HISTORICAL REVIEW. Note: The survey carried out by UNESCO from 1947 to 1951 on the operation of news agencies, the press, the film and the radio in the world did not include the Soviet Union. The information here given on TASS was consequently not obtained from the agency itself, as is the case for the other agencies included in this book. It was obtained from the few available sources (books, publications, articles, etc.), and its accuracy cannot be guaranteed. As far as possible, however, it has been checked in the various countries where TASS operates. Sources of information for this report included: Sobranie Zabonow (compendium of the official bulletin of laws of the Soviet Union, 1925-35); Editor and Publisher, December 1944-June 1945; Louis Menzer, "The Structure of the Soviet Foreign Propaganda Organization" (thesis at Chicago University, 1948); Joseph Marz, Die Moderne Zeitung, Kunstverlag Agathen, Munich, 1951.

The report on TASS was sent for checking to the agency's head office in Moscow. At the time of going to press, no reply has yet been received.

Before the first world war and until the revolution of October 1917 there existed in Russia a telegraphic news agency called Petersburger Telegraphen Agentur.

Shortly after the Bolshevik revolution of 1917 a news agency was created under the name of Rossijkoje Telegranfnoi Agenburo (Rosta). The purpose of this agency was to distribute official communiques and news items, as well as to send out propaganda material to the press in areas under Bolshevik control. In 1919 regular distribution began of a bulletin called Agit-Rosta, which consisted of propaganda on various themes (young people, women, agriculture, economy, etc.). The agency also assisted in various campaigns, such as the war with Denikin and the struggle against desertion, sending out special articles and slogans.

The Telegrafnoie Agenstvo Sovietskavo Soiuza (TASS) replaced Rosta on 10 July 1925. The federal system in the new State led to the creation in every Republic of the Union of a local agency; these were subordinated to TASS. Through TASS each of these agencies received news from the other Republics and from abroad, as well as Federal Government information.

SELECTION 10

BASIC DATA ON THE DAILY PRESS, BY CONTINENTS AND FOR THE WORLD*

The following chart prepared by UNESCO is included because it illustrates the gross disparities which exist around the world in the ratio of news agencies to size of population.

Area	Estimated million population (mid 1952)	Per cent of total world population	Number of daily newspapers	Per cent of total world number of daily newspapers
Africa	203	8.2	208	2.8
America, North	225	9.1	2,265	30.1
America, South	115	4.7	613	8.2
Asia (ex. USSR)	1,298	52.8	2,257	30.0
Europe (ex. USSR)	400	16.3	2,071	27.5
Oceania	14	0.6	106	1.4
USSR	205	8.3	...	...
World Total	2,460	100.0	7,520	100.0

* Reprinted from *The Daily Press: A Survey of the World Situation in 1952,* UNESCO, Clearing House, Department of Mass Communication, No. 7, December 1953, Table 2, p. 12.

THE PRESIDENT AND THE PRESS*

JOHN F. KENNEDY

The world's attention during April, 1961, was on events concerned with Cuba's Castro government, its adversaries, and its supporters. The adversaries had been defeated in an attempt to land on the island and overthrow Castro. The Soviet Union accused the United States of complicity; the United States accused the Soviet Union of complicity. The President of the United States discussed the attendant problems in a speech delivered on April 27 to the Bureau of Advertising of the American Newspaper Publishers Association, here reprinted without its introductory remarks.

My topic tonight is a . . . sober one of concern to publishers as well as editors.

I want to talk about our common responsibilities in the face of a common danger. The events of recent weeks may have helped to illuminate that challenge for some; but the dimensions of its threat have loomed large on the horizon for many years. Whatever our hopes may be for the future—for reducing this threat or living with it—there is no escaping either the gravity or the totality of its challenge to our survival and to our security—a challenge that confronts us in unaccustomed ways in every sphere of human activity.

This deadly challenge imposes upon our society two requirements of direct concern both to the press and to the President—two requirements that may seem almost contradictory in tone, but which must be reconciled and fulfilled if we are to meet this national peril. I refer, first, to the need for far greater public information; and, second, to the need for far greater official secrecy.

The very word "secrecy" is repugnant in a free and open society and we are as a people inherently and historically opposed to secret societies, to secret oaths and to secret proceedings. We decided long ago that the dangers of excessive and unwarranted concealment of pertinent facts far outweighed the dangers which are cited to justify it.

Even today, there is little value in opposing the threat of a closed society by imitating its arbitrary restrictions. Even today,

* *New York Times*, April 28, 1961, p. 14.

there is little value in insuring the survival of our nation if our traditions do not survive with it. And there is a very grave danger that an announced need for increased security will be seized upon by those anxious to expand its meaning to the very limits of official censorship and concealment.

That I do not intend to permit to the extent that it's in my control. And no official of my Administration, whether his rank is high or low, civilian or military, should interpret my words here tonight as an excuse to censor the news, to stifle dissent, to cover up our mistakes or to withhold from the press and the public the facts they deserve to know.

DISCIPLINE ASKED

But I do ask every publisher, every editor and every newsman in the nation to reexamine his own standards, and to recognize the nature of our country's peril. In time of war, the Government and the press have customarily joined in an effort, based largely on self-discipline, to prevent unauthorized disclosures to the enemy. In times of clear and present danger, the courts have held that even the privileged rights of the First Amendment must yield to the public's need for national security.

Today no war has been declared—and however fierce the struggle may be, it may never be declared in the traditional fashion. Our way of life is under attack. Those who make themselves our enemy are advancing around the globe. The survival of our friends is in danger. And yet no war has been declared, no borders have been crossed by marching troops, no missiles have been fired.

If the press is awaiting a declaration of war before it imposes the self-discipline of combat conditions, then I can only say that no war ever posed a greater threat to our security. If you are awaiting a finding of "clear and present danger," then I can only say that the danger has never been more clear and its presence has never been more imminent.

DANGER CITED

It requires a change in outlook, a change in tactics, a change in mission by the Government, by the people, by every business man or labor leader and by every newspaper. For we are opposed around the world by a monolithic and ruthless conspiracy that relies primarily on covert means for expanding its sphere of influence—on infiltration instead of invasion, on subversion instead of elections, on intimidation instead of free choice, on guerillas by night instead of armies by day.

It is a system which has conscripted vast human and material resources into the building of a tightly knit, highly efficient machine that combines military, diplomatic, intelligence, economic, scientific and political operations.

Its preparations are concealed, not published. Its mistakes are buried, not headlined. Its dissenters are silenced, not praised. No expenditure is questioned, no rumor is printed, no secret is revealed. It conducts the cold war, in short, with a wartime discipline no democracy would ever hope or wish to match.

Nevertheless, every democracy recognizes the necessary restraints of national security—and the question remains whether those restraints need to be more strictly observed if we are to oppose this kind of attack as well as outright invasion.

For the facts of the matter are that this nation's foes have openly boasted of acquiring through our newspapers information they would otherwise hire agents to acquire through theft, bribery or espionage; that details of this nation's covert preparations to counter the enemy's covert operations have been available to every newspaper reader, friend and foe alike; that the size, the strength, the location and the nature of our forces and weapons, and our plans and strategy for their use, have all been pinpointed in the press and other news media to a degree sufficient to satisfy any foreign power; and that, in at least one case, the publication of details concerning a secret mechanism whereby satellites were followed required its alteration at the expense of considerable time and money.

The newspapers which printed these stories were loyal, patriotic, responsible and well-meaning. Had we been engaged in open warfare, they undoubtedly would not have published such items. But in the absence of open warfare, they recognized only the tests of journalism and not the tests of national security. And my question tonight is whether additional tests should not now be adopted.

VOLUNTARY PLAN SOUGHT

That question is for you alone to answer. No public official should answer it for you. No governmental plan should impose its restraints against your will. But I would be failing in my duty to the nation in considering all of the responsibilities that we now bear and all of the means at hand to meet those responsibilities if I did not commend this problem to your attention, and urge its thoughtful consideration.

On many earlier occasions, I have said—and your newspapers have constantly said—that these are times that appeal to every citizen's sense of sacrifice and self-discipline. They call out to every citizen to weigh his rights and comforts against his obligation to the common good. I cannot now believe that those citizens who serve in the newspaper business consider themselves exempt from that appeal.

I have no intention of establishing a new Office of War Information to govern the flow of news. I am not suggesting any new forms of censorship or new types of security classifications. I have no easy answer to the dilemma I have posed, and would not seek to impose it if I had one. But I am asking the members of the newspaper profession and the industry in this country to reexamine their own responsibilities—to consider the degree and the nature of the present danger—and to heed the duty of self-restraint which that danger imposes upon us all.

Every newspaper now asks itself, with respect to every story: "Is it news?" All I suggest is that you add the question: "Is it in the interest of national security?" And I hope that every group in America—unions and business men and public officials at every level—will ask the same question of their endeavors, and subject their actions to this same exacting test.

And should the press of America consider and recommend the voluntary assumption of specific new steps or machinery, I can assure you that we will cooperate wholeheartedly with those recommendations.

Perhaps there will be no recommendations. Perhaps there is no answer to the dilemma faced by a free and open society in a cold and secret war. In times of peace, any discussion of this subject, and any action that results, are both painful and without precedent. But this is a time of peace and peril which knows no precedent in history.

OBLIGATION TO INFORM

It is the unprecedented nature of this challenge that also gives rise to your second obligation—an obligation which I share. And that is our obligation to inform and alert the American people—to make certain that they possess all the facts they need, and understand them as well—the perils, the prospects, the purposes of our program and the choices that we face.

No President should fear public scrutiny of his program. For from that scrutiny comes understanding; and from that understanding comes support, or opposition, and both are necessary. I am not asking your newspapers to support an Administration. But I am asking your help in the tremendous task of informing and alerting the American people. For I have complete confidence in the response and dedication of our citizens whenever they are fully informed.

I not only could not stifle controversy among your readers—I welcome it. This Administration intends to be candid about its errors; for, as a wise man once said: "An error doesn't become a mistake until you refuse to correct it." We intend to accept full responsibility for our errors; and we expect you to point them out when we miss them.

Without debate, without criticism, no Administration and no country can succeed—and no republic can survive. That is why the Athenian lawmaker Solon decreed it a crime for any citizen to shrink from controversy. And that is why our press was protected by the First Amendment—the only business in America specifically protected by the Constitution—not primarily to amuse and entertain, not to emphasize the trivial and the sentimental, not to simply "give the public what it wants"—but to inform, to arouse, to reflect, to state our dangers and our opportunities, to indicate our crises and our choices, to lead, mold, educate and sometimes even anger public opinion.

WIDER COVERAGE URGED

This means greater coverage and analysis of international news —for it is no longer far away and foreign but close at hand and local. It means greater attention to improved understanding of the news as well as improved transmission. And it means, finally, that government at all levels, must meet its obligation to provide you with the fullest possible information outside the narrowest limits of national security and in intent to do it.

It was early in the seventeenth century that Francis Bacon remarked on three recent inventions already transforming the world;

the compass, gunpowder and the printing press. Now the links between the nations first forged by the compass have made us all citizens of the world, the hopes and threats of one becoming the hopes
and threats of us all. In that one world's effort to live together, the
evolution of gunpowder to its ultimate limit has warned mankind
of the terrible consequences of failure.

And so it is to the printing press—to the recorder of man's deeds,
the keeper of his conscience, the courier of his news—that we look
for strength and assistance, confident that with your help man will
be what he was born to be: free and independent.

SELECTION 12

FREEDOM AND THE PRESS*

THE NEW YORK TIMES

*This editorial discusses the issues and considerations surrounding the
relations between the national interest and the publication of news in the
light of President Kennedy's speech (selection 11).*

An issue fundamental to the security and to the freedom of the
American people was raised last night by the President of the United
States in his speech to the Bureau of Advertising of the American
Newspaper Publishers Association. It is an issue that most immediately and directly affects the press in our free democratic society; and it is an issue that, especially since American participation
in the fiasco of the Cuban landings became publicly known, has
been deeply troubling thoughtful newspaper men throughout the
country.

It is the question of how to reconcile, in the context of cold war
and of the Communist technique of fighting that war, the basic
American principle of the public's right to know with the basic
necessity of maintaining the national security. In time of open and
declared war the question is regularly posed, but the solution is
relatively simple. Under such circumstances, the need for censorship,
even if it is self-censorship, as it was in this country during the last
war, is universally recognized and generally observed.

But cold war is different, and we are living in a period of cold

* *New York Times,* April 28, 1961, p. 30.

war. It is a kind of war, and yet it is not war. For the preservation of our democratic society in this time of "clear and present danger" it is more essential than ever that the people be fully informed of the problems and of the perils confronting them. This is a responsibility as much of the press as of the President. But it is equally essential that the secrets of military technique and—as the President said—of "covert preparations to counter the enemy's covert operations"—be kept inviolate. On matters affecting policy the people must know so that the people in the last analysis can decide; but the terrible difficulty arises in that twilight zone where the revelation of military secrets might affect immediately and adversely the security of the country, and yet where the withholding of information might involve deception of the public. This is a problem that no society but our kind of open democracy faces; and it is because the maintenance of our kind of open society is so precious that the dilemma is so terrible.

Naturally, when "secret" activities become matters of general knowledge in the community, there is no longer a secret—as to a large extent was the case in connection with the Cuban landings. But to dismiss the problem with that observation is to beg the question. For there are often real secrets, and they are often discovered. The President did not attempt to solve the problem, but he did ask American journalists to apply something more than the mere test of "is it news?" He asked that we also apply the test of "is it in the national interest?"—an unsatisfactory test because it is so subjective, and yet one that in the context of the present day must also be applied.

No formula can be entirely satisfactory. Certainly censorship is not, and complete license is not, either. The best for the moment is to take seriously the President's request for self-restraint. Along with this ought to go greater accessibility of officials, so that newspaper men may have frank and informed advice on the harm that might come from revelation of a discovered secret. No responsible newspaper would knowingly damage the national interest; and the greater candor in government promised by the President will materially help protect that interest.

Problems of Evaluating Information

Much of the information which one acquires needs careful evaluation in order to eliminate distortions which result from the observer's biases or the reporter's prejudices.

The six readings which are presented in this section can be divided into three categories.

(a) The article by Professor Wendell Johnson (selection 13) and the excerpts from Mr. Lowell J. Carr's book (selection 14) describe the "built-in" problems which all individuals have as they try to assess the nature of the world around them. The digest of William Buchanan's and Hadley Cantril's study (selection 15) indicates some of the results this natural bias produces when individuals evaluate the activities of persons in other cultures.

(b) The articles by Ben H. Bagdikian (selection 16) and Warren Breed (selection 17) describe some of the distortion which creeps into (or is intentionally injected into) available information sources.

(c) The concluding essay in the section (selection 18) analyzes some common methods of recognizing and classifying biases in information.

SELECTION 13

HOW EVERYONE FILTERS THE FACTS*

WENDELL JOHNSON

WENDELL JOHNSON, *speech pathologist and author, has been a Professor at the University of Iowa since 1931. He is widely known as a government and private consultant and has been awarded many academic and professional honors. Among his books is* Your Most Enchanted Listener *(1956).*

This is the problem of misevaluation and the part it plays in the process of communication. Whether a speaker talks to one other person or to millions of listeners he must select something to talk about and he must decide to make one set of statements rather than another about it. Faced with a vast expanse of reality—and fancy—he must discriminate, select, and discard, weigh, judge, and arrange

* Reprinted from *The Iowa Publisher* (August, 1954).

the details before him. For every detail he leaves in the field of his consideration, there are innumerable other details that he must leave out.

SPEAKER FILTERS FACTS

In carrying on this relentless evaluative process, the speaker intrudes himself as a kind of filter between the world he talks about and the other persons to whom he talks about it. And each of these other persons is also in his own fashion, a sort of filter through which only certain sizes and shapes of fact and feeling and belief, as it were, can pass—on their way to still other persons who, in their turn, filter what is conveyed to them, relaying on to still others only what passes through their own evaluative meshes.

It would seem that a great share of our trouble is due to the simple fact that most of us are, in large measure and most of the time, unaware of our own evaluative processes and of the ways, peculiar to us as individuals, in which they do indeed filter the world surrounding us as we try to describe and explain that world to our fellows. We simply do not realize how greatly our accounts of what we take to be reality are colored and formed by our personal evaluations of that reality, nor do we as a rule appreciate or understand the fact that the "same" reality may be evaluated very differently by two different persons, both honest and intelligent. Forgetting these things, or never quite knowing them at all, we interpret differences of evaluation as disagreements, and disagreements as conflicts, and we react to conflicts as though they were motivated by ill will, those with whom we are in conflict appearing to be unreasonable and, in the end, unacceptable to us.

GRAVE THREAT TO HUMANITY

These problems are in a sense inherent in the fact that men are unique among the creatures of the earth in being creators and users of symbols, and so they are problems that have always plagued mankind. There are, however, two very important considerations to be stressed. The one is that any difficulties arising in the use of language become increasingly serious in their effects as the means of communication become increasingly efficient. And, of course, in recent years communication has come to be greatly more efficient than it formerly was, so that today for the first time in history we can in the space of an instant spray the verbal spume of our hatreds over whole continents and befog the entire globe with our confusions and obfuscations. In this fact lies surely today's gravest threat to humanity's future.

The other crucial consideration is that these difficulties in the use of language are not beyond the limits of our understanding and of our ability to deal with them constructively. They are not part and parcel of language itself; the cure does not consist of plucking out our tongues. Nor does the fault lie with the world, as such—the world of not-words. The chief source of trouble—and the major reason for hope—would seem to be our lack of consciousness of our symbolic functions, and our ignorance of the role of language in our evaluative processes. *We have a most urgent need for awareness of the fact that each one of us necessarily filters the world in trying to present information about it.*[1] We need knowledge, far more knowledge than we now possess, about the effects of our symbol systems and of the process of symbolizing our experience upon the development of our individual personalities and of our ways of living together. But if we recognize these needs we should not find it impossible to meet them quite effectively by means of scientific research and the knowledge it so faithfully yields and by means of using this knowledge in the education of our children, most of all, but of ourselves as well.

SELECTION 14

SITUATIONAL ANALYSIS*

LOWELL J. CARR

LOWELL CARR *was Professor of Sociology at the University of Michigan from 1920 until his retirement in 1955. Among his numerous publications are* Delinquency Control *(1940) and* Analytical Sociology *(1955).*

As an ordinary person facing a social situation, you are a poor instrument to prepare a record for four reasons:

1. *You look at your social world through a set of colored spec-*

[1] Emphasis added—Editor.
* Reprinted from *Situational Analysis*, by Lowell J. Carr (New York: Harper and Brothers, 1948), pp. 5-7.

tacles. Everyone of us is the product of the culture in which he has been reared. Culture is the body of man-made things, symbols, relationships, ideas, beliefs, practices, and values peculiar to a population. That you bear your father's family name, that you believe every effect has a cause, that you eat with a knife and fork and pay for your food with money, that a man or woman is supposed to have only one mate at a time and then only after a certain binding ceremony called marriage—these are matters of culture. As we all know, culture has been evolving and accumulating for at least 500,000 years. You were born into a pre-existing culture, you have as a matter of course assimilated the beliefs and presuppositions implicit in your family and community culture, and you tend, therefore to see situations as your culture defines them for you, and to adopt the role, or set of behavior patterns prescribed by our culture for each situation. This is what we mean by looking at situations through "colored spectacles." Culture defines your world for you. Before you can become a dependable observer you must learn to discount your culture. . . . You must learn, in other words, to become keenly aware of the relativity of your own point of view in every social situation and to make allowance for that relativity. If you cannot overcome . . . your dominant expectations, at least you can become aware that you have them.

2. You are also a poor instrument to prepare an objective record because *you have a habit of wanting practical results, rather than mere objective data in any given situation.* . . . In nearly every situation you want some one specific outcome rather than another. Even at the movies you identify yourself with the hero or heroine and hope the villain gets what's coming to him. That attitude of wanting one thing to happen rather than another is not scientific detachment. In any situation in which your real interests are involved, you will find it very difficult indeed to discount the distorting effect of this tendency of yours to take sides. . . .

3. A third reason why you are a poor instrument . . . is that *you do not want to be objective, you do not want to dissociate yourself from the phenomena under observation.* In any situation involving another race, another social class, the other sex, or some idea that vigorously challenges one of your own pet ideas, you will cling tenaciously to your own stereotype (expectation) or desire. You will resist objectivity with every subterfuge and rationalization that you

can think of. And you will insist that the situation is what you say it is because that is what you want it to be.

4. Finally, *you are a poor instrument for the preparation of an objective record of any situation bigger than your immediate presence, for your contacts with such situations are bound to be more or less haphazard, incomplete, and subject to all kinds of distortions implicit in the processes of distance communication in modern society*. . . . Actually most of us have to take our definitions of beyond-the-horizon situations at second, fourth or tenth hand, and we can never know just how much arbitrary selection and distortion have gone into the process before the product reaches us. After all, no picture can be any better than the man who points the camera.

SELECTION 15

HOW NATIONS SEE EACH OTHER*

WILLIAM BUCHANAN and HADLEY CANTRIL

WILLIAM BUCHANAN *is Professor of Political Science at the University of Southern California and has taught at Mississippi State College. He was co-author with Herbert Krugman and Richard W. Van Wagenen of* An International Police Force and Public Opinion *(1954).*

A. HADLEY CANTRIL *is a psychologist who has taught at Dartmouth, Harvard, Columbia, and Princeton, where he has been a Professor since 1945. He served in the Office of War Information during World War II and has held several other government positions. He is the author of* Tensions That Cause War *(1950) and other works.*

The following selection was compiled from the findings of the authors by Charles A. McClelland of San Francisco State College.

The facts and conclusions contained in the book *How Nations See Each Other* were based on several surveys sponsored by UNESCO in 1948 and 1949. Those which are of greatest interest to us were in response to the following question in the UNESCO survey: From the list of words on this card, which seems to you to describe the —— people best? Select as many as you wish. . . . If you have no particular feelings one way or the other, just say so.

* Based on *How Nations See Each Other* by William Buchanan and Hadley Cantril (Urbana: University of Illinois Press, 1953), pp. 45, 49, 50, 56 and 59, 92 and 94.

The words were: hardworking, intelligent, practical, conceited, generous, cruel, backward, brave, self-controlled, domineering, progressive, peace-loving, impossible to characterize.

This questionnaire was given to people in eight different countries. Each group selected those words which they felt best described themselves and then selected those which they felt best described each of five other countries, the U.S., the Soviet Union, France, Britain and China.

The results of the survey clearly indicate that national stereotypes do exist. There was, however, a wide range of response shown in the "impossible to characterize" category. For example, 71% of the Germans tested selected this answer in description of the Chinese. But only 3% of the French and the Americans selected this answer in description of themselves.

The picture of the Russians is quite consistent from country to country but that of the Americans is somewhat less so. Consistencies, which surmount the translation barrier, suggest that stereotyped views of certain people are common property of the Western culture rather than the effect of bilateral national outlooks that differ from one country to another.

There is some evidence that stereotypes change. In 1942 the Office of Public Opinion Research asked a sample of 1200 Americans to select those adjectives (from a list of 25) which best described the Russians. Seven of these were also used on the UNESCO survey. The results of the seven which were used in both surveys were as follows:

	1942	1948
Hardworking	61%	49%
Intelligent	16	12
Practical	18	13
Conceited	3	28
Cruel	9	50
Brave	48	28
Progressive	24	15

This alteration over a period of time (plus some other evidence) suggests that stereotypes are less likely to *govern* the likes and dislikes between nations than to *adapt* themselves to the positive or negative relationship based on matters unrelated to images of the people concerned. It seems that the individual is first brought to a feeling of like or dislike after which he refocuses his mental image to correspond. Stereotypes should not be thought of as causative, but as symptomatic. "These people threaten us, they have fought against us, they are just across our border, we cannot understand what they say, hence they *must* be cruel, conceited, domineering, etc."

The results of the stereotype question indicate: (1) that there exists in all eight countries surveyed a tendency to ascribe certain characteristics to certain people; (2) that there is a uniform tendency of respondents of all countries, taken as a whole, to describe the Russians in the same terms (i.e. domineering, hardworking, cruel, backward), and somewhat less agreement on the Americans (i.e. progressive, hardworking, conceited, practical, generous); (3) that stereotypes of one's own countrymen are invariably in flattering terms (peace-loving, generous, hardworking, intelligent, brave, etc.) (Note: no people rate others above themselves); (4) that the prevalence of complimentary over derogatory terms in a national stereotype is a good index of friendliness between nations.

The survey accentuated a phenomenon that has frequently been remarked—the narrow limits of the individual's horizon. The individual respondent is quick and definite in answers about conditions that affect him personally—his job, his security, his location in the class structure.

There is an evident connection between the individual's position in his national life and his view of the world. Involved in this position are his income and "status," his occupation, his education and his feeling of personal security.

Respondents generally indicated that the "kind of life they would like to lead" involved economic advantages. Nations with higher standards of living were recognized as offering this life, by their own natives and by outsiders as well.

Whether respondents in one nation express themselves as "friendly" or "unfriendly" to other "people" seems to be influenced by proximity of the latter, their language, and the policies of their government which are discernible in the history of their neutrality or military and ideological alliances. These aspects determine how much attention a nation attracts and whether it stimulates confidence or apprehension. It appears that the individual, after deciding whether a nation threatens or reassures him, then fills in with a description of the people of that nation coloring them in predominantly attractive or predominantly unattractive characteristics to suit his purposes.

Peoples everywhere were prone to stereotype their own nationality in favorable terms.

SELECTION 16

THE NEWSMAGAZINES*

BEN H. BAGDIKIAN

BEN H. BAGDIKIAN *is* Washington correspondent and staff writer for the Providence Journal-Bulletin. *In 1950 he wrote "Pitchmen of the Press," a prize-winning study of four American columnists and commentators. In 1956 he was awarded an Ogden Reid Foundation Fellowship for a study of the press in England, France and Italy. The selection below originally appeared as a series of twelve articles in the* Journal-Bulletin. *It was later reprinted in the* New Republic *(Feb. 1959). The manuscript for the material in this collection was a reprint distributed by the promotion department of the* Journal-Bulletin.

1. EACH WEEK THE WORLD NEATLY RECONSTRUCTED

Each week a politically crucial bloc of American voters—perhaps as many as 10,000,000 men and women—have arranged before their eyes a neatly reconstructed picture of the nation and the world. This arrangement is through the pages of the Big Three among news magazines:

Time, Newsweek, and U.S. News & World Report.

Each magazine tells its readers it is devoted mainly to news.

Time's subtitle is: "The Weekly Newsmagazine."

Newsweek's name is augmented by its motto: "A Well-Informed Public is America's Greatest Security."

And the encyclopaedic title, U.S. News & World Report, is embellished with the legend: "The Complete News Magazine."

The 4,000,000 copies of newsmagazines that are picked off newsstands and delivered by mailmen go into homes and are read chiefly for what they have to report of the news of the world.

But their function is not the same as newspapers'. The

* Reprinted by permission of Mr. Bagdikian and the publishers of *The Providence Journal and the Evening Bulletin,* from the issues of *The Providence Journal-Bulletin,* October 5-17, 1958.

58,000,000 copies of daily newspapers that circulate every day among Americans record as quickly as possible the hard bricks of events that come flying through the air minute-by-minute, hour-by-hour, and day-by-day.

The magazines look back at the end of the week, pick up the random blocks where they lie, rearrange them into an architecture, add their own backdrops, landscaping, climate and sound effects.

How accurate is this weekly re-creation? How close to real life does it look a year afterward, five years afterward? How often are the bricks placed where they fit? How often are they left alone when, for the moment, they don't seem to fit anywhere? How often are the bricks of real events reshaped to build a scene more comforting to the public eye or more satisfying to a publisher's taste than the scenery of real life?

For whom is this weekly world prepared?

A Time magazine advertisement once said:

"America's leading educators, presidents of business corporations, members of Congress, the top men in practically every field vote Time their favorite magazine."

Newsweek recently said a survey found "65.4 per cent of Newsweek families are administrative and operating executives."

Many top men do read the newsmagazines. Yet, it is a cliché among many professional men that Time and Newsweek are interesting until they report something the reader happens to know about and then they are terrible. This is a criticism made of many other popular publications, but few interpret events with such dogmatic finality as the newsmagazines.

But there is even some evidence that not all "top men" favor the newsmagazines.

Five years ago some 700 scientists were polled by Marie Bestul of the University of Maryland as to publications they found congenial. Top response was The New York Times, 20 per cent; Harpers, 13 per cent; The Reporter, 12 per cent; The Saturday Review, 10 per cent; Atlantic Monthly, 10 per cent.

Almost at the bottom was Newsweek, less than one-half of one per cent; and U.S. News & World Report, less than one-quarter of one per cent. Time was not included by name in the study but failed to get a significant number of votes in a space left for write-ins.

There are some interesting variations in the pattern of sales of the weekly newsmagazines. In general, they sell more in cities than in rural areas. Time, for example, sells 12 magazines for every 1,000 persons in the country as a whole, but 19 for every 1,000 persons in metropolitan areas.

Education levels, literacy and incomes are higher in city areas, and in such locations there are more occupations—such as stockholders, government employes, and major merchants—affected by national affairs and therefore provide better markets for general news.

But not all city areas buy Time magazine in the same proportion. In Boston, for example, 30 copies of Time are sold per 1,000 Bostonians. But only 16 are sold per 1,000 in New York.

If one lists the metropolitan areas with a high proportion of newsmagazine sales he finds that one characteristic of such cities, with some exceptions, is that these communities are served by inadequate newspapers when it comes to national, international and cultural news and serious, rational commentary on the news.

The cities with low sales of newsmagazines tend to be those with better newspapers.

Average sales per thousand persons for Time in all major city areas is 19. Some places where the magazine does not sell so well are, with copies sold per thousand:

Baltimore	16	Louisville	12
Charlotte, N.C.	16	Nashville	15
Chicago	16	New York	16

Some places where Time sells at higher-than-average levels are:

Boston	30	Omaha	29
Los Angeles	28	San Francisco	28
Manchester, N.H.	29		

(In Providence Time sells 16 copies per thousand.)

Yet, plainly there are factors other than good and bad newspapers governing the sales of newsmagazines. Los Angeles, for example, has a relatively low output of serious news and commentary in its daily newspapers. Yet its high sales of Time could also stem from the splash Hollywood makes in the national news and the stake of so many of its citizens in how that splash is recorded in the mass media.

Washington, on the other hand, has good, serious newspapers, but also high newsmagazine sales (32 Times per 1,000). Here the sales are high, probably because the population is heavy with bureaucrats and other government employes who generate most national news and whose careers are affected by how this news is reported.

The fact that the sales of Newsweek follow the same general pattern as Time indicates more than an accidental influence at work. U.S. News & World Report varies somewhat.

Whatever the pattern, the popular and commercial success of the magazines is proof that they satisfy millions of Americans. Time, Inc., the parent corporation of which Time magazine is the foundation, grossed a quarter of a billion dollars last year and showed a profit of $25,000,000.

And no matter what criticism can be made of the magazines' contents, their success is based largely on the serious desire of readers to get an idea of what goes on in the world. In an era of instant communication, revolutionary change, new and alarming pressures and an endless stream of news, it is natural and encouraging that the serious citizen pauses occasionally and asks himself what it all means.

The newsmagazines tell him.

It seems legitimate to inquire into how fair, how accurate, how reasonable are the interpretations the newsmagazines present to their their public.

Most newspapers cling to the ideal—some say outmoded—that the reporter should let the news speak for itself, that the reporter should record the facts of an event objectively and not tell the reader what he thinks they mean.

The late Elmer Davis once said:

"The good newspaper, the good news broadcaster, must walk a tightrope between two great gulfs—on one side the false objectivity that takes everything at face value and lets the public be imposed on by the charlatan with the most brazen front; on the other, the 'interpretive' reporting which fails to draw the line between objective and subjective, between a reasonably well-established fact and what the reporter or editor wishes were the fact."

Thus, the success of the newsmagazines is based partly on the failure of newspapers, if the pattern of variation of sales in certain cities means anything. The magazines' growth is also a sign that there is an unmet popular demand for simple, dramatic interpretation of the news.

If the newsmagazines often make the news too simple and too dramatic, they survive, because the popular hunger is there.

The major question then becomes: who is the man who interprets the news, what is his record for accuracy, for integrity, for fairness, for rationality, for respect for the need of the citizen to know all the facts as they occur, pleasant and unpleasant?

It is one of the ironies of the Big Three newsmagazines that the proprietor with a reputation for the most extreme personal political bias, publishes a newsmagazine with a reputation for being the least biased of the three—U.S. News & World Report.

How justified is that reputation?

2. U.S. NEWS, FAST-RISING GIANT

On the last page of the fastest rising newsmagazine in America one finds in small print:

"This page presents the opinions of the Editor."

A study of six months of David Lawrence's U.S. News & World Report shows that these opinions run to the need to expel Russia from the United Nations and attack it militarily, the "illegality" (his quotation marks) of the Supreme Court decision on racial integration, the dangers of "New Deal experimentalism," the "dictatorship" of big unions, the "immorality" of stopping H-bomb tests, and the general perfidy of the Kremlin and left-wing Supreme Court justices.

On this same page is printed another sentence:

"The news pages are written by other staff members independently of these editorial views."

Are they?

One newspaper editor, answering a poll, referred to "Lawrence's reactionary weekly." Yet the survey of 144 editorial page editors, by Carol Donley of the Dept. of Journalism, University of Wyoming, resulted in easy first place in usefulness for Lawrence's magazine. Time was a poor second, Newsweek third.

This kind of recognition must be a source of deep satisfaction to the 69-year-old editor. The son of poor immigrants, he worked his way through Princeton as an Associated Press campus reporter, developed a close relationship with college president Woodrow Wilson. When Wilson went to the White House, his relationship made Lawrence a leading political reporter.

It is, perhaps, typical of Lawrence that he sacrificed this valuable professional contact and personal friendship by reporting—because he thought it important news—that Wilson had suffered a stroke that impaired his abilities.

Lawrence became a financial reporter, started a syndicate, and in 1926 began a rather dreary daily report of government decisions and announcements called "U.S. Daily." At the same time, he wrote an increasingly conservative daily column (it now appears in 250 daily papers). While a former employe, Drew Pearson, and friends Walter Lippmann and Joseph Alsop were commenting more or less sympathetically on the New Deal in the '30s, Lawrence became known as one of the most conservative commentators in the trade.

By 1940 Lawrence had considerable wealth and put much of it into the new "U.S. News," forerunner of the present magazine. What happened afterward may be depressing to some who admire impersonal news presentation. "U.S. News" had no visible bias. Ten years ago he married it to "World Report" and a bias, or point of view, began to be evident to many. It became successful from that time on.

The circulation was 354,000 in 1951, went to 922,000 in 1957, is thought to be over 1,200,000 today. This is about the same as Newsweek, half as much as Time. It is believed that U.S. News & World Report could make two or three times its present profits if it did not pour so much into news space. But its growth certainly is related to this generous allocation of space to the reader. (Lawrence's 60 per cent interest is held in trust, will go on his death to the employes, who already own 40 per cent.)

Among the features of this growing giant are:

Lengthy tape-recorded interviews with important news sources, printed verbatim in question-and-answer form without comment.

Generous use of full texts of important public declarations, speeches by politicians, and other spoken news, also without comment within the text. These plus the interviews may constitute as much as one-third of any one issue.

Competent on-the-scene reports by the magazine's correspondents.

Full-scale analytical pieces on a single theme, with heavy emphasis on economic reporting.

Outstanding use of graphic illustration to clarify economic and other complex news.

These all include many presentations plainly contrary to the opinions of David Lawrence himself.

In terms of quantity of reporting U.S. News & World Report is far ahead of its two major competitors. In 1957 it averaged 90 pages a week of news, double Time and Newsweek. In the first six months of 1958 it printed 297 pages on business outlook (Newsweek, 82; Time, 36); 103 pages on education (Time and Newsweek each 34 pages); and 91 pages on science and space (Newsweek 74; Time, 54). Total news pages so far this year average 69 pages a week for U.S. News & World Report, 52 for Newsweek, and 46 for Time.

This by itself is no measure of net value to the reader. Time and Newsweek summarize, which could conceivably be more useful than the lengthy primary documents published by U.S. News & World Report. And Time and Newsweek devote considerable space to cultural-intellectual-entertainment life, but U.S. News & World Report almost none.

But for political and economic reporting, Time and Newsweek plainly are outdistanced in space and detail by their younger rival.

A study at the University of Syracuse School of Journalism of the 1956 political campaign showed that Time printed 34,000 words of campaign news, Newsweek some 14,000 and U.S. News & World Report, 150,000 words. Searching for bias, the survey said Time's words were 75 per cent biased toward the Republicans, Newsweek's 28 per cent toward the Republicans, U.S. News & World Report only one per cent toward the Republicans, the rest neutral.

But this study evidently looked only for editorially inserted words of bias. U.S. News & World Report deals heavily in exact reproduction of the words of others. The Syracuse survey did not measure a pertinent factor: how balanced and fair was the selection of persons whose words were accurately reported? And in what editorial surroundings were these words placed?

A study of this year's U.S. News & World Report shows that it uses sources who are individually legitimate and interesting focal points of news and opinion. But it also shows that taken together they do not form a balanced picture of informed opinion.

In the first six months of this year, for example, there were verbatim interviews with 27 representatives of large corporations. There were almost none from labor or the opposite wing of domestic economics. On auto workers' demands there were textual reprints from heads of the car manufacturing corporations, none from the union. On prices, wages and profits there were full texts from Harlow Curtice, head of General Motors; Roger M. Blough, chairman of U.S. Steel; and Benjamin F. Fairless, president of the American Iron & Steel Institute; but none from the opposite side.

Where the magazine searched out unusual sources, they tended to be on the side of the editor's opinions. For example, on March 21 the magazine reprinted as news the monthly newsletter of the First National City Bank of New York. Its message was that Germany is more prosperous than England because Germany has a free enterprise economy and England a semi-socialist one. No presentation was made of the obvious additional or even contrary factors in understanding the two economies.

Politically, the personalities and space are biased toward the Lawrence view. Of speech texts from 12 politicians, 11 are conservatives or conservative-moderates (Styles Bridges, Harry Byrd, Lyndon Johnson, John Stennis) and only one (Hubert Humphrey) from the other side of the Congressional spectrum.

On Jan. 21 a series of texts on the political campaign formed a Republican-versus-Democratic debate by way of speeches selected by the editors. The three Republicans (President Eisenhower, Nixon and Sherman Adams) started off with three and three-tenths pages; the three Democrats (Sam Rayburn, Humphrey and Dean Acheson) were at the end with seven-tenths of one page, or only 18 per cent of the total space for that feature.

Typically in the magazine there is hard news, there is give-and-take, and typically, there are legitimate individual sources accurately reproduced who add up to a solid net profit in space and emphasis for the Lawrence opinions.

This is not to say that anti-Lawrence opinions are excluded. In actual wordage, there are probably more in U.S. News & World Report than in Time, Newsweek, or, indeed, in the liberal New Republic and The Nation. But in balance and net impact, the total effect is heavily weighted in his favor.

This weight is enhanced by editorial handling of otherwise neutral or unbiased reportage. For example, on May 23 the issue was devoted to the cover theme: COMMUNISTS FORCING SHOWDOWN?

To carry out this Lawrentian theme, it was necessary to torture much of the first-rate material that did not fit the editorial mold. There was no evidence of fiddling with reports themselves, only their immersion in contrary surroundings.

This was the week of the Latin American mobs attacking Vice President Nixon and of the French Army revolt in Algeria. The lead introduction said: "Violence flared last week on four continents . . . Back of almost all of it was Communist direction."

Yet, it was plain that the French Army revolt was not Communist inspired. And Vice President Nixon was the first to say that Communism was not the basic explanation for the mobs in Latin America. In fact, these points were borne out by the reports of the magazine's own correspondents.

Over the first-hand story of Robert Kleiman, U.S. News & World Report correspondent, the magazine headline read: "Communist-supplied arms . . . played a major part. Communist political tactics in Paris played still another role. It was in this situation that French officers finally rebelled . . ."

But the story this headline described made almost the opposite point. Kleiman made much of "intimidation by right-wing leaders . . ." The only material in his story the headline could refer to was one sentence in the 17th paragraph: "To win the Algerian war, General Massu maintained that the flow of rebel arms from neighboring Tunisia must be halted. Some of these arms come from Communist sources."

A boxed display thrust into the midst of the Kleiman report announced: "TREND OF CONFLICT: Rebel attacks have been increasing recently, as Communist arms flowed in from next-door Tunisia . . ."

Even in the standing feature, "Business Around the World," the theme was "supported" by: "Busy as their firebrands are with brickbats, the Communists still have time to poke around in the trouble spots of the business world . . ." Fifteen lines later it added that Communist bloc nations may not be aiming primarily at weakening Western markets so much as getting rid of their own surplus problems.

The bristling supernationalism of Lawrence appears in a dramatic display on Page 43 entitled: "When U.S. Is Insulted Now and 44 Years Ago." It noted that 44 years ago when Mexico arrested seven American sailors and then refused to apologize or to raise the

U.S. flag and give it a 21-gun salute, American soldiers invaded Mexico and occupied Vera Cruz for seven months. The display then reported that by contrast when the Vice President was spat on by mobs, American soldiers were sent only to nearby countries, not right into Venezuela.

The magazine repeated the theme again on Sept. 5, 1958, in an article on the murder by Iraq mobs of three Americans. It printed a two-thirds-of-a-page display recalling 19th century American enforcement of payments by other countries, with the title—"In the Past: When Americans Have Been Killed Or Attacked Abroad—"

The theme: COMMUNISTS FORCING SHOWDOWN? is over another piece of text that does not support it:

"On the spot, in South America, the answers come quickly from leaders, from the people:

"Are South Americans going Red? No.

"What bothers them then? U.S. neglect, the U.S. recession, U.S. trade barriers.

"What else? U.S. ties with dictators.

"Result? Angry neighbors."

Thus, two distinct lines appear in U.S. News & World Report:

1. Accurate reprints of interviews and public statements, plus first-hand reports by the magazine's own correspondents, many of them unbiased reporting:

2. A selection process of the reprints and interviews which heavily weights them in quantity, number and presentation on the side of Lawrence's personal convictions, and an embellishment of the first-hand reports which carry out the Editor's themes in headlines, introductions and other presentations even when these embellishments are contrary to the reports themselves.

Many years ago, Delbert Clark said:

"In some ways Lawrence is the most skillful of all the Washington columnists: he has the ability to appear sweetly reasonable while making the most highly prejudiced statements of opinion . . ."

Clark was talking of Lawrence's personal column, but a study of U.S. News & World Report leads one to much the same conclusion. It also causes doubt as to the validity of the claim:

"The news pages are written by other staff members independently of these editorial views."

[Article 3, "U.S. News and Its Wound," deals with the treatment by *U.S. News & World Report* of the integration-segregation issues in the United States, and is therefore not included in these readings in International and Intercultural Relations.]

4. U.S. NEWS AND CRYSTAL BALL

"Don't never prophesy—onless ye know."

This is a grandfather's advice by James Russell Lowell and a commandment in ordinary news reporting.

Forecasting is a weakness to which journalistic flesh is prone, and so fervent an apostle as David Lawrence in his U.S. News & World Report is guilty of this minor transgression.

The magazine, more than any of the Big Three news weeklies, is devoted to heavy portions of full texts, verbatim interviews and serious news. But here and there in the pantries of its growing mansion it sips at the wine of prophecy.

This is, perhaps, a natural weakness for a magazine that started as a financial report. The financial newsletters that proliferate from Washington and New York indicate that businessmen have a special appetite for forecasts printed in imitation typewriter type, giving the impression that the editor has just received a tip so hot he sat right down, typed it out and ran it to the mailbox.

Thus, a number of pages in U.S. News & World Report are tinted paper filled with imitation typewriter type and filled with a pot-pourri of news flashes, general background conditions, and forecasts. They are called such names as "Tomorrow, Newsgram," and "Washington Whispers," and "Trend of Business." U.S. News & World Report is said to have been the first to introduce the colored-page, imitation-typewriting to regular magazines.

Has it been a noteworthy contribution to public information?

The magazine's general business forecasts have a good reputation among businessmen, and in 1957 it had the satisfaction of having predicted quite accurately the current recession. (Although, like many a prophet, it began to get nervous when the time came and began to hedge: Jan. 3, 1958—"There was a growing opinion that the drop would prove as brief as it was sharp, with the trend starting to level off early in the new year.")

But when it moves out of the business arena into the political and diplomatic world, the magazine's crystal ball begins to cloud.

Early in 1957 it devoted its cover article to "What's Coming in Ike's Second Term."

Among other things, it assured the reader, ". . . American influence and power will be felt throughout the non-Communist world . . . Communism in this period is more likely to decline rather than grow in its appeal and influence . . . It is entirely possible that, at the end of a second Eisenhower administration, the United States will be without a real rival in all the world in point of military and political and industrial power . . . In this period, too, American power and influence is to push into the Middle East . . . Money from U.S. taxpayers and a warning that the United States will fight . . . are counted on to bring stability to countries of that area and to stop the Soviet Union from overt moves . . . A broad measure of prosperity is probable during the second term . . . Unemployment is not expected to become a major problem at any point in the four years ahead. Jobs will be quite plentiful . . ."

The second term is not yet over, so it seems safest to suspend judgment on the above forecast and merely wish the prophet luck. But one may be forgiven for questioning the magazine's vision when on May 23 this year it said: "Worldgram, From the Capitals of the World . . . Violence in little Lebanon is expected to die down in the face of U.S. power" and the next week added: "In Beirut, odds are against any call for U.S. to send in troops to help Lebanon's pro-Western Government." One week after that the prophet looked up and said crisply: "Don't expect peace to break out in Lebanon right away."

Not many weeks before, the magazine had said flatly: "Washington Whispers . . . Marshall Tito of Yugoslavia is going to retire next May as President of the nation and as Communist Party secretary."

On Dec. 27, 1957 "Washington Whispers" said: "Christian Herter, under secretary of state, is reported by his friends to be unhappy over the fact that he does not play a larger role in policy making . . ." One week later, Washington whispered back: "Christian Herter, under secretary of state, has no intention of giving up the State Department post he holds, despite reports to the contrary indicating dissatisfaction with his job."

For the benefit of any misinformed readers, U.S. News & World Report said May 30: "It turns out that the Central Intelligence

Agency knew about the Communist plans in South America to embarrass Vice President Nixon . . ." The misinformed reader could conceivably have got the idea from U.S. News & World Report the week before when it said: "Washington Whispers . . . This country's Central Intelligence Agency, counted upon to know in advance what is to happen in foreign countries, missed completely the Communist plans for attacking Nixon in South America."

The reversals in world events and the prophetic whispers tell something. They indicate that unlike most prophets, those of U.S. News & World Report set the record right when the world insists on going its own way.

They tell of the weakness for forecasting as another crotchet from the magazine's past. Other harmless editorial peculiarities, plain throw-backs to the "U.S. Daily" 30 years ago when Lawrence recorded government pronouncements, are features like "Newslines —What You as a Businessman Can and Cannot Do, as a result of recent court and administrative decisions." On May 23, for example, readers learned: "You cannot, as a producer of sugar, avoid paying the manufacturers' excise tax on sugar sold for use on a ship." In a section called "Trend of American Business," the magazine reported that a Texas physician said it is all right to feed infants cold milk, a wife can be taxed on her alimony, and "There are 55 kinds of cockroaches in the U.S."

These are minor inventions on an otherwise formidable structure of the magazine, like the prophecies.

The forecasts indicate another lesson, perhaps not quite learned as yet.

On March 21 of this year, the lead prediction in "Tomorrow" read:

"A tax cut now appears to be as certain as anything can be in this world."

On June 27, "Tomorrow," shifting to the past tense, reported: "A cut in taxes was not required to reverse a downtrend."

They teach that perhaps death and taxes, but, alas, little else, including a tax cut, is certain in this world.

5. NEWSWEEK . . . READS THE PAPERS

On Page 21 of the April 21, 1958, Newsweek magazine, the Editor-in-Chief in a message to readers said:

"Somewhere, at every moment of every day, the men and women of NEWSWEEK are at work on missions of many kinds . . . in a hut in the jungles of Cuba or Indonesia, a literary salon in Europe, at the White House in Washington, or a machine shop in Ypsilanti."

There are, indeed, Newsweek correspondents who travel to sources of news all over the world, but the Editor-in-Chief may have slighted a key man: the intrepid editor who each workday takes the elevator to his office in the Newsweek Building at 152 West 42nd Street in New York and fearlessly reads The New York Times.

The correspondents in Cuba, Paris, and Ypsilanti produce some first-rate articles in Newsweek, but the editor reading The New York Times produces more than all the others combined.

The use of so sturdy a source of news as The New York Times is admirable, but Newsweek, as does its uptown senior rival, Time, tends to present this same information not so much as fallible words from identifiable human sources as The Revealed Truth recorded in Holy Writ.

Both Time and Newsweek have human beings covering news, many of them competent. Time has 53 fulltime correspondents listed in 15 American cities outside New York, and 32 in 15 foreign cities. Newsweek has 29 in six American cities outside New York, and 11 in seven foreign cities. Both maintain additional "stringers," local reporters, usually newspaper men, who are available to cover specific items on a fee basis. And both maintain large staffs in their New York headquarters to compile, write and edit the stories.

Yet, David Cort, who worked on Time magazine from 1932 to 1946, says that 75 per cent of the material in Time came directly from The New York Times and the New York Herald-Tribune. Staff members at Newsweek say the percentage there is at least as high as at Time.

Newsweek is the middle magazine of the Big Three, at least for the moment. Its net paid weekly circulation in 1957 was 1,119,000. But it was being approached rapidly by U.S. News & World Report, which has tripled its circulation in eight years and this year is reported to be over 1,000,000. Time has twice that circulation.

Newsweek has struck many of its readers as being the middle magazine in another way. To some it has appeared to be an imitation of both its rivals.

There are signs in recent years that it has copied features of its competitor, U.S. News & World Report: verbatim interviews, graphic display of economic and social data, and possibly a more conservative political slant.

At the same time, Newsweek has had the reputation in the trade of being a kind of downtown edition of Time magazine. It has used the same basic cover color, red. Its format is almost the same. The departments into which the magazine is divided have only minor variations from Time. And its picture captions and the style of its text writing have followed the creations of Time, usually without much skill.

Some of the similarities may stem from the effect Time has had on all popular journalism. It was Time, for example, that changed the prevailing style of picture captions from the lugubrious cadences of the National Geographic to the crisp, cryptic, teasing phrases commonly attempted in newspapers and magazines today.

Time's writing style, known as "Timestyle" during the Brass Age of the magazine, went through several stages, taking some journalistic literature, including Newsweek's, with it. But in the beginning it sounded like a small town weekly. An item from Vol. 1, No. 1, of Time magazine, dated March 23, 1923, said:

"Mrs. H. H. Votaw and Miss Abigail Harding, sisters of the President of the United States, arrived at Buenos Aires from Montevideo. They were received by representatives of the American Embassy and the Argentine Foreign Office."

Fifteen years later such an event would have taken on the dramatic air of a subequatorial rendezvous. By that period Time was using "Timestyle," an artificial, super-dramatic form of writing that used manufactured words placed in upsidedown sentences. This was the era of Time obituaries that always tolled the melodramatic phrase, "As it must to all men, death came last week to . . ." It was the era of "cinemaddict" for "movie fan" and the formula whereby an archaic or rare word was used every few hundred lines with a footnote explaining what it meant (the idea was to give the middle-brow reader of Time the feeling that by reading the magazine he was in the intellectual big leagues—but with no strain on his intelligence).

In recent years Time has achieved literary respectability. While it still tends to pronounce the news in tones of Divine Authority, it usually does it in recognizable English prose, some of it highly effective. It could describe the late Senator Bilbo of Mississippi:

"He was a wretched, sick and snarling little man. But he had the voice of a brass trumpet blaring venom and racism."

Newsweek has appeared to imitate these styles. But where Time used imaginative, precise words, Newsweek tended to use flat and tired ones. Where Time confidently issued the news like Moses Revealing the Divine Word inscribed on his tablet in the Madison Avenue dialect, Newsweek's Moses often seems to carry a curbstone instead of a tablet and the message comes out in the idiom of Main Street.

This is the significance of the magazines using conventional sources for news. In Newsweek, for example, the facts can come from The New York Times, the New York Herald-Tribune, the Associated Press, United Press International and Reuters, but often the reader sees it as absolute truth souped up with a few 42nd Street adjectives. On June 9, Newsweek wrote:

"On Memorial Day at Indianapolis, hard-bitten mechanics tuned up the powerful, low-hung cars and 33 taut drivers roared out . . ."

Or else routine news and publicity releases find themselves draped in the metaphors that burden bad newspaper copy, freshman themes and other transgressions on the English language:

"Esther's company is International Swimming Pool Corp. which, like all others, is splashing its way to new records. This year . . . a gurgling $100 million more . . ."

Or in the August 11 issue a brewery official explained a transaction, or as Newsweek put it, "quickly blew the mystifying froth off the glass."

Another feature of Newsweek that detracts from its value as a news organ is its persistent self-promotion. It is constantly telling the reader what a splendid job Newsweek is doing presenting the news, perhaps on the newsmagazine theory that readers have trouble judging the facts for themselves.

It is not unusual for the editors of Newsweek to use 10 per cent of the space in an important international story telling the reader about Newsweek. History could conceivably look back with awe at the American offer to ban nuclear bomb tests. But if it looks back to Newsweek it will find that on September 1 the magazine used the first 30 per cent of its lead page on the story to tell the reader that Newsweek had said this was going to happen.

On the other hand, Newsweek's approach to the news often is more conventional and thus more readily judged by the reader than is Time's. The magazine often produces first-rate special articles on large themes. And it is unique among its rivals in regularly printing reports under the signatures of real, identifiable human beings.

U.S. News & World Report, except for some of its foreign reports, usually ascribes even eye-witness stories to its "Board of Editors." Time is a collective effort, and unlike even the Bible, offers the reader no clue as to who wrote stories that express highly individual value judgments.

Newsweek and Time both have back-of-the-book departments reporting and commenting on special fields in American arts, sciences and entertainment that provide material usually overlooked in the daily press. (While there is evidence that Newsweek, for example, reads the New York Herald-Tribune carefully for information, it was also able to note in its Press section that the Herald-Tribune had omitted any stories about the pecadillos of the son of the dictator of the Dominican Republic at about the same time that the newspaper was printing heavy advertisements from the Dominican Republic, a noteworthy sidelight on American mass media that probably would have gone unnoted in the daily press.)

Newsweek does not seem to be so dominated by a single strong set of political-social opinions or a powerful personality, as do Time and U.S. News & World Report.

The leading figure of Newsweek is Malcolm Muir, Editor-in-Chief since 1937, who has been in publishing all his life, with heavy emphasis on business and sales. He had been president of McGraw-Hill Publishing Co., where he was influential in the creation of several trade publications and of the now highly successful magazine, Business Week. His strength was said to be salesmanship. Speeches and papers for which he was known in publishing circles were, "Breaking Down Sales Resistance in Industrial Selling," "Shadows of State Socialism," and "National Dangers of the Thirty-Hour Week." In 1937 Vincent Astor and Averell Harriman headed Weekly Publications, Inc., which had been printing a magazine called News-Week since 1933. They brought Muir to head the enterprise (Astor became chairman of the board and still is. Harriman became a director, no longer is). Muir took out the hyphen and upper case "W" in the title and added the formula of news commentary and special reports. During the war and immediately afterward the magazine produced some notable special articles. But the elder Muir has always remained interested primarily in the fiscal and managerial strength of the publication. He is a director of the National Association of Manufacturers and other prominent business organizations.

Executive Editor of the magazine in his son, Malcolm Muir Jr., who spent the early years of his career with the United Press and with newspapers.

Thus, Newsweek appears to many to reflect the economic and political conservatism of its chief. At the same time Newsweek shows hesitancy in plunging completely into personal dogma in the news, which some ascribe to the conventional news disciplines learned earlier by the executive editor.

The magazine appears less unified and more loosely edited, and this, too, seems to add to its reputation of being less biased in its presentation of the news than Time.

Nevertheless, Newsweek seems compelled to duplicate Time's air of knowing it all. Yet, the holy wars of Time and self-congratulations of Newsweek arise for the most part from the same human world of news as the imperfect daily press.

Taking one issue of Newsweek at random, June 16, one finds that the main news section, National Affairs, carries information which is 53 per cent identical with news in The New York Times for the days during which Newsweek was being compiled. There is a heavy concentration in the magazine of Times items from the days Wednesday, Thursday, Friday—in which Newsweek is selecting its major stories.

In that issue of Newsweek there is one story in which the order of facts and a stretch of language is identical with The New York Times, although this conceivably could be coincidence.

In addition, the interpretation that Newsweek puts on news events, particularly foreign events, appears to follow closely The New York Times editorials of that week.

One can speculate on the hungry eye of the editor who reads the Times. On Page 33 of the June 16 issue of Newsweek there is a story entitled: DISASTER, Toll of the Wreckers. It blends three separate news items into a single theme. Two are of tornadoes striking Wisconsin (the facts in Newsweek match exactly those in an Associated Press report), and of a grasshopper plague in the Southwest (the facts for which match those in The New York Times report). A third item was far-fetched for the DISASTER theme, reporting that volunteer hurricane watchers had started their seasonal duties. One may speculate that the Newsweek editor saw the grasshopper story on Page 21 of The New York Times of June 7 and just below it, by chance on the same page, a routine story on the hurricane watchers (with facts that match exactly those that appeared in Newsweek).

A reasonable reader could hardly argue with the use by Newsweek and Time of reliable, conventional sources of news, like The New York Times and the Associated Press. But one might question the air of superior knowledge, the self-promotion and the dogmatic judgments of news displayed by the magazines without providing the reader with some sign of the source. Unlike the newspaper and wire service sources of much of the magazines' facts, Newsweek and Time leave the reader with a set of opinions and almost no room to judge the meaning of news for himself. They provide little clue as to whose opinion he is reading.

6. THE DOGMA OF OMNISCIENCE

A recent issue of Newsweek magazine declared:

"Lifting the Curtain, East Berlin—Red China . . . is calling now for an early trial of Imry Nagy, Premier of short-lived free Hungary . . ."

The date on Newsweek was June 23, 1958. The execution of Nagy had been announced on front pages everywhere six days earlier, on June 17.

Didn't the editors of Newsweek see on Tuesday, the 17th, the news of the death of a man they reported alive six days later?

Undoubtedly they did, and no doubt with considerable chagrin. For on the Tuesday that Tass, the Russian news agency, announced the execution of Nagy, the Newsweek editors were on their Monday-Tuesday "weekend." They had sent the magazine to the presses Sunday night with the "news" of the demand for Nagy's trial, Tass announced Nagy's death on Tuesday: the magazine first hit the newsstands on Wednesday—and the date on it was the following Monday. The news inside is eight days older than the date on the magazine.

Like most magazines, Newsweek put an advanced date on the magazine for understandable commercial reasons: It is easier to appear up-to-date by changing the calendar; and when a prospective buyer looks at the magazine he is less apt to think that it is "last week's issue."

All the Big Three newsmagazines have an eight-day gap between the date they send news to press and the date on the magazine, and all of them have a five-day gap between the day they appear and the date on the cover. It is no major sin. It is of interest chiefly because it is part of the news magazine mystique that makes it necessary to know everything, or to appear to know everything, and to give the reader the feeling that he is privileged to peer with the editors into the future, or at least into the secrets of the past and the inner soul of the present.

Many of the correspondents who provide material for this mystical insight are competent men highly regarded within the trade. And on more than one occasion they have dug out newer, better and more important news than the daily newspapers.

But in their daily operations the editors of the magazine ignore the dreary rules of conventional news reporting whereby the reader is supposed to be told where the news comes from. This is a discipline on reporters, preventing mere rumors, planted items and reporters' wishes and opinions from being presented as facts. And it provides the reader with some basis for judging the seriousness, significance and reliability of the news.

All news organizations from time to time use material with only a vague source specified: "a high official" or "diplomatic sources." These are sometimes first-hand official statements of importance given on condition that the correspondent not give the source, for diplomatic reasons. Or else in the judgment of the correspondent a story is basically sound and important to print, even though no individual will let his name back it up (in which case the reputation of the correspondent gives the reader a guide). But these are special cases in most news organizations, and the whole weight of professional practice is to tell the reader both the news and where it came from.

Unhampered by such rules, the newsmagazine editor can write news that is more readable, and legitimately so. Few persons, for example, would argue with the scrupulousness and usefulness of The New York Times's Review of the Week. But the lack of restraint in the news magazines often permits the news to look more titillating and more authoritative than the facts warrant, giving the reader little hint as to when the news stops and the editorial titillating begins, or when the facts end and editorial dogma takes over.

In the June 23, 1958, Newsweek, for example, one reads:

". . . the extreme rightists not only are largely uncontrolled in Algeria but are rapidly gaining strength in France itself."

The same week in Time one reads of the same rightists:

"Abandoned by their idols and outflanked by the Army—which has quietly taken over almost all key posts in the Algerian civil administration—the diehards had little choice but to make what amounted to a humiliating confession of defeat."

In Newsweek: "rapidly gaining strength."

In Time: "a humiliating confession of defeat."

When Secretary of State Dulles appeared before a hostile Senate committee, Newsweek reported Feb. 4, 1957:

". . . . Dulles flushed deeply, then went pale. He stopped his restless doodling and his pencil fell from his fingers."

Time, the same week:

"Dulles scribbled heavily at his doodle pad, his face beet-red."

Newsweek concluded:

". . . John Foster Dulles had reached a crisis in his relations with Congress."

Time concluded:

". . . Fulbright and his Senate friends were plucking political fiddle strings."

U.S. News & World Report said of Dwight Eisenhower's first political appearance in 1952:

"Voice . . . Harsher than expected. Not much warmth."

Time the same week said:

"They liked him for his strong, vigorous manner of speech."

Two weeks later U.S. News & World Report said:

"Dwight D. Eisenhower . . . found himself deep in the bewildering wonderland of big-league politics . . . so far as neutral observers could tell, the Eisenhower side seemed to be losing as many skirmishes as it was winning."

Time at about the same period on Eisenhower:

"They like him because he turned out to be an amazingly good campaigner . . . for his quiet control . . ."

In the June 13, 1958 U.S. News & World Report:

"Why are six Soviet fishing boats stationed constantly off the

East Coast of Canada? . . . That riddle has puzzled U.S. and Canadian officials for some months."

In Newsweek, dated three days later:

"Pentagon Pipeline, Navy Headquarters—Top officials here insist there is no indication that those Soviet trawlers off Newfoundland are on any sinister mission.

. . . As for recent press reports that the trawlers are up to no good, a well-informed officer says: 'Things must have been quiet over the holidays.' "

Two weeks later U.S. News & World Report had an answer to its riddle: It said "Western intelligence officials" report "Why Red Subs Prowl U.S. Coasts—Russians Mapping Ocean Floors Around America . . ." explaining that the trawlers merely supply the subs.

That week, Newsweek had a new version. In a redlined special display it said:

"THE REDS SNOOPING CLOSE TO HOME—WHY? While the Navy still publicly insisted that the Soviet 'fishing' fleet off the Newfoundland coast (see Periscope, June 16, above) was only interested in fish, intelligence reports were somewhat more candid. It seems that (they) . . . are serving as floating headquarters for Russian subs which are jamming U.S. radar in Iceland, and eavesdropping on experimental electronic installations in the Boston area . . ."

On June 23 Newsweek displayed its June 16 item proudly as a sign of its authority, although its June 23 story was the reverse of the one on June 16.

Where does this leave the reader? First, U.S. News & World Report says "U.S. and Canadian officials" are puzzled."

Newsweek at the same time says "top officials" and "a well-informed officer" are not puzzled at all, that the boats are just fishing. Then U.S. News & World Report, which had previously reported "U.S and Canadian officials" puzzled reported that "Western intelligence officials" are not puzzled but know the boats are mapping the ocean floor (presuming U.S. and Canadian officials were still puzzled, the "Western intelligence officials" must be Western European or Latin American, a grave commentary on North American intelligence). But Newsweek, which failed at the time to tell the reader its "top officials" and "well-informed officer" were not being "candid," finally told the reader that "intelligence reports" have the boats jamming radar.

Using the same vague references, Newsweek in May explained why President Eisenhower lost his temper and responded angrily to a reporter. Quoting "intimates of the President," Newsweek said:

"Far from getting him down, they said, the press conference blowoff was an indication that Mr. Eisenhower felt genuinely confident about the Administration's ability to handle problems facing the nation. . . ."

A normally skeptical reader might ask more documentation for the claim that a man loses his temper because he feels so good. And a reader of the news magazine might be excused if occasionally he becomes skeptical when the glib, authoritative, rootless conclusions change from week to week, and from magazine to magazine.

The important point is not that interpretations and conclusions differ. Honest, reasonable men often differ in their view of the same scene. In the handling of news this ordinarily acts as a discipline: there is an obligation to let the reader know what is documented fact, what is rumor, what is wishful thinking, and what is personal opinion. In the newsmagazines, particularly Newsweek and Time, little distinction is made. The operating rule is that the world must be presented as clear, black-and-white, and interpreted with positive authority.

Above all, it must also be highly readable. As the publisher of Newsweek reported of a survey in his weekly column on Nov. 7, 1955:

". . . Articles in Newsweek are more readable than those in other news and business magazines. . . . In another phase of the testing, it was found that the Newsweek test article was more thoroughly comprehended than articles from the other magazines. . . ."

"That is," the Publisher added, apparently uncertain that he had been thoroughly comprehended, "the reader retained more of what he read in Newsweek."

7. NEWSWEEK: PERISCOPE'S PROGRESS

In Newsweek of May 3, 1954, the Publisher told his readers in a column entitled "Periscope Progress."

"The Periscope, the first feature of its kind to appear in any publication, was first carried in Newsweek in 1937. . . . Remarkable for its accuracy, The Periscope's outstanding reputation is the result of the combined efforts of a well-integrated editorial group and a large corps of strategically placed confidential correspondents. It is closely read throughout the world and its influence is considerable."

Since prophecy seems to be a compulsion that newsmagazines find hard to resist, it is rewarding to study Newsweek's, particularly in the issue reporting "remarkable . . . accuracy." In that May 3, 1954, Periscope section, for example, one finds:

"The Inside Story, The White House—The inner circle here is predicting that ex-Sen. Henry Cabot Lodge Jr., now U.S. Ambassador to the U.N. will replace Sherman Adams as Ike's White House chief of staff."

Four years later this "inside story" had failed to reach the outside world. Ultimately, Sherman Adams did resign, some 1,500 days later, but was not replaced by Mr. Lodge.

The efficiency of the "well-integrated editorial group" can be seen in another Periscope item that same week:

"Military Straws, Tokyo—Look for Brig. Gen. Don Zimmerman of the Far East Air Force . . . to head up the faculty at the new Air Force Academy."

The editorial group could look in the future for this, or it could have looked behind 10 days to the April 23 New York Times, which carried an official announcement of General Zimmerman's appointment as dean of the faculty of the Air Force Academy.

The same Periscope column said:

"Behind the Curtain, Oslo—It's becoming more and more clear here that Franz Josef Land, in the Arctic Sea, is the most likely jumping-off place for any Russian airborne attack against the U.S."

The item neglected to specify behind which curtain the strategically placed confidential correspondent found Oslo, Norway.

Of all the Periscope forecasts and inside tips on national and international affairs of the "remarkable . . . accuracy" issue of May 3, 1954, 52 per cent were too vague or were impossible to judge or check and therefore useless to the reader (such as the Franz Josef Land item).

Ten per cent were printed elsewhere first.

Eighteen per cent were correct. (This included items like one saying President Eisenhower would spend two months in Denver "this summer." The general rumor had been printed elsewhere first, and the President spent two autumn months there, but the item was counted correct.)

Twenty-nine per cent proved wrong.

In addition to world affairs, the Newsweek Periscope rises from the depths and looks at the sunlit world of Music, Movies, etc. The May 3 issue had three items on "Periscoping TV-Radio" of which one was wrong, one was partly wrong (and the remainder obvious), and the third had been printed elsewhere first and was based on a publicity release.

The issue also "Periscoped" music. Of three items, two were wrong, one partly wrong.

In Periscoping movies, of four items, one was totally wrong, one mostly wrong, one was from a Hollywood release, and the fourth was partly right.

These are the results from one issue, selected at the urging of the publisher. If one takes a broader sample—the first three months of 1957—the percentage of success and usefulness is not much different.

Of the main Periscope section during this period, 17 per cent was accurate and apparently printed first in Newsweek.

Some 46 per cent consisted of items so obvious or so vague or so beyond confirmation that they were useless to the reader. An example is the March 18 item: "You can look for the coming investigation of the AFL-CIO Bakers Union to be even more lurid than the Teamsters' hearings." It is perfectly accurate that the reader could look for this, if he chose. If he did look he might have trouble deciding that the bakers' operations were more ghastly yellow than the Teamsters'. But this item was counted in the too-vague-or-impossible-to-check category rather than wrong, as later Teamster disclosures might justify.

Ten per cent of the items had been printed elsewhere first, one of them two months earlier.

Twenty-seven per cent were wrong.

Some wrong items: "Democratic Chairman Paul Butler has finally and definitely tipped intimates he plans to resign in May." Eighteen months later this final and definite tip had failed to materialize.

Another was the prediction that David Beck, the teamster official, would stay in Europe, a forecast printed in the Newsweek dated the day after Beck returned to the United States.

On Feb. 11, 1957, Periscope said, "Satellite Shadows, Budapest —Don't be surprised if State Security Minister Ferenc Muennich . . .

succeeds Janos Kadar as Premier of Hungary shortly." Readers were not surprised: Muennich didn't succeed Kadar; Kadar is still in office at this writing, nineteen months later.

On March 18, 1957 another Periscope said:

"The Diplomatic Wire, New York City—Private advices of the highest quarters reached NEWSWEEK on the eve of the Bermuda conference that British Foreign Secretary Selwyn Lloyd will be out soon. . . ."

Eighteen months later, with Selwyn Lloyd still British Foreign Secretary, Newsweek mailed out a promotional letter offering, among other things:

"ACCURATE FORECASTS. You'll be the first to know what's ahead, with uncanny 'Periscope' predictions."

8. TIME MAGAZINE AND THE TRUTH

Henry R. Luce, co-founder, editor-in-chief and largest single stockholder of Time magazine, once told a school of journalism:

"The owner-editor cannot honorably evade his personal confrontation with every aspect of truth in every aspect of his paper."

The problem of Truth in the news is an old one. In the process of struggling with it, Time magazine has, at least, solved the problem of success. It is the biggest, brightest and most powerful of the Big Three newsmagazines. It has a paid circulation of 2,173,000. It is the foundation for the publishing empire of Time, Inc.: Time, Life, Fortune, Sports Illustrated, Time International, Life International, Life en Espanol, House & Home, Architectural Forum and a complex of paper mills and radio-TV stations.

For millions of middle-class Americans it is the interpreter of national and world affairs. Thousands of foreigners get their major impression of the United States from it. The United States Information Agency last year distributed 1,800,000 copies free in 56 foreign countries as part of the American propaganda effort.

The magazine has 500 carefully selected, well-paid staff members capable of the most skilled performance of almost any publication in the country. It has the most effective network of information gatherers in the United States, in terms of intensive coverage of particular subjects. On occasion its work is distinguished, showing by contrast the superficial coverage of other magazines and of many newspapers.

Time frequently answers in its stories the simple human questions that the hard-boiled types of journalism ignore.

When it has a mind to, Time can develop the possibilities of a news event more imaginatively than almost any other news organization in the world.

The magazine's writing and editing is bright, sometimes brilliant.

But is it The Truth?

The elusiveness of Truth in terms of contemporary men and current policies must have worried the editors of Time occasionally. But if so, they have spared the reader this human doubt. Each week the world is created absolute and dogmatic, the good guys on one side, the bad guys on the other, with Time holding the only scorecard. Only when the reader checks back does he discover that the simple world of one year develops messy complications the next, or that the good guy of October may be the bad guy of January, that Truth and Time change.

For example, was it the Truth, when Time reported Dwight Eisenhower's appearance at the start of his 1952 campaign in Abilene in the June 16, 1952, issue:

"They saw Ike, and they liked what they saw.

"They liked him because he turned out to be an amazingly good campaigner . . . They liked him for his strong, vigorous manner of speech, for his quiet control . . . It was a crashing conquest."

Or was it the Truth when, after the campaign was over, Time in its issue of Nov. 3, 1952, described that same week in Abilene:

"At first the echoes were not strong. Ike . . . as a political candidate . . . did not quite 'come across' . . . his voice was flat; he looked like an old man on TV . . ."

Time, during the 1952 campaign:

". . . Stevenson tore into this straw man . . . the Democratic candidate made a careful pitch . . . In the same speech, Stevenson got in a reference to aid to India, which is getting to be the stock Democratic way of changing the subject on China."

Time, four years later:

". . . Stevenson of 1952, a man meticulously concerned with facts . . ."

Time, before Adlai Stevenson became a presidential candidate:

". . . Illinois has a good governor now: Adlai Ewing Stevenson . . . In his three years . . . Stevenson has . . . sent state police out to stop commercial gambling downstate . . . Lopped 1,300 political hangers-on off the state payroll . . . he didn't think State's Attorney John Boyle of Chicago was a good candidate. Stevenson has largely kept hands off law enforcement in Cook County, on the theory that local authorities are better staffed to handle it. But he didn't like the way Boyle had done the job . . . promptly dumped Boyle . . . If Lincoln Steffens was right, corruption is the norm of U.S. political life . . . But men like Adlai Stevenson have dedicated themselves to a more hopeful and dynamic proposition: that the U.S. is not a static pattern but an experiment, among other things—in good government."

Time, after Stevenson became a presidential candidate, eight days before election day:

"Stevenson . . . has himself cited his record as governor to support his argument that he can deal with corruption; he tells his audiences that he knows about corruption because he followed 'eight years of magnificent Republican rascality.' He never so much as slapped the wrist of the Cook County Democratic organization, the most corrupt and powerful of existing big-city machines. . . ."

Time, Aug. 1, 1955, on President Eisenhower's accomplishment at Geneva:

". . . If Geneva was to be measured by the spirit, as all the participants insisted it should be, then quite a bit was achieved . . . the chances of a war started by the Russians is continuing to diminish. This was the reading of Geneva."

Time, May 19, 1958, quoting Dean Acheson approvingly to support Time's thesis a summit conference should not be held:

"From former (1949-53) U.S. Secretary of State Dean Acheson came two forceful, well-argued statements on U.S. foreign policy. . . . The 1955 Geneva Conference, said Dean Acheson, 'was not merely a failure; it was a fraud and positive harm. . . .' "

The changeability of Truth in the pages of Time was noted in 1955 by a Harvard student, Milton S. Gwirtzman, who listed in the Harvard Crimson some Time truths which seemed to change with political administrations:

Time, March 10, 1952, on the income tax under a Democratic administration:

"This week, once again, the American taxpayer . . . was working over his income tax return. He did not do the job happily ... The blow, in full and crushing measure, now lands each March 15 on the chin of a fellow named John Q."

Time, April 18, 1955, on the income tax during a Republican administration:

". . . 60 million Americans have by this week signed their 1954 income tax forms ... They did this, wonderful to tell, without riots or protest ... It has become more and more unfashionable to criticize the income tax level."

Time, Aug. 12, 1946, on the character of George E. Allen under a Democratic administration:

"Last week . . . the President (Truman) eased his croniest crony, George E. Allen, into the Board of Directors of Reconstruction Finance Corporation." And on Jan. 28, 1946: "George is all the more remarkable because, to the naked eye, he is a clown."

Time, Dec. 14, 1954, on the character of George E. Allen under a Republican administration:

"Last week . . . the President (Eisenhower) chatted quietly with . . . golfing companion George E. Allen, Washington lawyer and friend of Presidents."

Time throughout the 1956 campaign ridiculed public questions about the risk of having a sick President in office. During the politically crucial times for the President (and the American electorate), Time took the President's decision at face value, or as it said in the July 22, 1956, issue on the President's decision to run again: ". . . settled the issue with the simplicity and finality of a one-foot putt."

During the illnesses and during the campaign it took the words of Press Secretary James Hagerty at enthusiastic face value. Only afterward, Jan. 27, 1958, in an admiring profile of Presidential Press Secretary James C. Hagerty, "the best . . . White House press secretary in U.S. history," did it tell in a boys-will-be-boys context how Hagerty "at least once handed a Cabinet member a statement to read about how well Ike looked—before the man had even been in to see the President."

And 16 months after the last campaign in which the President can run, under the Constitution, Time raised the question, in its Mar. 3, 1958 issue:

"President Eisenhower is 67; the cumulative effect of his three major illnesses has sapped his second-term strengths ... Most of the work curtailment had come in the field of domestic affairs . . . if allowed to slide, small problems can snowball into major cases: e.g., the present economic recession, and it is this area that the President's inability to ride constant herd is most felt."

The late William Allen White, once wrote:

"I think on the whole, sooner or later, the American people do get the truth. But they often get it when it is cold potatoes and does them no good."

9. TIME: "THEY DEPEND ON ITS ACCURACY"

Time magazine once claimed that the top men in their fields of work in America vote Time their favorite magazine: "They depend on its accuracy."

Some surveys show that this may be less than accurate, since many top men say they do not have confidence in Time's accuracy.

Yet, "accuracy" is not always easy to judge in journalism. In a simple event it may be so elementary as the correct names of people in an accident. But in a worldwide social phenomenon it may be a matter of judgment, knowledge and the integrity of the reporter.

The dominant rule in American journalism is objectivity, or the reporting of facts with a minimum of the reporter's own opinions about them. This, too, has difficulties. As Time once said in its Press section in a piece entitled, "The Fetish of Objectivity."

One of the most treacherous journalistic cliches is that a news story should always let the facts speak for themselves. Thoughtful newspapermen know that the facts alone seldom can, that they speak clearly only when they are told in proper order and perspective—and thus interpreted by an honest journalist.

The question is does the reporter collect all the facts he can and then draw a picture based on the facts? Or does he have a preconceived idea and collect only the facts that bear it out.

There is abundant evidence that in its National Affairs and Foreign News sections Time's mind is made up before the events begin. But ordinarily its departments in the back of the magazine—Art, Books, Cinema, Education, Medicine, Music, Press, Religion, TV & Radio, Science, Sport, Theater—score high in imagination and taste.

In these departments Time's inherent talent seems to operate without the distorting lens that focuses on politics and Asia policy.

In American politics and foreign news, Time's reporting appears to be governed by an iron rule: when the facts fit the mold of Time's wishes, the reporting can be superb; when they do not fit the mold, Time's reporting can be so distorted as to raise serious questions about responsibility in mass communications.

It was interesting then, on March 17, 1958, to see the conclusions-first-or-facts-first problem appear in the back of the magazine, in the Press Section. Here, in a piece entitled "Silver-Lining the Slump?", Time concluded that in general American newspapers were suppressing news of the recession, or as it said: "Newspapers from Seattle to Savannah were doing their unlevel best to bull their way through one of the nation's biggest—and most botched—running stories: the recession."

Was this true?

It is certainly possible.

What evidence did Time present?

It did not report that for months businessmen, economists and politicians had been complaining that the daily press was sensationalizing the slump and therefore deepening it. Time itself has called such reports "gloomsayers."

(Time, reporting clouds, also found silver linings, as on Nov. 11, 1957: "Fundamentally, the U.S. was still more productive and prosperous than any nation in history . . . The economy was—and would continue to be—a husky and growing thing . . ." Time, Dec. 2, 1957: "The uneasy sign in the nation's economic picture is not the statistical droop but the mood. . . Despite the recent drops, the U.S. economy still has a long way to go before it approaches the slump of 1953-54—which economists now refer to as the 'gold-plated' recession." Time, Dec. 9, 1957: "THE PROFIT SQUEEZE, It Is More Apparent Than Real" Time, Dec. 30, 1957: "Anticipation of recession was scarier than the realization . . .")

To support its conclusion that daily newspapers were suppressing news of the recession, Time offered the reader 14 specific items of evidence.

No. 1 was its lead sentence: "DECLINE HERE? DON'T BELIEVE IT! headlined the Fort Worth Star-Telegram on Page One last week." This was a correct quotation of the headline and it was a story on the rosy side, listing aircraft and defense contracts in effect locally. Time did not report that the same newspaper was regularly running even bigger headlines on Page One, like the eight-column, 72-point banner:

TEXAS OIL ALLOWABLE SLASHED TO ALL-TIME LOW and the five-column, 72-point: 5,200,000 JOBLESS. While Time praised a few papers for running financial columnist Sylvia Porter, who, it said, reported the slump realistically, it did not say the Fort Worth Star-Telegram carries Sylvia Porter.

Item No. 2. "Though more than 50,000 workers are out of jobs in Georgia's four largest cities, the Atlanta Journal has zealously kept the state's slump off the front page, and until last week, even banned the word recession from the paper." This appears to be inaccurate: The Atlanta Journal earlier sent its own reporters through the state and then ran on Page One their stories telling of a serious depression in agriculture, Georgia's major activity. The term, "current business recession" is found on Page One months before the Time story.

Item No. 3. "In Los Angeles, where layoffs have idled nearly 6 per cent of the work force, Hearst's Herald & Express whooped: ROSY L.A. ECONOMY SEEN." That paper has been looking for a silver lining, such as the story quoted (which also had as a part of its headline the factual matter "Multi-Million Projects to Boost Business.") If the Herald & Express "whooped" with the story, it "whooped" on Page Eight. Other recession and unemployment stories had appeared on more prominent pages.

Item No. 4. "Scripps-Howard's Memphis Press-Scimitar last week ran a glowing story on expansion plans for a local Firestone Tire & Rubber Co. plant—without mentioning that 2,600 of its 3,600 employes have been laid off." This appears to be entirely inaccurate. The paper ran no story, "glowing" or otherwise, about Firestone expansion that week. A statement by a company official on past expansion ran six months earlier. The Firestone company says that at no time did it have 2,600 employes laid off. An official said: "In no month during that period were as many as 10 per cent of that figure laid off."

Item No. 5. "In Atlanta, the Journal suppressed the news of a layoff of 2,000 Lockheed Aircraft workers last fall until it could report that the factory had found other jobs for them." The Lockheed company announced the layoffs Aug. 15. The Atlanta Constitution, morning side of the Constitution-Journal combination, ran the story on Page One the morning of Aug. 15. The Journal ran it with a three-column headline on an inside page that afternoon. Its story on the factory finding other jobs for workers ran four months later when the company announced it.

A check of the 14 items of evidence of suppression shows almost the same pattern throughout. In one case it reported the opposite of what an editor, noted for his integrity, says he told the Time reporter. In a display of headlines clipped from newspapers, which Time presented as "HOPEFUL HEADLINES," "We don't want to scare advertisers," it used headlines that accurately summarized speeches and public statements: in one case the headline quoted was sarcastic, stressing by irony that times are bad; in others it showed small, inside-page headlines while ignoring Page One 96-point headlines in the same paper saying, "SLUMP WORSE . . ."

In another case it took part of a headline display and did not reproduce the main portion, which gave the total an opposite impact. In another it reproduced a Page Two headline over a report of a national speech; to cut this out it must have been necessary to pass the scissors a quarter of an inch from another 36-point headline on a report of a speech reading: GOP IS GETTING SLUMP IT PLANNED.

Thus, of the 14 "facts" Time presented to the reader to support its conclusion, one was correct; two were apparently wrong (based on what men later say they said, granting they could conceivably have said something else in private earlier); six were so unrepresentative as to give an essentially false impression; and five were demonstrably false.

It is possible American daily newspapers did play down the recession, but it has not been proved by Time in any evidence it gave the reader.

One month after Time's story, its competitor, Newsweek, reported: "HOW U.S. NEWSPAPERS ARE COVERING THE RECESSION . . . Wire-service logs showed that, in quantity of copy and the play it was getting, the recession was easily the biggest story of the spring season . . . Syndicated writers shuttled in and out of hard-hit industrial centers . . . Most newsmen agreed it was their duty to report the story as they found it, whether the news was good or bad."

This, too, could be unrepresentative, since the magazine drew its own conclusions from its own collection of facts.

It gives added significance to the Time statement:

". . . the facts . . . speak clearly only when they are told in proper order and perspective—and thus interpreted—by an honest journalist."

10. TIME, TONE, AND TAINTED WORDS

While Time has been known to be inaccurate in its facts, this is not the key to its reportage.

The key is not what Time says, but how it says it. It is not the hard news reported to it by The New York Times, the New York Herald Tribune, the Associated Press, United Press International, and its own staff in the field.

The key is how it is written in the high reaches of the editorial offices in Rockefeller Center, New York.

Noel Busch, cousin of the late Briton Hadden, the man who co-founded Time magazine in 1923 with Henry R. Luce, says of his experience on the magazine that Time regards as ideal that:

"Writers should not witness the events they write about."

It is the writer away from the scene, passing the story back and forth among the editors, who gives to the Time story the impact it will have on the reader. When it comes to domestic policy and foreign affairs, this impact often seems to be unrelated to the facts. The hard core of known events can be immersed in an impenetrable fog of emotional judgment. The reader can lay down a story with a point of view and never know precisely how he got it.

If one isolates the facts from the tone words added by Time's editors, the pattern appears. It is typical of Time's political reporting that the political world is generally divided into the forces of evil and the forces of virtue. If a political figure is a devil—in Time's perdition—he helps an elderly lady across the street just to impress the neighbors. If he is a political angel—floating in Time's heaven—his hand at the aged elbow is evidence of an innate kindness.

In 1951, the secretary of state, Dean Acheson, was a Time devil, an outstanding culprit of the Truman-Acheson Gang. While Time was not alone in characterizing Acheson as a menace, it was perhaps the most sophisticated and effective organ in destroying public confidence in Acheson. It did this not so much with rational argument and fact, as with the tone words added in Rockefeller Center. Such words from its cover story on Acheson on Jan. 8, 1951 include:

". . . This week . . . he expanded his gloomy note. . . . What people thought of Dean Gooderham Acheson ranged from the proposition that he was a fellow traveler, or a wool-brained sower of 'seeds of jackassery' or an abysmally uncomprehending man, or an appeaser or a warmonger who was taking the U.S. into a world war, to the warm if not so audible defense that he was a great secretary of state, a brilliant executor of the best of all possible foreign programs . . . tall, elegant and unruffled . . . either rode to work in a department limousine, or walked with little Justice Felix Frankfurter . . . In his fifth floor office in . . . Foggy Bottom he tried not to listen to the criticism . . . with his blue slightly protuberant eyes studied his foreign policy. It was not a very encouraging study . . . to what extent was Acheson to blame . . . Acheson's involvement . . . Acheson therefore inherited some of the policies and problems which he had helped create . . . was well on the way to becoming an immeasurable disaster . . . one of the major decisions and disastrous phases that have boomeranged to plague him . . . The one reason . . . was to provide Acheson's State Department with an alibi for its share in China's tragic disaster . . . State Department by its acts and by its failures to act . . . had bribed . . . thrown China's door open to Russia . . . Acheson's State Department continued hopefully to stroke the fur of the Red leader . . . most notable survivor among the architects of the 'China mistake' is Secretary Acheson . . . The case against Dean Acheson . . . policy has disastrously failed in Asia. The misreading of the Red Chinese . . . he must take full responsibility . . . the old animus against Chiang Kai-shek . . . On the record, U.S. policy in Europe is in a crucial state of hesitation . . . Acheson and the Administration . . . could not get around the fact of Western Europe's anguished resignation . . . Acheson had been invariably punctilious and polite . . . in the end . . . he had too frequently let himself be pulled down to the level of his hem-hawing, tiptoeing fellow conferees . . . The question was whether a different secretary of state might have done more . . . He possesses some of the intellectual arrogance . . . a highly civilized man, an intellectual snob . . . No blood, no sweat, no tears ever smudge the neat laundering of Acheson's sentences, or the mannerisms of his theories . . . the U.S. people . . . cannot quite tune in on him . . . Has Dean Acheson become . . . a national danger? . . ."

In its Jan. 3, 1953 issue, Time did a cover story on Secretary of State John Foster Dulles. Like Acheson, Dulles had become a matter of bitter dispute in the United States. The tone words and phrases from that story: ". . . John Foster Dulles looked squarely at the man . . . pressed Molotov with greater skill and force than any U.S. diplomat had ever shown . . . one sharp stroke after another . . . Dulles rescued other millions from gullibility . . . trips to reinforce the free world outposts . . . develop cohesion and strength . . . Dulles played the key role . . . Dulles' patient year of work and travel . . . Dulles both drew upon and nourished U.S. confidence . . . this emphasis on U.S. interests had a wholesome effect of stimulating the national prides of other Western nations . . . he played the year's most effective role . . . he was nimble in disentangling himself from his errors . . . after long and careful negotiation . . . Dulles . . . played goalkeeper in the free world's two major setbacks . . . Dulles has said quite pointedly. . . . A smaller man than Dulles might have insisted . . . had a brilliant career . . . applied Christian principles to historic realities . . . soundest bit of diplomacy. . . . He has explained . . . he has demonstrated . . . Dulles' restraint was deliberate . . . his highly practical analysis . . . Dulles analyzed . . . was all the more forceful because Dulles' line had already been proved right. . . . At that kind of diplomatic opinion-molding, John Foster Dulles is a master. . . . He recognizes the importance . . . works hard . . . tries again, tirelessly . . . gained new confidence . . . remarkable for their sweep and clarity . . . goes tirelessly about that business . . . displays a tremendous capacity for concentration and work . . . depth of the concentration . . . Dulles is providing direction . . . cleared the ground . . . stop epidemics of fear . . . Dulles disregarded the cries of those . . ."

These words, into which are inserted matters of fact, penetrate the reader's emotions ahead of the facts.

They are, in the main, opinions and characterizations by Time editors.

Both Acheson and Dulles were centers of bitter controversy at home, and Dulles abroad. It would be unrealistic in the extreme to expect any news to make a mathematically or emotionally precise division pro-and-con. And in commentary one is dealing with opinion and judgment.

But it is interesting that of about 640 lines on Acheson in the Time story, about 74 per cent is directly negative and critical; in the 670 lines on Dulles, only 4 per cent.

What is, perhaps, more important is that in dealing with facts which Time itself accepts, the impact on the reader is emotionally manipulated. One way is by innuendo and subtle reference. Time did not repeat directly the common anti-Acheson phrase of the time recalling that Acheson had said he would not turn his back on Alger Hiss. But it did use the phrase obliquely twice in the story: "Although he might have preferred to turn his back on the East" . . . and "Asia on which he had turned his back."

A major method of loading the story is to mention the positive arguments for a devil and follow with material wiping it out. Thus, of the 640 lines on Acheson, 23 are devoted to the major achievements which Time attributed to Acheson's regime, which on reflection, appear considerable: Lend-Lease, UNRRA, World Bank, Export-Import Bank, Truman Doctrine, Marshall Plan, NATO. But though it took 17 words to describe that "Acheson presided over the signing of the North Atlantic Treaty creating (on paper) a collective defense system," it then took 22 words immediately afterward to say, "The idea had not been his; it had originated in a resolution presented by Senator Arthur Vandenberg, approved by a Republican Senate. . . ."

Again, when it mentioned his "new anti-Russian policy," it followed by saying that it fell short of the need.

In the case of Dulles, some 96 per cent is devoted to approving and positive declarations. Curiously, it made some damning statements—but these consisted of 14 lines inserted after the first 430 lines followed by 210 lines of more praise, then 12 lines of criticism, and a final conclusion of high approval. The two small negative insertions might strike a reader as somewhat underemphasized: "Despite these attempts . . . the free world came to a year's end with a net loss and a troubled outlook in Asia." And "After two years in office, the Eisenhower Administration has failed to plug the yawning gap in its foreign policy . . ."

Time did not exclude unpleasant fact completely. In the case of a man it condemned, Acheson, it buried 62 lines of his considerable achievements in an avalanche—477 lines—of emotionally loaded words that stained the image. In the case of a man it approved of, Dulles, it buried 26 lines of grave and fundamental criticism, in an avalanche, 617 lines, of words that glowed with heroic praise.

Underneath it all, the reader could extract the basic facts if he worked at it. But the basic facts could conceivably come in a form which does the Time reader—a citizen who votes—no good.

If, on the other hand, one grants that Time has a right to its opinions, one may judge how the opinions hold up.

In the Dulles profile, Time's opinion was:

"Regionally, 1954's greatest area of success for American diplomacy and the man who runs it was the Middle East. There, a number of old problems were solved by new approaches . . . the status of the Suez Canal area was settled more firmly than ever before . . . the settlement was skillfully midwifed by the U.S. State Department."

According to some observers, Suez resulted in one of the gravest disasters for the West and for American diplomacy in this decade, and Hungary brought a disillusionment with America's "liberation" policy. Yet during this period, Time, on Dec. 13, 1956, told the reader that things were never better for the United States position abroad:

"The world's gaze and the world's hopes were directed toward Washington as rarely before. . . . In time of crisis and threat of World War III, President Eisenhower had cast U.S. policy in a role to reflect the U.S.'s basic character . . ."

Walter Lippmann that same week said "the initiative and the power are not in our hands, and we found ourselves doing what we did not want to do . . ."

James Reston, chief of The New York Times Washington bureau, said that the general feeling in Washington was that "the Soviet Union and Egypt have scored a tremendous victory."

Obviously, Time disagreed with both. The magazine said Reston "reported nonsensically."

Later, Editor-in-Chief Henry R. Luce of Time wrote to Reston apologizing. Mr. Luce wrote that Reston was not nonsensical, he was only wrong.

11. 'IKE'S PROMISE' VS. 'ADLAI'S PITCH'

A symbolic word for the discriminating reader of Time magazine is "cry."

In the normal vocabulary it is a verb meaning to make a loud call, to utter lamentations, or to weep.

But in the special lexicon of Timestyle it means: A Fool is Shouting Hysterical Nonsense.

For in Time villains "cry;" the heroes "solemnly state."

There are other words the student of Time learns. The modern Republican President of the United States when irritated "snaps" back an answer. "Snap" means that the question has been in bad taste or stupid, and the President is showing manly spirit. But a New Deal-Fair Deal Democratic President "snarls" or "sputters" or "spouts."

The outstanding characteristic of the political reporting of Time magazine is that without telling the reader why, the magazine surrounds personalities with an emotional aura, sometimes with adjectives, sometimes with verbs, sometimes with figures of speech.

Stylistically, the result is the most dramatic, crisp and evocative language in the news profession. But politically it is a vapor of bias that seeps into the text, clouding facts and bypassing the normal critical judgment of the reader. It is a highly artistic technique, but a study of Time's behavior in recent political campaigns shows that it is used as a partisan political weapon.

A study of the magazine during the 1952 and 1956 Presidential campaigns leaves the impression that Time magazine was the most effective propaganda printed for the benefit of the Republican National Committee.

The bias appeared in the balance of space, in the selection of facts, and in the use of pictures and illustrations. But the chief weapon was the emotional prejudgment with which it surrounded the news.

A reader cannot argue long over a strictly personal selection of adjectives by a writer. But if these selections fall into a clear political pattern, the reader has a right to know it.

In the Sept. 1, 1952, issue, under "REPUBLICANS, The Rediscovery," a story about Dwight Eisenhower—leaving out the news core—began:

"A great American soldier disclosed political greatness . . . rediscovered courage as a policy for a nation. Out of his own wide experience with the fateful issues of the 20th century, Dwight D. Eisenhower phrased a definition of the peril besetting the U.S. . . . a definition so compelling . . . it displayed . . . his credentials as a candidate for President . . . a good speech, in both the moral and political sense. . . . Ike calculated with grim arithmetic . . . turned to the kind of shrewd analysis . . . which the U.S. seldom hears from its officials. . . ."

In the same issue, under "DEMOCRATS Away From It All," a story about Adlai Stevenson—leaving out the news core—began:

"Candidate Adlai Stevenson climbed into his state-owned two-engined Beechcraft last week and flew off to the Wisconsin woods . . . hours loafing . . . a little half-hearted casting. . . . Evenings he lolled in the bearskin-draped living room before a fieldstone fireplace big enough to take 7-foot logs, which were hauled automatically from the basement at the touch of a button . . . he did little work. . . ."

On Oct. 10, 1956, Time reported the appearance of both Stevenson and Eisenhower at a farmer's gathering:

"Here, on rolling land near Newton, Iowa, some 8,000 American farmers and townsmen, their wives, kids and relatives assembled . . . giving their attention to their honorary chairman—President Dwight Eisenhower—honed to intellectual sharpness . . . dwelt on a theme . . . his own inner peace. . . ."

"From the same giant platform . . . Adlai Stevenson made a major bid for the farm vote at Newton . . . Stevenson promised the farmers everything but the moon on behalf of the Democrats. . . . From the past, Stevenson dragged out a familiar Democratic tactic . . . contended Adlai, in an astonishing defense of. . . ."

The title of the Eisenhower story was : "Ike's Promise."

The title of the Stevenson story was: "Adlai's Pitch."

This relatively subtle technique does not mean that Time neglected the blunt instrument of loaded pictures. In the 13 issues covering the 1952 campaign, Time printed 21 photographs of Eisenhower, all of them showing him in a favorable light—heroic, or friendly, or earnest. Stevenson's face in these issues appeared only 13 times, the two largest facial shots from photographs taken 30 years before, and 40 per cent of the total showed Stevenson in unflattering poses, eating, drinking, or grimacing.

Eisenhower's picture appeared on Page One of National Affairs in Time three times, on Page Two four times during the campaign period. Stevenson's never appeared on Page One of National Affairs.

Time carefully preserved the image of Eisenhower in the 1956 campaign, although in the Democratic past it had shown marked irreverence for political sacred cows. In 1956 it dealt heavily in cartoons. In the 13 pre-election issues it showed 10 cartoons involving the personal figure of Stevenson, all of them derogatory. It showed none that portrayed Eisenhower personally in a derogatory way.

Time's treatment of the campaign in 1956 was so consistently biased that it would be reasonable to label it campaign literature. While Eisenhower regularly "dwelt" on subjects or stated them, Stevenson "cried" or, as Time said Oct. 8, 1956, ". . . Adlai Stevenson went whirling across the U.S. landscape last week, spouting sparks and smoke. . . ."

Time's severest distortions are in the area of national politics and China policy, where Time's reporting is biased almost beyond use, in many instances. Both appear to be matters of deep conviction on the part of Editor-in-Chief Henry R. Luce. He is involved more deeply in the present administration than any other American publisher. And as the son of missionaries in China, where Luce grew up, it is said that the Editor-in-Chief retains the dream of Christianizing China and insists on unflagging support of Christian Chiang Kai-shek.

The bias does not usually keep important facts out of the magazine. But sympathetic facts are presented with dignity and joy; unsympathetic ones with ridicule and contempt. One imagines, for example, that when Time describes the Modern Republican candidates there are 500 voices raised in "The Battle Hymn of the Republic." But when it describes the Fair Dealing Democrats the editors are making Bronx cheers.

Describing the visiting dignitaries at the 1952 Republican convention, Time said:

"And there was former President Herbert Hoover . . . the old gentleman smiled a cautious smile . . . Time had whitened his hair . . . and softened the lines of his face. For 20 years he had suffered with dignity and without complaint an auto da fe of criticism such as few men . . . have ever endured . . . But this was his night among friends . . ."

Describing the visiting dignitaries at the 1952 Democratic convention:

"Hefty, hearty India Edwards . . . a woman with an eye on the

vice presidency . . . tramped to the speaker's stand splendidly corseted
. . . fogged in some fast opening lines . . . Mrs. Franklin D. Roosevelt,
whose new frizzy hairdo made her look like a genial golliwog . . ."

One need not be unkind to Mr. Hoover nor emotional about
Mrs. Roosevelt to note that Time had whitened Herbert Hoover's
hair, but only made Mrs. Roosevelt's look like a golliwog.

The difference in the descriptions of these two persons in Time
is unimportant. What is important is that the corset-golliwog content of Democratic stories was always high during the campaigns
and practically absent in Republican stories; and the "suffered with
dignity" content was high in Republican stories, absent in Democratic.

Time, one suspects, has political bifocal glasses, that its editors
look downward at the corsets of Democrats and upward at The
Higher Things in Life among the Republicans.

Nor need one be pro-Democratic or anti-Republican to question
the ethics of such political reporting in a publication that tells the
reader he is getting news in "Time, The Weekly Newsmagazine."

Time pursues its political enemies and boosts its friends by
another technique. If facts are damaging to friends, it mentions the
facts briefly and then rebuts them at length or dismisses them with
editorial contempt. If they are damaging to enemies, Time dwells
on them at length, may even base its entire reportage on them and
accepts them as proved conclusions.

When, for example, the 1952 Republican convention compro-
mised the civil rights issue, Time reported, ". . . one of the convention's youngest and prettiest delegates was the central figure in a
struggle over civil rights. Mrs. Mildred Younger, a 31-year-old Los
Angeles housewife, presided over the civil rights subcommittee with
an intelligent, calm hand . . . The subcommittee was bitterly divided . . . As a result . . . came out with a plank that each side
could construe as it wished."

A short time later the Democrats did the same thing:

"To satisfy two men with such divergent views on civil rights
as Russell and Harriman was a real triumph in fence-straddling for
Stevenson."

Pretty Mrs. Younger presided with an intelligent hand; Stevenson fence-straddled.

Often during the campaign, Time did not trust the Republicans to make their own arguments, but provided the reader with its own. When television viewers saw that the Republican delegates at the convention paid no attention whatever to the platform, Time volunteered: "The delegates' inattention was not necessarily evidence that they did not care what was in the platform. They knew that the resolutions committee. . . ."

Another technique is to concentrate on the mechanics or the messy details of an enemy operation, but to dwell on the spiritual side of a friend. When Sen. John Sparkman was nominated Democratic vice presidential candidate in 1952:

"John Jackson Sparkman, who had just been nominated for Vice President of the United States, stopped grinning, fished a cough drop out of his mouth and slipped it through a crack in the platform floor. 'There,' commented an unsympathetic observer bitterly, 'is a man who has every quality a Democratic candidate for Veep needs: he's from the South.' This comment contained considerable truth . . . Sparkman, in fact, is so resolute a compromiser that it takes a political micrometer to tell just where he stands . . ."

But apparently Time had no unsympathetic observers at the Republican convention: "The meeting quickly settled on California's Richard Nixon. No deal was involved. Nixon was a logical choice . . ." Its description of Sparkman during the campaign was minimal but repeated many criticisms made by others. Its treatment of Nixon did not, although Nixon had been bitterly criticized by many Americans:

". . . the most up-to-date attraction at the Illinois State Fair last week was a good-looking, dark-haired young man with a manner both aggressive and modest, and a personality to delight any political barker. He seemed to have everything—a fine TV manner, an attractive family, a good war record, deep sincerity and religious faith . . . He was Richard Milhous (pronounced mill house) Nixon, Republican nominee for Vice President . . ."

Time tended to take Republican statements at face value, and where the Republicans failed to say things, Time volunteered them; if the Republicans said embarrassing things, Time explained them away. Yet what Democrats said usually was looked at critically, or cynically, and then rebutted. During the 1956 campaign, for example:

"One day last week Stevenson . . . was disturbed, he said,

that the Republicans might be trying to fob off Eisenhower upon a docile, complacent, carefree people all happily chanting, 'Peace, Prosperity and Progress—ain't it wonderful' . . . Candidate Stevenson obviously felt he had a point . . ." Time then went on to explain on its own—in a report of Democratic campaign activities—"The U.S. has learned to live with its crises with equanimity . . . if there seems to be little interest in it as an election-year issue, it is only because the search is constant and the U.S. is always new."

Time regularly in the campaign drifted from Republican statements into heroic prose affirming those statements. And it regularly devoted part of the space under its heading "DEMOCRATS" to Republican (or its own) attacks on Democrats.

In a cover story on Vice-Presidential candidate Kefauver it started with a reference to Kefauver pitching manure and thereafter put the word "shovel" and "pitch" in the text describing his speeches. Aside from this, directly derogatory material constituted 30 per cent of the story, with Time adding editorial agreement. The companion story on Nixon was an almost unbroken epic of approval, brushing past criticisms to ever higher praise: ". . . while he is a politician to his fingertips, Nixon is a man of consistent principle, whose values are as sound and fundamental as any in U.S. politics today . . . Had Nixon been the weak, unprincipled character that his more choleric enemies make him out to be, he might well have given up . . ."

In an October, 1952, profile of Stevenson, 55 per cent was unflattering, derogatory or otherwise damaging, much of that 55 per cent being used to counter or nullify positive material. The Eisenhower cover story had only three per cent derogatory lines and with these Time took the initiative to answer:

"One of the Democratic charges against Eisenhower is that he is vague on issues. Actually, while Ike's prose is vague in style, his speeches are highly specific in content . . ."

Time's treatment of domestic politics is dramatic political polemics and it is certainly identifiable as free political opinion. But it is not reliable political reporting by any non-partisan standard.

An analysis of its behavior during the 1952 and 1956 political campaigns casts serious doubts on its own early prospectus:

"There will be no editorial page in Time.

"No article will be written to prove any special case."

12. NEWSMAGAZINES: A SERVICE AND A THREAT

The newsmagazines—Time, Newsweek, and U.S. News & World Report—constitute one of the most encouraging phenomena in American political development and one of the most discouraging in American mass communications.

The spectacular growth of the magazines undoubtedly reflects a greater public interest in world affairs and an increasing desire to understand what the news means.

The rise of the magazines has been dramatic ever since the mid-1930's. Time began in 1923, Newsweek in 1933, and U.S. News & World Report in two stages, 1940 and 1948.

In 1937 Time's net paid circulation was 670,000. Newsweek's forerunner, News-Week, had 278,000. Last year the American population had increased 30 per cent since 1937, but the combined newsmagazine circulation had gone up more than 300 per cent.

All news media became more popular during this time, including newspapers, for a number of reasons: The Great Depression and the New Deal brought politics close to the life of the average man; so did World War II and the constant postwar threat of World War III. During this same period, literacy, educational levels and income increased steadily.

Thus, while only eight news magazines were sold for every 1,000 Americans in 1937, 25 were sold in 1957. This three-fold increase in the per capita reading of news interpretation should encourage anyone anxious for a democratic people to keep informed and maintain understanding of what is happening in the world.

But at the same time, the magazines have presented national and world events as "news" by new, special techniques ranging from dramatic oversimplification to full-fledged partisan propaganda.

Each of the three magazines has had its particular interests in the news and has tended to fit the presentation of the facts to those interests. Sometimes this has permitted good, clear narration of events. But over the years it has been a narration that has to fit a mold.

The general bias of the three magazines is all on the same side of the American political arena. U.S. News & World Report has a net impact that agrees with its editor's ultra-conservative political and social opinions. Newsweek appears to fluctuate between orthodox business-and-trade interests and straight news. And Time is religiously committed to Modern Republicanism.

The generalizations have to be conditioned. When Time's dominant political interest is not threatened, it takes independent lines on civil liberties and other nonpolitical matters. Newsweek's apparent lack of unity makes it less dogmatic. And the technique of U.S. News & World Report of printing large quantities of primary documents in public affairs means that opposing points of view see the light of day, even though overbalanced by material agreeing with the editor.

This same kind of problem afflicts American newspapers in another way. In their stated commitments and their endorsements of candidates, the majority of American daily newspapers are pro-Republican.

The difference lies in the operating traditions of newspapers that call for strict separation of news and opinion. This tradition has been strong and overwhelming during the last generation. It holds that news will be presented without comment by the reporter or the editor, and without a political slant. Where political bias is expressed, it should be on the editorial page or in signed columns whose authors can be judged by name and reputation.

Certainly, this tradition is not upheld all the time on all papers. Some biased stories are printed in all newspapers from time to time because reporters and editors are human and vary in their competence and discipline. And a few newspapers consistently have biased news because their proprietors reject the tradition.

But on the whole, American newspapers have produced an audience used to generally objective stories on politics and social affairs. This is augmented by the heavy use of the relatively unpolitical wire services—Associated Press, United Press International, and Reuters. The rule of objectivity is followed so rigidly on so many newspapers that many serious students of mass communications think the newspapers overdo it.

The problem of the American newsmagazine is that it presents a subtly loaded political story or a dramatically oversimplified one to an audience conditioned to having outright political argument labeled. The problem is compounded by the fact that the newsmagazines go largely to middle-class readers who probably do not have a high interest in literary analysis and political sophistication.

The weekly is a solid institution in England. But the weeklies in England are presented as analysis not straight news; they cover the entire political spectrum from Socialist to Tory; they go largely to the highly educated reader who is in the habit of reading critically and they are, on the whole, written as rational analysis.

The bias of the American newsmagazines is not stated. They all imply they are news. Henry R. Luce, of Time, insists personally that his magazine does have a point of view and tells the reader what The Truth is, but he continues to call the publication, "The Weekly Newsmagazine." And the point of view is generally not presented in rational analysis but by the emotional coloration of personalities and events in a subtle, indirect manner to an audience traditionally unprepared for such manipulation.

It may be encouraging to some that the newsmagazine closest to the journalistic tradition of objectivity, U.S. News & World Report, has been growing the fastest in recent years. Its predecessor, United States News, had 10 per cent of the Big Three circulation in 1947 but had 22 per cent in 1957. And Time, which is the most loaded of all, had 70 per cent of the circulation 20 years ago and only 51 per cent last year.

But the total combined circulation has risen so fast that it still includes absolute gains of a large magnitude for all the magazines. The newsmagazines had 948,000 circulation 20 years ago, have 4,200,000 now. The numbers who read each issue are greater still. The magazines have multiple attractions for the whole family, they are printed on attractive, durable paper, and they are engagingly illustrated.

Some of the peculiarities of the newsmagazines have only passing importance. The compulsion to prophesy in U.S. News & World Report and in Newsweek, for example, builds up the illusion of an overly simple world to which each magazine has the only keyhole. Time avoids formal forecasting of events, possibly because its commercial inheritance includes the old Literary Digest. Time bought the Digest after the Digest had destroyed its reputation in 1936 with a widely ballyhooed "scientific" prediction that Alfred Landon would defeat Franklin Roosevelt by carrying 32 states. Mr. Landon got two states. But in any case, prophecy is a relatively unimportant weakness.

What is more important is that the newsmagazines are a new

phenomenon in American politics. They have arisen in the present form only in this generation, a generation unprepared for the special forms of influence which the newsmagazines use.

In many respects, this influence is comparable to modern advertising techniques of depth probing and psychological motivation. By using many of these methods in the presentation of news interpretation, the newsmagazines are influencing a generation of middle-class voters who are extremely sensitive to conventional bias in newspaper stories but almost totally unaware of the new techniques in newsmagazines.

For example, during the 1952 and 1956 presidential campaigns, Time magazine probably was read by most of its subscribers as a source of news on American politics. Most of the subscribers had grown in the tradition of separation of news and opinion in their daily newspapers. Few of them had any analytical experience with the literary presentation of news. But what they read in Time during these crucial months was campaign literature of an extremely skillful, almost artistic, nature which manipulated emotions under the implication that it was providing "news."

The retelling of the news at the end of the week and its interpretation from a particular point of view both are legitimate and useful.

But there would appear to be a need for public recognition that in the area of national politics and economics and in certain other special issues (such as Time's Asia policy and U.S. News & World Report on integration) they are confronted not with simple news or rational interpretation, but with magazines of opinion.

The major problems would seem to be that the combined bias of all the newsmagazines is all on the same general side of American politics, and that they pursue this bias with nonrational techniques with which the average reader has had no previous experience and against which he has little defense.

Consequently, the newsmagazines constitute both a problem in normal development of American politics and in the dissemination of news and interpretation of world events.

SELECTION 17

NEWSPAPER "OPINION LEADERS" AND PROCESSES OF STANDARDIZATION*

WARREN BREED

WARREN BREED *is Professor of Sociology at Tulane University. He has written "Social Control in the Newsroom, A Functional Analysis," which appeared in* Social Forces, *and many other articles. The selection below was originally his doctoral dissertation in sociology at Columbia University.*

More than twenty years have passed since Marlen Pew, on returning from a trip across the country, remarked that "Hundreds of newspapers, though published in cities scattered from coast to coast, were as like as so many peas in a pod."[1] This uniformity, or standardization, of the content of American newspapers has often been noted, and deserves analysis.

Standardization signifies that various papers (1) contain the same or similar items, and (2) that these are styled and arranged in the same or similar ways. One particular aspect of standardization, which will be the focus of the present article, is the tendency of many papers to feature the same stories atop their front pages, to the exclusion of others.

Several factors contributing to standardization come easily to mind: wire services and syndicates, supplying different papers with identical material in great quantities; publicity handouts distributed widely; chain ownership; and the tendency of most publishers to maintain a conservative political policy. The present essay will suggest a series of further factors which have received little attention.

It is true of course, that these individual newspapers are indeed reporting the events of the same nation and the same world. Thus one would expect that *every* editor would feature an obviously "big" story such as the outbreak of a war, the outcome of a crucial congressional action, or a policy-making speech by the chief executive. Critics of standardization feel, however, that the press often exhibits conformity hardly justified by the value of the particular stories displayed at the top of page one by hundreds of editors.

* Reprinted from *Journalism Quarterly*, Vol. 32 (Winter 1955).
[1] In *Editor & Publisher*, April 22, 1933, p. 82. Pew was long the editor of *Editor & Publisher*.

What seems worthy of study, then, is the *process* by which editors select the top stories they will feature on a given day. If, as may be assumed, individual editors are not entirely dependent on their own personal criteria of selection, how in fact are the top stories chosen? Who, or what, constitute the guides of editors? Certainly editors do not follow governmental leaders' suggestions as to top stories, and would resent such an inference. It is basic in the ideology of the free and responsible press that each editor is free to decide what his paper will feature or ignore. The existence of standardization, however, especially as regards the featuring of certain "top" stories rather than many alternative stories, may have consequences for the working of democracy. These possible consequences will be discussed, following an account of some further and little-recognized factors promoting conformity.

That these factors exist appears evident from the writer's study of the processes of newspaper control[2] (as differentiated from content, audience and effect). During this study some 120 newspapermen—editors and staffers—were interviewed with relation to "control," or editorial production, of the paper. The interviews took a conversational form, and averaged well over an hour each in duration.

Several "standardizing" processes were discerned.

As the observer watches newsmen at work, he notices that they are great readers of newspapers.[3] In the newsroom, if a man is not working or chatting, the chances are that he is reading a paper. This rather pedestrian truth entered—and advanced—the investigation, however, only when in an early interview a Michigan editor (30,000)[4] said, in response to the routine question about which papers he read fairly regularly:

> I look at the New York *Times* and the *Herald Tribune,* too, to see how they handle the news.

---

[2] Warren Breed, "The Newspaperman, News and Society" (Unpublished Ph.D. dissertation, Department of Sociology, Columbia University, 1952; and Ann Arbor, University Microfilms). Another phase of the study is reported in Warren Breed, "Social Control in the Newsroom: A Functional Analysis," *Social Forces,* 33:326-35 (May 1955).

[3] Staffers interviewed said they read about five newspapers a day, editors claimed seven. Breed, "The Newspaperman, News and Society," pp. 103, 134. The term staffers embraces reporters, rewrite men, copy readers, etc.

[4] Figures given after a newsman's locality indicate the circulation range of his paper.

Fortuitously, the interviewer asked, "Does this help you in playing *your* news?"

Yes. (Pause.) But we don't necessarily ape them; we always give a local story the biggest play . . . .

This became a consistent pattern in the interviews. An editor would be asked if the "play" of other papers helped him decide which stories were worth page one. Regularly, he would agree, then rapidly would back out, usually to affirm that he didn't copy the other paper, and that local stories, or later big stories, always rated over those featured in the paper read. Two forces seemed to be at work upon the editor: he wanted to acknowledge the aid from other papers, yet as a professional, he wanted to maintain his autonomy.[5]

While it is clear that many editors are independent, or "inner-directed" about their decisions regarding news judgment, it also seems evident that one paper influences another, as regards the journalistically vital matter of page one play. The influence goes "down," from larger papers to smaller ones, as if the editor is employing, *in absentia,* the editors of the larger paper to help "make up" his page.[6] How true this is in any particular case is an empirical question; some editors are surer of their judgment than others.

The pattern of influences seems to assume an "arterial" form, analogous (although in reverse) to the dendritic geological pattern by which rills, runnels and freshets flow into brooks and streams which in turn join the great river. For instance, we would expect that, say, a county weekly in Iowa will "look up to" the nearest daily for some guidance as to news values. The small daily, in turn, will scan the nearby big-city papers which are checking the Des Moines *Register's* front page. *Register* editors will be reading papers (we would expect) from such regional centers as Chicago, Minne-

---

[5] This response pattern is analogous to that of congressmen, who displayed some reluctance to admit that opinion polls correctly portrayed and measured public opinion (and, presumably, the influence of polls on themselves and their votes). George F. Lewis, "The Congressman Looks at the Polls," *Public Opinion Quarterly,* 4:229-31 (June 1940).

[6] A gross form of influence was seen in the early days of radio in the 1920's. "In the good old days, news commentators got their material largely by buying late editions of the afternoon papers, jotting down a few notes and marching up to the microphone." T. R. Carskadon, quoted in George L. Bird and Frederic E. Merwin, *The Newspaper and Society* (New York: Prentice-Hall, 1942), p. 542. The pattern also occurs in this form in communities moving from "folk" to "urban" status; the writer once watched a radio news broadcast in Saltillo, Mexico, in which the announcer simply read news from a newspaper.

apolis and St. Louis. In addition, they, together with most other editors, will also see one or two of the near-national papers: the New York *Times,*[7] the *Herald Tribune,* and the *Christian Science Monitor.* These journals are so widely mentioned by newsmen as "papers they see fairly regularly" that they take on new significance as "opinion leaders" for hundreds of smaller papers. Similar patterns could be found in other areas of life, especially other vehicles of mass culture (movies, radio, advertising, etc.), and in business, family and educational activities.[8]

Actual proof that the arterial pattern exists, of course, would require experimental study. The front page of a "big" paper would have to be checked against several "satellite" papers in its area, and an accurate count kept of similarities and differences for equivalent time-intervals. Especially close watch would focus on "breaks" in the news pattern to see whether the smaller papers "switched" to the play taken by the leader. Distant papers would serve as controls. Short of such an experiment, however, the following evidence can be marshalled to substantiate the arterial hypothesis.

1. *The great amount of newspaper reading by newsmen.* This does not prove influence, but it is logical to expect that newsmen read papers not purely for information alone, but also to apply their reading to their own work. Continued exposure to a set of stimuli predisposes the individual to developing a favorable frame of attention, at least when the source of the stimuli (in this case, other papers) is valued by the individual.[9]

2. *Interview responses.* No editor flatly stated that he did *not* check other papers for their news-play. Most, in fact, tended to acknowledge the arterial effect. Here is what some said:

[7] Thus the *Times,* with some 500,000 circulation, may have far greater national *influence* than the New York *Daily News,* with its 2,000,000 circulation. Also, of course, the two papers are read for different purposes, and the *Times* is probably read more by "important" people (opinion leaders) .

[8] For the influence stemming from larger to smaller cities in other ways, see R. D. McKenzie, *The Metropolitan Community* (New York: McGraw-Hill, 1933) , chap. 8. It is quite clear, incidentally, that news, in the American sense, is heavily weighted in favor of urban, rather than rural activities. The phrase "opinion leaders" was originally suggested in Paul F. Lazarsfeld, Bernard Berelson and Hazel Gaudet, *The People's Choice* (New York: Columbia University Press, 1948), chap. 5.

[9] For a systematic discussion of this principle and related principles, see Charles E. Osgood and Percy H. Tannenbaum, "Attitude Change and the Principle of Congruity," in Wilbur Schramm, ed., *The Process and Effects of Mass Communication* (Urbana: University of Illinois Press, 1954), pp. 251-60.

Definitely. You want the help of other people—other men who have had lots of experience in preparing their front pages. It's a must. For example, the news editor and I will go to the exchange desk, and compare the handling of stories in various papers. (Managing editor, Ohio, 90,000.)

I rely on these other good papers for help in news judgement, and on the better radio broadcasts. (Editor, Ohio, 25,000.)

To a certain extent, you get a consensus, particularly in state stories. I don't check them with that in mind. But if I'm in doubt sometimes, I check an early edition of a (state capital) paper, so I can keep with my hunch, or change. (Editor, Midwest, 30,000.)

Sometimes I will see the (Philadelphia) *Inquirer,* and get ideas for my headlines. (Wire editor, Pennsylvania, 25,000.)

Sure, like everything else, you learn from the good points of others. There's a herd instinct over the American press; they follow a certain line to succeed—the line which seems successful for the bigger papers. (Editor, Midwest, 40,000.)

You always study the other guy's front page. (Editor, East, 40,000.)

A comment by a managing editor to his wire editor, overheard by the researcher while observing city desk action on a Pennsylvania daily (30,000), was: "What did the New York papers do with this story?"

3. *Scattered suggestions from the literature.* Rosten was struck by the influence exerted by such papers as the New York *Times* and *Herald Tribune,* the Baltimore *Sun,* the Washington *Post* and the *Star,* and also by columnists—Clapper, Mallon, Krock, Allen and Pearson. "The influence exerted by writers for the New York *Times,* for example, is thus very great: the facts in a New York *Times* dispatch will be copied widely and incorporated—in whole or in part—into news accounts going to papers all over the country."[10] Elsewhere, Rosten added: "Newspapers supply a reporter with information which he incorporates, consciously or not, into his own dispatches; they influence his personal political attitude and his professional activity."[11] T. R. Cawley of the Gannett group has opined that perhaps what a newsman considers news is "measured by his reading of the big dailies."[12] Smith and Rheuark quote a Pennsylvania editor as saying that "the best news tips come from

[10] Leo Rosten, *The Washington Correspondents* (New York: Harcourt, Brace, 1937), pp. 94-5.
[11] *Ibid.,* p. 169.
[12] In *Editorially Speaking,* Rochester, n.d., IV, pp. 14-17.

newspapers themselves . . . A building boom in Pittsburgh . . . may reveal a tiny boom in the correspondent's own community."[13] Allen, while confining his statement to editorials (but presumably news-play would operate similarly), said, "For 40 years the great editorial page of the New York *World* was the textbook of editorial writers throughout the country. It was consciously imitated by newspapers everywhere."[14]

Speculation as to some possible reasons why newsmen do so much newspaper reading may add some clarification to the pattern: (1) Many editors require staffers to be acquainted with late developments on reporting for work, ready to "follow up" in later editions what happened in time for an earlier paper. (2) It is professionally advantageous for a staffer to keep up, both on the news itself and on newspaper techniques. (3) Newsmen are not busy at all times during their eight-hour day, newspapers are inevitably present in all newsrooms, and it may "look better" to be seen reading than to be merely sitting. (4) News becomes a "value" to the newsman, a phenomenon he rates highly and identifies with; this is possibly so true that he prefers to read papers than, say, to work in his spare office time doing research or planning a local feature. (5) If there are any characteristics common to the emotional and mental make-up of the newspapeman, one may be a tendency to restlessness, a searching for something he cannot pin down. One could "search forever" in newspapers. (6) Reading newspapers probably fills certain needs of relaxation and a sense of adequacy (as when he discovers a story which he could have handled better). In any event, the newsman does much newspaper reading, and one would be hard put to claim he is not influenced by this repeated experience.

There are some situations which limit, or even negate, the working of the arterial effect. The big local story generally outranks the big national or world story, and here the local editor has his own decision to make about relative newsworthiness. The more recent story is preferred to the top story in the big city paper, which was printed hours earlier and at some distance.

In a city with competing papers, an interesting pattern may

[13] C. R. F. Smith and Kathryn M. Rheuark, *Management of Newspaper Correspondents* (Baton Rouge: Louisiana State University Press, 1944), p. 55.

[14] Eric W. Allen, "The Editorial Page in the Twentieth Century," in Bird and Merwin, *op. cit.*, p. 310.

occur. If one paper breaks a story of less than paramount interest, the other will sometimes ignore or de-emphasize it. An excellent example was found in Trenton. The researcher, in checking five weeks' issues of both papers, noted that the *Trentonian* in several issues featured, on page one, news of federal aid to a local slum-clearance project amounting to some $700,000. The Trenton *Times* barely noted the development with a few lines at the bottom of its weekly city council stories. City hall reporters on both dailies were aware of this discrepancy. The *Trentonian* reporter, on being interviewed, said that he had "broken" the story (i.e., published it first), figured it was big news, and followed it up. He believed the *Times* was not using it because he was "riding" it. The *Times* reporter corroborated this, indicating that it was *Times* policy not to play second fiddle to the other (much newer and smaller) paper. Thus readers of the two papers received a markedly different version of the slum clearance situation.

The arterial effect can also work in reverse, where the bigger paper is suspect. One wire editor (eastern 30,000) said, "If I see Hearst giving a story a big blast, I'll double check it for a phony angle." Similar attitudes among some Midwest newsmen were voiced concerning the Chicago *Tribune*.

Several kinds of suggestive evidence have been advanced that the arterial process in fact exists. A further set of data which could support the argument deals with the career pattern of newsmen. Respondents were asked where men went on leaving their paper. By far the greatest proportion went to larger papers, or to wire services. The associate editor of a Midwest paper (40,000) said that in 31 years only two departing staffers had gone to smaller papers. Here we have another reason why newsmen follow larger papers: they may work for one some day.

The existence of such a phenomenon prompts the question "Why?" Why is it that many editors seek guidance from larger papers? Here again some tentative suggestions will be essayed, as points of departure for further research.

1. Journalism lacks a body of tested knowledge about news judg-ment. The learned disciplines—medicine, science, engineering, etc.—have built up, through research, a body of systematic theory and principles. Journalism, with few exceptions, has not. Therefore, what criteria of relative newsworthiness can the small-city editor

apply?[15] Which of the scores of stories reaching his office any day merit page one? At best, he has certain traditional rules of thumb concerning news values (names, money, sex, scandal, war, conflict, etc.). He does know, however, that the New York *Times* employs many experienced specialists to make decisions about relative news importance. It is a short step for him to follow such a paper as the *Times*.

2. Following the news judgment of larger papers furnishes the newsman on a smaller paper a feeling of satisfaction, or a rationalization, that he has performed his job adequately. An eastern staffer said that the wire editor of his paper compared his own news decisions with those of the *Times* as "proof he's O.K." The staffer then asked, "Is this why front pages all over the country look the same?" A second staffer noted that if an editor questions a newsman's judgment, the latter can point to a larger (and thus prestigeful) paper and show that the big-town editors "agreed with him."

3. There is scattered evidence that many papers are understaffed. Costs of publishing are up and profits are down. Staffers consequently have little time to examine each piece of news for its intrinsic worth. Only the big papers employ editors who do nothing but sift and evaluate dispatches. The small-town man, aware of this, places faith in the larger paper and the validity of its news judgment.

4. A final—and more tenuous—line of reasoning to explain the pattern of "follow the opinion leader" would stem from something we might call the drive toward cosmopolitanism. Small cities show signs of yearning to be bigger; small papers often seek to increase their size or appearance of size. They may do this by employing big-city "circus" make-up and featuring world, rather than local, news. No American city is isolated from larger cities. Urbanism, through the mass media, travel and migration has spread its influence widely into non-urban places. Bigness has often been termed an American value. That the small paper may try to simulate the

[15] Walter Lippmann noted the editor's dilemma in his classic *Public Opinion*, first published in 1922. "Without standardization, without stereotypes, without routine judgments, without a fairly ruthless disregard of subtlety, the editor would soon die of excitement." *Public Opinion* (New York: Penguin, 1946), p. 267. The problem of news judgment has yet to receive adequate study. An interesting empirical study is Walter B. Pitkin and Robert F. Harrel, *Vocational Studies in Journalism* (New York: Columbia University Press, 1931), Part I.

bigger one, then, is not surprising. One hears small-town people speaking apologetically about "our little town," "our little police force," "our little newspaper here in town." Small city institutions *are* small, and in American culture bigness is coveted. From such considerations of American values about bigness and status, it could follow that the arterial pattern is a normal response.

What about the reverse pattern of influence: do small papers influence big ones? Available data indicate that they do not. Newsmen, asked which papers they read regularly, seldom mentioned smaller papers. Frequently one reporter is assigned to check the smaller papers of the surrounding shopping area, to clip items for rewriting. This varies inversely with the number of "string" (part-time) correspondents maintained by the paper. An example of the "big city" orientation of newsmen is the case of the county editor of an eastern paper (30,000). Although responsible for news in the environs, he had never seen a copy of the weekly paper from a town 15 miles away, but he knew well the papers from larger cities.

It seems significant that while newsmen will perhaps not be surprised about a discussion of the arterial pattern, it generally exists below the threshold of their conscious mind. Only one newsman contacted in the survey verbalized a statement of the pattern before it was broached by the interviewer. In much the same way, pre-literate people may be unaware of the functions of some of their folkways.

There are other factors encouraging uniformity in news selection:

The wire budget. This device is a list of the stories that wire services send to subscribing papers at the start of each news-day, stories they believe will be "tops" that day. National budgets (the United Press uses the term "editors schedule") list some ten stories. These are supplemented by occasional later notes about "upcoming" big stories, and by regional and state budgets. The practice dates from the early 1920s.

Some wire editors use the budget more than others. It would seem that, as with the arterial effect, the smaller and less experienced editors use it most. All editors contacted, however, looked at it each day. Some comments:

> It is used religiously. It immediately enables you to look forward to what's coming—makes make-up easier. You can almost make up your

paper without seeing the news—just by using the budget. (Ohio managing editor, 90,000.)

You *know* they're (budgeted stories) important, so you can use 'em. (Ohio editor, 30,000.)

Each day the wire service sends out its budget of the big stuff, and the boss follows that. (Assistant wire editor, eastern, 40,000.)

The managing editor . . . makes up the paper, but doesn't see the story—he depends on me for that. But he makes up the paper without reading the copy—either local or wire stuff. Just uses the budget, and the report on what the city editor has about local stuff. (News editor, eastern, 60,000.)

More independent editors allowed that the budget was a handy device but that they had their own sense of news values and judged accordingly. The comments given above, however, suggest how critical the items listed on the budget can be. One wants to know, who selects the budget items?

Interviews with AP executives in New York disclosed that the decision about budget items is made by the general news editor, who works an eight-hour shift, and his two assistants who take the other shifts. AP bureaus send to New York a budget line or budget offering, suggesting their biggest stories for the day. The general news editor decides which will form the budget.

The service message on page one display. The "service message," or "play message," is close kin to the budget, but less prominent. The New York *Times* syndicate sends to clients a report of the stories it is featuring on page one that night, and also which stories the *Herald Tribune* is featuring. It would be expected that a New England editor, say, who changed his make-up after receiving the *Times* message, would skew his shifts in the indicated direction. Wire services also sometimes transmit notes about the play being given by big papers. One editor (eastern, 15,000) said:

The UP sends out play messages at night . . . we do some studying and soul-searching if the big papers are playing something up and we've minimized it. (So you do revamp in this case?) Well, we do plenty of analyzing and considering about it.

Clipping and pasting. An "old-timer," a reporter who had drifted from paper to paper in pre-Guild years, made this remark:

A newspaperman never thinks up anything new; he copies stuff from other papers.

City editors are still observed clipping items from other papers for re-working. Sometimes a reporter will simply re-write the same material with a new twist; sometimes he will use the clip as a point of departure and gather new material on the story. A reporter (eastern, 25,000) said:

> I'm the early man in the morning. I . . . clip the morning paper for each man's beat . . .

Another reporter (eastern, 60,000) showed a reason for the practice, and criticized it a moment later:

> Around 8 a.m., the local officials aren't on the job yet . . . you can't call them, so we'll just copy it right out of the morning paper . . . Every morning the boss gives me the morning paper's stories of the day . . . Confidentially, if nobody's watching, I toss 'em in the wastebasket. Burns me up to think I can't cover my beat . . .

Local handling of wire copy. Wire stories are seldom changed significantly by local papers. When the copy arrives on a "ticker," the copy editor generally confines his efforts to marking capital letters, and "chopping" from the bottom for space reasons. In recent years wire copy is sent to many newspapers in coded tape form which automatically activates the local typesetting machine; any changes would require considerable work. The technological innovation is thus insuring even closer conformity to the national pattern. On only one paper visited did editors do any considerable altering of wire copy; this was a "liberal" daily near Washington and New York, thus in a position to check wire stories, when suspect, with sources in those news capitals.

It appears, then, that standardization of newspapers exists. Now we can ask: How does standardization jibe with the ideals of democracy? Specificity requires that we briefly characterize democracy. For the present purposes, the following six characteristics of democracy may suffice:

1. Elective, rather than appointive, officials.
2. Reliance on discussion over policy issues, which in turn means that the channels of discussion must be kept open to all: good government is not an acceptable alternative to self-government.
3. Belief in the essential dignity of the individual, regardless

of his status, and the belief that the individual is rational and therefore capable of intelligent discussion.

4. The opportunities and freedoms of the civil liberties, including the freedom of speech and the press, the freedom of the human personality to develop to the fullest, and the freedom from the inhibitions of orthodoxy and conformity.

5. The separation and balance of interests, to the end that no one group dominates the activities of others.

6. The process of peaceful change, in which forms of government and the economy are not fixed, but subject to modification.

It will be seen that standardization, as seen in the arterial effect and other devices short of autonomy, falls short of achieving the level of performance required by the criteria of democracy. In each of the six characteristics, except the first, democratic norms would demand more independence of the individual editor.

Criticisms of the press from the point of view of democracy usually point to the class basis of press ownership ("the one-party press," etc.),[16] or to the increasing number of one-publisher cities ("monopoly").[17] In contrast, the present criticism focuses rather upon editors and the processes of editing, *independent of* the structure of ownership. In other words, the present hypothesis holds that the arterial and other "journalistic" processes would obtain even with competing cities *and* with less oligarchic press ownership and control. All these conditions, separate and combined, are non-democratic. For the future, one can hardly hope for more democratic ownership or for more competition; but one can always hope that the trend toward better reporters and editors will continue, and that this professionalism may reduce the editor's dependence upon arterial aid.

What this analysis reveals is a gap between the ideals and the working of democratic information processes, at the point of the

[16] For an old and coruscating blast on this thesis, see Upton Sinclair, *The Brass Check* (Pasadena: The Author, 1920). For a recent study, see Nathan Blumberg, *One-Party Press?* (Lincoln: University of Nebraska Press, 1954); the interpretations based on data in this study are open to argument.

[17] See, for instance, Morris L. Ernst, *The First Freedom* (New York: Macmillan, 1946), chaps. III and IV. For a strikingly effective rebuttal to this hypothesis, see Stanley K. Bigman, "Rivals in Conformity," *Journalism Quarterly*, 25:127-31 (June 1948), and Raymond B. Nixon, "Implications of the Decreasing Number of Competitive Newspapers," in Wilbur Schramm, ed., *Communications in Modern Society* (Urbana: University of Illinois Press, 1948), pp. 42-57.

editor's decision as to which stories shall be displayed on page one. While some are undoubtedly independent and use their own news judgment, many "follow the opinion leader." It is clear, however, that editors of small papers are not necessarily to be blamed for their abdication of autonomy. Rather, a set of institutional conditions causes them to follow the arterial pattern. Under these conditions editors may actually be serving their readers (but not ideal democracy) better by adhering to the news judgment of specialists in the big cities.

The danger is the potential influence of a small number of persons in deciding what millions of citizens will read. Great responsibility rests upon those few. In effect, editors of large papers, and "general news editors" of wire services, hold more responsible posts than even they perhaps realize, as *absentee* guides of the news display policies of hundreds of newspapers.

SELECTION 18

LIBERALISM, CONSERVATISM, AND INTERNATIONALISM

URBAN G. WHITAKER, JR.

The following selection was prepared by the editor to bridge a gap in the available material for his classes at San Francisco State College. It has not been previously published.

Terms like "liberal" and "leftist" have been so maligned in the cautious atmosphere of recent American politics that their continued usefulness has been challenged. To eliminate them, however, would be impossible even if it were desirable. They are useful words which describe a common and proper orientation of attitudes toward a particular problem. Instead of avoiding such words, we will best contribute to a clearer understanding of the modern world by sharpening our definitions and encouraging their accurate use.

A close examination of the attitudinal spectrum may be of value for numerous purposes. This essay is particularly concerned with the orientation of attitudes toward international affairs. First, the spectrum itself will be defined and examined carefully from the "radical" far left to the "reactionary" far right. Principles governing the inter-relationships and general functioning and application of the spectrum will be identified and discussed. Finally these principles will be applied to specific examples of the orientation of attitudes toward international affairs.

I. THE NATURE OF THE ATTITUDES SPECTRUM

There are four stopping places or common orientations on the spectrum or continuum of general attitudes. Reading from left to right they are: radical, liberal, conservative and reactionary. They are probably best defined in terms of *change*. The radicals to the extreme left stand for a *radical* or *root* or *basic* change as the word itself suggests. The liberals just to the left of center are ready to move forward but they are reformers rather than revolutionaries. They are willing to change what *is* but without completely destroying it. The conservatives just to the right of center are content with things as they are. Again as the word itself suggests, the conservative wants to save what is; he wants no change at all. At the extreme right the reactionary alone wants to change *back* to what once was.

The radicals and liberals are called *leftists*. The conservatives and reactionaries are called *rightists*.

Sometimes the communists or socialists are associated with the far left because of their radical economic idea that the ownership of the means of production should rest with the community as a whole rather than with private individuals. The facsists are associated with the far right because of their reactionary idea that the means of production should be concentrated in the hands of a few private individuals (as used to be the case before the *liberal* idea of economic democracy began to displace the old system).

But if the communists' *economic* ideas are of the radical left wing their *political* ideas often tend to be of the reactionary right wing. While the communists move away from older economic practices toward the *new* idea of community ownership, they move back toward the *old* idea of strict controls on speech, assembly and the press.

This suggests a basic fact about the spectrum: it must be applied separately to politics and economics. There is no necessary correlation between economic liberalism and political liberalism.[1]

[1] Willard Kerr demonstrates this in reporting a study of several students at Tulane University. Kerr, "Untangling the Liberalism-Conservatism Continuum," *Journal of Social Psychology*, Vol. 35, 1952, pp. 111-125.

In fact we can identify a number of attitude areas to which the spectrum applies: clothing, food, automobiles, social manners, education, religion and many others.

Most people are probably conservative in some things, maybe reactionary in a few, liberal in others and perhaps rabidly radical in their attitudes toward still other things. The writer of this paper, for example, is often called a liberal. That is true perhaps of his general economic and political orientation. However, he dresses quite conservatively (plain ties, solid color socks, a simple gold wedding band, etc.). He has resisted the invasion of his home by television, he almost never goes to a movie, and he favors keeping the U.N. as it is (conserving it) instead of converting it into a world government (a *radical* move) or abolishing it (reactionary). About some things he is even reactionary. For example, he prefers the older model automobiles without all the chrome and the false fenders.

Almost every person is intimate with every position on the spectrum in one way or another. Rare indeed is the person who is a pure radical wanting to revolutionize everything, or the complete liberal unsatisfied with the way anything is, or the absolute conservative who likes everything that is, or the total reactionary who prefers all that was.

Thus when we apply the conservative or the liberal label to a person, a policy, or a publication, we should carefully specify the particular sub-spectrum (economic, political, religious, etc.) which is intended.[2] In common unspecified usage the terms usually assume either an economic or a political emphasis. It may even be useful and possible to identify a *general* socio-political or socio-economic inclination which justifies the application of certain labels to individuals, groups or publications.

The *New Republic* calls itself a "liberal" journal and it exhibits consistent willingness to progress in economics, politics, religion and international affairs. The CIO is often tagged as liberal, usually meaning in economics. Fulton Lewis, Jr. is never called a liberal and often is labeled "reactionary" by his opponents because of his consistent opposition to such things as income tax, foreign aid, and international organizations.

[2] Professor Kerr describes five sub-spectra (which he calls "continua"): political, economic, religious, social, aesthetic and finds no meaningful correlation in an individuals' attitudes (liberal, conservative, etc.) from one to another. See *ibid.*, conclusions, p. 121.

This leads to a further observation about the attitudes spectrum. It is subject to distortion depending on the viewer's own attitude. To the radical, the liberal at his immediate right often looks like a conservative and the conservative seems quite reactionary. To the reactionary on the other end of the spectrum, the liberal usually appears quite radical and the conservative seems too liberal.

Thus it is difficult to place any specific person at some definite place on the spectrum because the outlook of the person who judges him is, itself, a source of distortion. President Franklin D. Roosevelt is a good example. To his right-wing enemies he was a full-blown radical. But in his own estimation he was "a little bit left of center."[3] To the communists he was a conservative (conserving the capitalistic free enterprise system). And to most historians he was, through most of his public life, a liberal.[4]

President Eisenhower was considered by most liberals of the opposite political persuasion to be a conservative. "Modern" Republicans call him a liberal and at least one right-wing reactionary has called him "the most radical" President in our history.[5] He himself preferred the phrase "moderate progressive" which neatly straddles the center line between conservatives and liberals.[6]

There is a dominant American value which holds the center line in particular respect. "Objectivity" and a willingness to listen to all sides are considered *good*. This feeling can be used either to support a cautious consensus somewhere near the center of the spectrum or it can support the idea that a healthy democracy must tolerate all four attitudes. The latter thought seems particularly appropriate. If we did not have the radicals' dreams to point the way for the liberals, we would be without our vision and our hope. If we had no liberals to stimulate and to manage progress, our hopes would never become accomplishments. If we were short of conservatives to guard and preserve the accomplishments of progress, both our economic and cultural wealth would be endangered. And if we had no reactionaries to remind us of past accomplishment, we

[3] *The Roosevelt I Knew*, by Francis Perkins (New York: Viking Press, 1946), p. 168.

[4] See also *Roosevelt, Dictator or Democrat?* by Gerald W. Johnson (New York: Harper & Bros., 1941), pp. 10-11.

[5] J. Bracken Lee at the Governors' Conference in Chicago, August 1955. See the *New York Times*, August 10, 1955, p. 14.

[6] *The Eisenhower Years* by Richard Rovere (New York: Farrar, Straus & Cudahy, 1956), p. 352.

would be minus an important corrective to the excessiveness of the radical, the pessimism of the liberal and the overconfident laxity of the conservative.

Individuals who accept this idea that a healthy democratic society requires all four kinds of attitudes are likely to feel the same way about themselves. An individual who is willing to entertain any of the possibilities offered by the radical, liberal, conservative, and reactionary is flexible. He has burned none of his bridges and has the maximum number of alternatives for a "good" solution to the particular problem at hand. It is wise procedure for anyone to consider *all* the possibilities. This flexible attitude itself is a *liberal* one—very close to "willingness to change." It is tempered by another, equally proper, *conservative* attitude: the wisdom of caution. Together the two general attitudes, liberal flexibility and conservative caution, have a kind of "corner" on the attitude market. The liberals are the Ushers of Progress; the conservatives are the Guardians of Goodness. What the liberal acquires, the conservative retains and both win the plaudits of mankind in general.

All this suggests a certain movement of the spectrum itself. Time does not stand still. As time passes the spectrum moves constantly to the left. What was radical yesterday is only liberal today and will be conservative tomorrow. In a little while it may even become reactionary. Social Security is a good example on the U.S. domestic scene. In 1890 the 1935 Social Security Act was a radical dream. By the early 1930's it was a liberal proposal. After 1935 it was a fact and its proponents could become conservative about it. But anyone in the 1960's who favors the 1935 Act exactly as it was was passed during the first FDR term is a reactionary. Time has passed him by. The Act has been amended by the efforts of new liberals and its new version is supported by new conservatives.

It is helpful to imagine what would happen to a single person with a mission (such as the passage of the 1935 Social Security Act) who maintains a constant view. Without changing his own idea about his mission he moves to the right by the leftward progress of society around him, from radicalism through liberalism to conservatism *because he is successful in achieving his goal.* If his original idea was ultimate perfection (i.e., could not, in the opinion of the society, be improved upon) then conservatism becomes a stopping place. Reaction would be bad. Progress would be impossible. If, on the other hand, his idea was not quite perfect when it was finally achieved and the society decided to improve on it the author must either become a liberal again for the period of further progress or, if he adamantly refuses to relinquish the original vision, become a reactionary as society moves forward beyond him.

This explains at once the attractiveness of progress and the appeal of success. Society applauds both the liberal who stimulates the former and the conservative who maintains the latter. In theory any individual, group, or entire society, will tend to become more conservative with the passage of time because of the successes of its liberal programs.

This theoretical conservatism, however, will develop only with *final* and *perfect* liberal achievements. Whether there are such things is a matter of disagreement. Freedom of speech may perhaps be an example. We usually associate the liberals with this value but it is not clear exactly why. It may be because the freedom is only recently won or because it is not yet completely achieved. More likely it is a product of spectrum distortion as the reactionaries— who want to withdraw the freedom and return to a past situation —tack the liberal label on conservatives. One who fights for freedom of speech in the U.S. in the second half of the 20th century *is* a conservative. Our common thinking habit makes us reluctant to associate conservatism and "fighting for rights." But a logical analysis of the process requires that we will always have "fighting *conservatives*" as well as "fighting *liberals*" and that a "fight for right" may be either a fight to *initially attain* (the liberal's struggle) to to *firmly retain* these rights (the conservative's battle).

Many liberals will be unhappy with this analysis. They don't like the suggestion that it is conservatives who lead any part of the civil rights parade. The conservatives, too, are disturbed at the thought that only liberals can care about freedom of speech, freedom of worship, and everything else in the Bill of Rights. What should be pointed out to them is that they as individuals are not "liberals" or "conservatives" but proponents of free speech. As proponents of that value they may all have been liberals at one time or another and they may all be conservatives now.

One of the troubles with the general labeling of persons as liberals or conservatives is that it must blur either the meaning of the label or the value framework of the person labelled. Every individual believes—it is so by definition—that his choices are good. If it is inconsistent to be a total liberal (*everything* should be changed) and at the same time to be in favor of *existing* benefits such as freedom of speech, the inconsistency can be resolved in either of two ways: (1) the "liberal" can be against freedom of speech in favor of something new and different; or (2) the general applicability of the "liberal" label can be denied and the person can admit to being a conservative *in this situation*.

What all this means is that the four attitudes of the common spectrum are not substitutes for value choices. They are nothing more than possible attitudes which a single individual may believe to be appropriate in different combinations of time, place and circumstance. *The individual must choose according to some other scale of values which of these four attitudes he feels proper in any given situation.* Any careful, thinking person who makes a serious effort to support all of his beliefs about various subjects will notice that he slides back and forth on the attitudes spectrum according to whether the things he values are still just dreams (radical), are the possible prize of a current contest (liberal), have already been achieved (conservative), or have been passed by and need retrieving (reactionary).

It is not the purpose of this essay to describe or to classify those basic values which govern general choices of alternatives. It is sufficient here to point out that liberalism and conservatism are *not* themselves such basic values; that they are instead merely the attitudes about change which may result from application of basic values to human problems. The purpose of this writing is to see what benefit we can derive from applying our knowledge about these attitudes. Particularly we are interested in seeing whether radicalism, liberalism, conservatism, or reaction are helpful descriptions of certain forces in international relations.

II. THE ATTITUDES SPECTRUM IN INTERNATIONAL AFFAIRS

Radicalism and liberalism as attitudes toward change are most likely to be present when there is dissatisfaction with both the present and the past. Even though the dissatisfaction itself stems from applying certain values about poverty, war, and disease rather than from hoping for radicalism or conservatism as ends in themselves it is clear that international relations have yielded unsatisfactory results in the past and that only a *new* set of circumstances will be considered *good*. Thus some premium attaches to international *progress*. This is another way of saying that we don't have very much to be properly conservative about in the international affairs field. Thus, although we have seen that conservatism may be a natural stopping place, that the success of liberal progress may make conservatives of all of us some day, there has been so little accomplished internationally that international liberalism seems in no danger of becoming passé.

True there are some who look back on the "golden age" when we Americans could afford to ignore the rest of the world and be ignored by it. Those days of isolation—if indeed they ever really existed—have passed and that minority which yearns for them is reactionary. But few modern Americans look with longing on the international environment of the 19th or even of the early 20th century.

For the vast majority of us we have not yet reached a state in international history where there is very much agreement as to the merits of what *is*. There is plenty of room between here and the millennium for many, many more processions of radicalism, followed by liberalism, succeeded by conservatism.

Within this framework many specific questions present themselves. As we discuss each one in turn we may perhaps find some sort of consistently liberal or consistently conservative viewpoint so that there may be some real meaning in the label "a liberal in international matters." On the other hand we may discover that there is so much basic difference between "liberalism" applied to international economics and the same attitude applied to international organization that little real meaning attaches to the term.

Internationalism: Among the persistent international issues about which it is possible to be liberal or conservative the most significant is that of nationalism versus internationalism.

Each of these terms has multiple meanings. Nationalism, for example, can refer to that *radical* movement which seeks to establish a new nation-state in displacement of colonialism or as a partial replacement of some larger more encompassing nationalism. "Algerian nationalism" is a good current example. But the term can also be applied to that *conservative* feeling that an existing nation-state must be preserved against the growth of *supra*-national institutions.

Internationalism usually carries this latter connotation. It suggests the erosion, if not the outright elimination, of national sovereignty. Insofar as the present world is accurately described as a world of sovereign nation-states, any internationalism which seeks to change this system is perforce "liberal." Thus when the term "liberal" is used with reference to international relations it usually means to describe persons, publications or policies which promote international or *supra*-national rather than national development. This is the most usual liberal-conservative distinction in international affairs and most of the others spring from it or are clearly associated with it.

International Organization: General ideas about the process of international organization or about the role and activities of specific organizations are closely related to this common dichotomy. International organization may, in fact, be the embodiment of internationalism which radicals and liberals seek as a successor to the nation-state system. On the other hand present organizations such as the U.N. are clearly *inter-* rather than *supra*-national and they may contribute to the preservation of the state system as much as to the creation of a successor to it. While the existence of an *inter*national structure may have been a liberal step forward from a less formally organized system it is also a conservative retainer for the system against the possibility of *supra*-national organization.

It is clear that the proponent of today's United Nations Organization would have been a radical in the 1890's and that he was a liberal in the 1930's and early 1940's. But it is equally apparent that he is presently conservative. Thus when Eleanor Roosevelt who, as a liberal, favored the creation of the U.N. becomes satisfied with its existence, she joins with Herbert Hoover who, as a conservative, opposed its creation, but became accustomed to it. If Mrs. Roosevelt had remained consistently liberal she would have been immediately dissatisfied with that which she sought to create. Had Mr. Hoover remained consistently opposed to the United Nations idea he would have become a reactionary.

Liberals of the early 1960's are again clamoring for something new—newer than the original United Nations of 1945. Mrs. Roosevelt will be with them. Her conservatism is transitory. Mr. Hoover may join them after they succeed. His is basic and close to being a value in itself.

Foreign Aid: Programs of assistance to other countries are a further elaboration and refinement on the theme of liberal internationalism versus conservative nationalism. Liberal support created the aid program and generally favors its expansion and development. In addition it is the liberals who propose the diversion of aid through *international* rather than bilateral channels. Conservatives originally opposed aid but most of them have been convinced of its utility and at least will tolerate if not support a basic program. Their energy is mostly spent in "holding operations" opposed to liberal extension proposals. It is left to the reactionaries to oppose the basic idea of aid. And the radicals tend to be put out of business as the spectrum progresses to the left, achieving as it goes the radicals' dream of years not long passed. The distinction is rather arbitrary and perhaps monetary. If our aid program is 3.9 billion dollars annually any proposal for less than that amount is reactionary, suggestions for moderate increases are liberal, and a plan to double or triple the amount may be radical.

III. CONCLUSIONS

Composite liberal and conservative positions seem to emerge from an investigation of general international problem areas. The liberal in international affairs is willing, in general, to support the growth of internationalism at some expense to the state system *status quo*. Specifically he is likely to favor increasing the powers of the United Nations, extending the scope of international law, and both increasing and internationalizing programs of foreign aid. The radicals to his left propose more sweeping reforms such as conversion of the U.N. into a federal world government, compulsory jurisdiction for the International Court of Justice, and international control over the entire foreign aid apparatus.

To the right the conservative attitude is generally dedicated to the maintenance of the nation-state system and opposed to *supra*-national or further international developments. Specifically, conservatives like the U.N. *as it is,* prefer voluntary international law, and don't want to rock the boat with increases in foreign aid. Reactionaries at the rightist extreme still dream of abolishing the U.N., of anarchic isolation, and of economic egocentricity.

Whether these attitudes tend to be consistent within single individuals, organizations, or publications who can accurately be described as "liberal" or "conservative" has not been determined by careful investigation. Close observation indicates, however, that at least among interpretive news periodicals there is significant correlation.

The value of the attitudes spectrum for students of international affairs would not disappear, however, even if it were shown that individuals do not tend to be radical, liberal, conservative or reactionary "across the board." So long as a careful distinction is made concerning the particular policy or policy area it is helpful mental shorthand to describe general attitude orientations with one of the four spectrum labels. Such classifications are of particular value for instructional situations where it is desired to present a balanced picture or to provide the tools for acquiring one.

Problems of Organizing and Using Information

Given the immense problems of acquiring and evaluating information relevant to international relations a major question emerges: What kind of study is the study of international relations? Are so many pieces always missing from the puzzle that the process becomes an enormous game of chance? Or, is enough known—or knowable—that international relations can be studied with reasonable expectation that they can be understood, predicted and controlled?

Feeling on this question of whether international relations is an art or a science runs high among those who teach and do research in the subject. Some are adamant that the only way to improve the prospects for world peace is to take a scientific approach to the development of international relations theory. They think this is possible and that international relations scholars should put a heavy emphasis on the behavioral sciences for guidance in theoretical development.

Among the prominent writers displaying this point of view are Professor Quincy Wright of the University of Virginia and Professor F. S. C. Northrop of Yale.

Professor Wright believes that, "International relations is a field extraordinarily difficult for science to enter," but that "nevertheless science has often been able to solve such difficulties." He concludes that, "All disciplines have tended in the modern period to become sciences, however resistant their material may be to such treatment."* His book offers some examples of the way a developing science of international relations might use a mathematical system of coordinates to plot such national capabilities as "energy and lethargy" and such value orientations as "objectivity and subjectivity." He even offers a table which assigns numerical measures to these and other qualities of existing states, nations, governments and peoples. Students who have strong interests in this field of study will want to read Professor Wright's treatise carefully and will find it useful as a reference work.

In the first chapter of his book, Taming of the Nations *(selection 19), Professor Northrop is more definite about the science of*

---

* *The Study of International Relations* by Quincy Wright (New York: Appleton-Century-Crofts, 1955), pp. 115 and 119.

international relations. It not only can be developed but it already is. We need only call on the appropriate experts to describe for us the "normative inner orders" of each society with which our own has relations.

If our government were to agree with Professor Northrop's position, the State Department would hire a team of cultural anthropologists and sociologists and get to work putting together a scientific theory about the relations between nations. There would be a very direct link between the theoretician and the policymaker and there would be no further need for those "practitioners of the art" of international relations whose feelings are reported in the next article (selection 20) by Kenneth Thompson.

Mr. Thompson's report does not completely eliminate the role of theory makers in the conduct of international relations. It recognizes a legitimate function for the theory makers and even encourages them to formulate their ideas about regularities and recurring patterns in international affairs. But it emphasizes the uniqueness of those affairs and the ultimate necessity for making decisions by "rational hunch" rather than by scientific deduction. In short, the Thompson report says that international relations is a game which must be "played by ear."

The final reading on this question (selection 21) is by Professor Harold Guetzkow of Northwestern University. Although his article was written several years before the other two it offers an effective compromise between them. Where Northrop is radically innovative and Thompson is reluctant to believe that much progress toward a science of international relations is possible, Guetzkow is a liberal innovator proposing the careful, step-by-step construction of a theory of international relations.

SELECTION 19

TAMING OF THE NATIONS*

F. S. C. NORTHROP

F. S. C. NORTHROP *has been Sterling Professor of Philosophy and Law at Yale University since 1947. He has been a visting lecturer at many universities and colleges and has received many academic honors. Among his*

* Reprinted from *Taming of the Nations*, by F. S. C. Northrop (New York: The Macmillan Co., 1952), Chapter I, used with their permission.

best known books are The Meeting of East and West *(1946) and* Taming of the Nations *(1952) of which the following selection is the introductory chapter.*

If open diplomacy openly arrived at is to succeed, the people, without whom the statesmen cannot be effective, must be informed. It is with the provision of this information that this book is concerned.

The problem is much more complex than even most statesmen have assumed. All too often issues of domestic politics have been regarded as decisive and sufficient for the determination of foreign policy. Others have regarded national self-interest as the ruling factor. Still others put its basis in the idealism of one's own country or in an undefined ideal of all.

In an imperialistic age, an international policy based on national self-interest has some chance of succeeding, since the imperialist is able to determine in major part what happens. But the contemporary world is not congenial to imperialism. Everywhere it is on the wane. The masses of men are against it. Every sign indicates that its day is done. This means also that the days of foreign policy based on national self-interest are over.

Even if this were not the case, national self-interest will not work in foreign affairs. There are at least two major powers in the world today. Moreover, one of these powers, as the sequel will show, is dominated by an ideology that commits it and its allies to revolutionary world conquest by resort to force. Already this power has put this program into effect throughout the whole of eastern Europe and in Asian Korea. No nation in the world today, not even the United States, is able alone to defend itself and its different ideological and cultural values against this major power. Thus even national self-interest is forced to generate its opposite. Nations must learn how to cooperate or else they perish. Also, there is the atomic bomb. It is not likely that any nation can survive an atomic world war. Again the choice is between collaboration and suicide.

Collaboration requires that nations and their statesmen must learn new ways. We have both to act and to go to school in order to learn how to act. The statesman must also be a scholar. But if statesmen are to be scholars, international relations must become more than a speculative program or an art. It must also be a science, for when death is the fruit of error, one can ill afford to err.

But can there be a science of international relations? In this field are we not in the presence of imponderables? Yes. Imponderables are involved. In fact imponderables are crucial. But this need cause no dismay. For, as the sequel will show, imponderables can be specified. Moreover, when specified they become prodigious sources of strength.

The specification of imponderables calls, however, for new methods of inquiry. The old techniques of the traditional students of international relations and the accepted institutes of foreign affairs will not do. For their ways of approach to the subject matter of the meeting of the nations cannot specify the imponderables; they cannot locate the decisive, causal factors which can determine the pathways from war the nations not only may take but actually are taking.

The problem of a science of international affairs is not unlike that of the science of chemistry. No one would suppose that he had created a science of the chemical elements if he approached the subject from the standpoint of the properties of merely one of the chemical elements. An objective, sympathetic description and understanding of all the different kinds of chemical materials in the universe is obviously necessary for a chemical science. The same is true for any science of international relations which can pretend to be adequate. Before any theory of the way to relate the nations can be even attempted, the character of at least the major individual nations must be determined.

Like the chemical elements these national elements are not identical. Their properties and respective reactions vary from nation to nation. To suppose, therefore, that a trustworthy theory for relating nations can be grounded upon a mere balancing of them as power factors is like treating the ninety-odd chemical elements with their radically diverse reactions in different combinations as if they were identical physical entities determined as to their behavior by one physical property only, namely their respective masses. Once this obvious characteristic of nations as of chemical elements is noted much of the mysticism of the imponderables evaporates. Just as the unexpectedness of the reactions of chemical materials becomes expressible in scientific terms when the individual properties of the ninety-odd chemical elements are specified, so the imponderables in the actions of the eighty-odd nations become amenable to scientific treatment when the differing specific properties of these nations receive the attention which is their due.

The method for determining the properties of the elements of chemistry is well known. What is the corresponding method for specifying the properties of the elements of international relations? Fortunately recent investigations in the sciences of cultural sociology, cultural anthropology and the philosophy of culture give us the answer to this question.

A nation is a society responding as a unit. What is it that gives a society this national unity? The answer is common norms. Except as the people of a society agree upon at least some common norms that society cannot respond as a national unit. The key, therefore, to the understanding of any nation and to the specification of those of its properties which will determine its international reactions is to be found when the major common norms of its people are determined. For unless the people of a nation have a dominant ideology there is no consistent dominant response.

In fact without this dominant common ideology there is no domestic, to say nothing about an international, policy. The present weakness of international law causes us to overlook the fact that there has not always or everywhere been domestic law. Force and war have ruled within nations as well as between them. This reminds us that the science of international affairs is of a piece with the science of domestic relations. In ancient Greece and Rome, as in much of Asia today, law was restricted to the patriarchal joint family; between families, apart from the mediation of the village elders, there was often no law.

These historical reflections are important for another reason. They indicate that the way to peace in international affairs is not to apply between patriarchal families and between city-states but to extend from nations to the world the rule of law after the manner in which the rule of law was successfully extended from the patriarchal joint families and the warring city-states to the nation. Precisely how this is to be done will concern us in the sequel.

The method to be used, however, can be made clear now. It is the method for gaining effective law anywhere. This method has been specified within this century by the distinguished Austro-Hungarian sociologist of law, Eugen Ehrlich. He investigated what it was that distinguished law in his own society which was effective from law which was ineffective. He noted first that one never has law in any community without norms. He noted secondly that these norms are never given by any particular facts in any society such as the economic ones, the political ones, the ethnology or the climate. The norms are determined instead not by any particular facts given inductively by observation but by what he termed "the inner order" of all the facts. This means that there is never a legal, political or economic society except when all the facts of that society are ordered by certain common normative or, in other words, ideological principles. Law and its political institutions, and one may add also economics and its business institutions, are effective only as they correspond to and express this ideological or normative inner order. Hence, there can be no science of any nation or of the relation of all the nations without a specification first of the normative inner order of each particular nation and then of the relations between the many national inner orders.

The sociologist Sorokin in the case of many cultures and the anthropologist Kluckhohn for the society of the Navaho Indians have shown how the scientific determination of the normative inner order of any specific society is to be achieved. It consists in specifying the meanings or philosophy held in common by the leaders and majority of the people of a given society. In fact, the philosophy of any society is but the name for the basic concepts and assumptions agreed upon by its people for organizing the data of their experience and ordering their relation to nature and to one another.

Once the normative inner order of each nation is specified, then the relations between the different nations can be given with similar objectivity. Thus, there is no more need for speculation about the *de facto* relationship between the eighty-odd nations of the world than there is for speculation concerning the normative inner order of the society of a given nation. Both can be determined providing one will examine ideological normative factors with scientific objectivity. In fact, the science of international relations may be defined as that subject which specifies the normative inner order of each nation and the relation between these national normative inner orders.

Ehrlich called this normative inner order of any society or nation its living law. The order specified by the constitution and rules on the statute books of a given society he called its positive law. What he found was that positive law is only effective when it corresponds to the underlying living law of the society to which it refers. Law is effective in any society when the norms which it introduces correspond to the underlying normative inner order habits of the living law of the people to whom it is applied. Law is ineffective, and to law may be added foreign policy and foreign economic aid, when the norms for ordering the relations between people which it prescribes contradict or depart too far from the norms and ideals built into the beliefs and bodies of the people as given in the inner order of their total behavior which is, to use Ehrlich's language, their living law.

To achieve, therefore, a trustworthy guide for international policy in the contemporary world we shall have to do three things. First, the normative inner order of beliefs and habits which is the living law for each national or cultural group in the world must be specified. Second, the relation between the normative ideology of each nation or culture group and that of all other nations and cultural groups must be determined. In certain cases this relationship will be found to be one of compatibility. In other cases it will be found to be that of logical incompatibility and contradiction. This means that no single theory of the way to relate nations can be specified as a universal policy or panacea applicable to all nations. Nor should this surprise us. For if nations differ from one another with respect to their properties, just as do chemical elements, certain combinations of nations will produce a peaceful response whereas certain other combinations of nations, if pressed, will issue in an explosion. We shall find, for example, that Gandhiji's rejection of any use of force in relating men and nations is a correct program for any group of individuals or nations who hold the norms for the inner order of their society from which Gandhiji's pacifism issues. To apply this method, however, to nations whose normative inner order is the antithesis of this is to produce war rather than peace. Just as to put one chemical together with a second chemical may produce a healthful food and to combine the first chemical together with a third chemical may create dynamite or an atomic bomb, so to put Gandhiji's inner order for society with that of Confucius will issue in peace whereas to combine it with that of Premier Stalin will result in something quite different. Programs of peace abstracted from the individual ideological living law properties of the nations are not merely vacuous; they are positively dangerous.

Having specified the normative living law of each individual nation or cultural group and having specified also the respective relations between these diverse national normative inner orders, the third task will be that of framing foreign policy and international law in the light of these international living law findings. Providing this is done, Ehrlich's criterion assures us that the results will be effective. . . .

SELECTION 20

TOWARD A THEORY OF INTERNATIONAL POLITICS*

KENNETH W. THOMPSON

The following selection was prepared by KENNETH THOMPSON *as a report to the profession of an informal conference which included: Robert Bowie, Dorothy Fosdick, W. T. R. Fox, Walter Lippmann, Hans Morgenthau, Reinhold Niebuhr, Paul Nitze, Don K. Price, James B. Reston, Dean Rusk, Arnold Wolfers, and George F. Kennan. The footnotes refer to unpublished papers presented to the conference by the participants.*

. . . Reformers, in contrast to historians, make their theories explicit. They focus, however, on international relations not as they are but as they ought to be. Hence reformers, like historians, are not primarily theoreticians. Practitioners look to the present more than do reformers; statesmen, at least some of the greatest, conceive of international relations in terms of a generalized picture of the international scene. They see concrete cases as examples of more general or theoretical principles. They are inhibited, however, in their concern with the theoretical by the imperatives of practice and policy and only rarely when these immediate demands recede into the background can they afford to make their theories explicit. Statesmanship, as history, can serve as the handmaiden of theory for "those engaged in practice may have insights derived from concentrated experience and thought on particular nodes where action was significant and possible, which can both assist the theoretician and serve as test checks on his theories."[1] Their practical concerns,

* Reprinted from *American Political Science Review,* Vol. 49 (September 1955), pp. 733-746.
[1] Paul H. Nitze, unpublished paper, "The Implications of Theory for Practice in the Conduct of Foreign Affairs," p. 4.

however, prevent them from developing theories general enough to account for behavior on the international scene. Only scholars who analyze, compare, and evaluate the words and deeds of leaders like Bismarck, Churchill, or Wilson can uncover the essence of their approach, i.e., their theory.

THE PURPOSE AND FUNCTIONS OF THEORY

Observers can point to intellectual activities which are not primarily theoretical more readily than they can define or identify theory. Those who assert the possibility of theory for the field of international relations confront the same obstacles, ambiguities, and contradictions on which all past theories of history and politics have suffered shipwreck. The material with which the theorist must deal confounds and frustrates his task at almost every point. The substance of theory is history, composed of unique events and occurrences. An episode in history and politics is in one sense never repeated. It happens as it does only once; it is nonrecurrent in that it has never happened before nor will it be repeated again. In this sense, history is beyond the reach of theory. Underlying all theory, however, is the assumption that these same unique events are also concrete instances of more general propositions. The wholly unique, having nothing in common with anything else, is indescribable, for we know that all analysis (and even description) is made in terms of predicates, class concepts, and repeatable relations. Both recurrence and uniqueness are present in history as in everything else, and the logical difficulty in reconciling them is neither greater nor smaller in international relations than in other fields.

The purpose and function of theory is not to provide a "substitute for the art of decision-making in foreign affairs, which, in view of the infinite number of combinations of multitudes of variables that form any concrete solution must always remain in part a matter of risky choices based on more or less rational hunches."[2] Theory may serve to enhance the rationality of choice of decision-makers by helping them in the articulation of a more fully consistent view of the factors of the external environment. Yet the statesman is bound to a world of contingencies and pressures. He must express his philosophy from time to time as rough guides and rules-

---

[2] Arnold Wolfers, unpublished paper, "Theory of International Politics: Its Merits and Advancement," p. 1.

of-thumb that can only be limited and restricted in character. Whether this is a permanent condition, the conference was not agreed. It was suggested that the field of medicine offers an interesting parallel to decision-making. The medicine man of an earlier age was turned into a physician as philosophical and scientific inquiry gave him new insights and resources. In the same way the policy-maker today is handicapped by the fact that his rough generalizations are sometimes drawn from a single experience. With better data and more accurate theories he can become more nearly "a physician of policy." It should be noted that this analogy was not accepted by those members of the conference who resisted the notion that the realms of nature and human behavior can be readily equated.

The function of theory as conceived and discussed by the participants is threefold. First, and perhaps most basic, it makes possible the ordering of data. It is a useful tool for understanding. It provides a framework for systematic and imaginative hypothesizing. It gives order and meaning to a mass of phenomena which without it would remain disconnected and unintelligible. This function is one emphasized particularly by Professors Fox and Morgenthau. The ordering of data can help the observer to distinguish uniformities and uniquenesses. In one scheme of analysis, for instance, it helps us to understand and distinguish the relatively fixed, the changing but uncontrollable, and the manipulatable aspects of world politics. In another, it guides us in considering the manifold social configurations of politics by offering an organizing principle founded on the most distinctive characteristic of politics, the struggle for power. Theory holds out the tools whereby the observer can discover in the welter of events that which is recurrent and typical. It satisfies man's need for intellectual orientation in a vital sector of existence.

Second, theory requires that the criteria of selection of problems for intensive analysis be made explicit. It is not always recognized that whenever a particular problem is selected for study and analysis in some context or other, there is practically always a theory underlying the choice. The idea of a presuppositionless social science has often been warmly embraced by prominent and aggressive research groups, but has tended more to mislead than to clarify the true nature of most research. It must be obvious that while social scientists should steel themselves to be as objective as possible, the notion that one band of observers goes about its task with a heavy baggage of biases and preferences whereas another starts free from all theories and presumptions is of course a grotesque caricature of social studies. Theory can serve to make more fully explicit the implicit assumptions underlying a research design and thus bring out dimensions and implications that might otherwise be overlooked.

Third, theory can be an instrument for understanding not only uniformities and regularities but contingencies and irrationalities as well. It can make possible "the creative elaboration of fruitful hypotheses which bear on the relationship between specified variables."[3] In modern politics there is a need for specific knowledge of contingent factors. It is argued, for example, that an anatomy of tyranny that deals only with general laws and similarities cannot adequately illuminate the difference between a nihilistic philosophy like nazism and a utopian one like communism. Present-day ideologies and revolutionary forces are variables that complicate the traditional roles of the major powers and must therefore be seen as they relate to other constants and variables. The function that theory serves will be determined by the problem and the intellectual interest of the observer.

THE NATURE AND CONTENT OF THEORY

The content of theory is also a consequence of the particular aim and interest of the student. The author of one of the papers for the conference suggests that at least four elements should go to make up a comprehensive theory.[4] The first element in a theory must be the "givens" on the world political scene, such as the ruling conception of politics, the geographic factors, and aggregates of natural resources. Another element involves long-run basic changes, such as the rise of nationalism or the spread of the coal-and-iron technology. A third element, not to be overlooked, consists of the contingencies consequent upon state policies over which comparatively little rational control is assured. The policies of other states and of one's own state as they are shaped and influenced by domestic forces and political systems are illustrative. A fourth element concerns those areas of choice involving levels of preparedness, patterns of alliances,

[3] *Ibid.*, p. 5.
[4] William T. R. Fox, unpublished paper, "International Relations Theory and Areas of Choice in Foreign Policy," p. 3.

and use of organizations for peaceful change that arise as part of a free and rational decision-making process. A theory that included these four elements would exhaust the basic relevant factors of international politics.

In practice, of course, no single existing theory at any significant level of abstraction does justice to all these elements. Insofar as the variables and contingencies of international politics can be understood and discussed at all, it is as concrete and limited theoretical propositions. For instance, the irrationalities of state policies over which we can have little rational control stem in part from the tendencies of differing forms of political organization. If we introduce the notion that totalitarian governments consistently overestimate their own power and underestimate that of others, we are dealing with a specific theoretical problem. Theory in its present state cannot handle complex bodies of variables in any complete sense. There are specific theoretical statements which can be observed and tested, however, and the resulting findings can be employed in the building of more complex theoretical models.

We are still left with the dilemma of uniqueness and recurrence unless we can arrive at a more coherent view of the nature of a theory of international relations. It should be clear that the influence of public opinion and domestic politics on foreign policy is always uncertain, usually unpredictable, and rarely subject to significant theorizing. By contrast, the choices that are open to a policy-maker in formulating a nation's foreign policy are in general limited in character and rooted in the historic policies that his predecessors have followed. The choices of statesmen are limited by the range of national objectives; national interest is susceptible of theoretical understanding. The fact is inescapable that individuals with quite different personal and political philosophies, like Bevin and Churchill in England or Acheson and Dulles in this country, conduct foreign policies that in practice are similar if not identical in basic objectives. This fact makes a theory of international relations possible. It reflects the rational character of international relations uniting the observer, the statesman, and the international scene.

"A theory of international relations is a rationally ordered summary of all the rational elements which the observer has found in the subject matter. Such a theory is a kind of rational outline of international relations, a map of the international scene."[8] It is grounded in the assumption that foreign policy is pursued by leaders who if successful must be conscious of objectives which are essential to national security. Because of this characteristic, it is possible for the political analyst and historian to retrace the steps of past decision-makers and anticipate those of statesmen of the future to the extent that state behavior is rational. The national interest is the least common denominator of rational foreign policy and the most general level of theoretical understanding. Everyone is of course aware that nations are in practice deflected from a rational course by errors of judgment and emotional preferences. A theory of international relations thus points to the contrast between the empirical reality of the international scene and what it tends inherently to be but can never completely become. The difference between a wholly empirical and a theoretical conception of international relations is like the difference between a photograph and a painted portrait. "The photograph shows everything that can be seen by the naked eye. The painted portrait does not show everything that can be seen by the naked eye, but it shows one thing that the naked eye cannot see: the human essence of the person portrayed."[9]

A theory which deals with the rational elements of international politics can come to terms with the "givens" in the world political equation, the long-run basic changes, and the areas of choice in foreign policy. It can take account of the areas of state policy over which there can be slight control—such as domestic politics—only by showing how through these influences actors can be deflected from the course that rational theory would indicate they should follow. Theory provides a base or fixed point upon which analysis can be founded in the face of irrationalities and contingencies that no theory can deal with at this stage of our intellectual development.

THE LIMITATIONS OF THEORY

Thus theory can at best portray the essence of international politics. The practitioner who must labor in the vineyard of

[8] Morgenthau, p. 5.
[9] Ibid., p. 6.

empirical reality, however, finds its functions limited for him in a threefold way. In the practitioner's realm thinking must focus on concrete actions, while theory attempts to deal with a full continuum of thought. No one theory can be adequate or relevant to all his tasks. The subject matter of theory and practice is essentially ambiguous, and the practitioner is often required to take up where the theorist, because of his material, is obliged to leave off.

The first limitation is possibly the most serious. Some decision-makers prefer "to prick out a policy" case by case. They are distrustful of formal theory which is often too general for their purposes. They are skeptical about carrying any theory too far. They point out that a "wrong theory, an oversimplified theory, or a theory applied out of context can produce disastrous results."[10] Too often theory gives no apparent guide-line for practice and the best the policy-maker can do is to avoid commitments that would oppose a new line of action if the first fails to work out.

Another persistent obstacle to the application of theory in practice is the inherent limitation of any one theory. Even for the scholar "no one theory may be equally accurate in explaining the cycle of peace and war, the rise and fall of great states, the extent to which the future is already implicit in the past, why certain states are 'great powers' and so forth."[11] Yet even if such a theory were intellectually possible, it might not be particularly useful in aiding the statesman having to deal, for instance, with the threat of a Russo-German coalition. For his purposes, a theory of less architectonic proportions which revealed something about historic Russian and German foreign policy could be more helpful.

The theorist, as we have seen, faces problems that set inherent limits to this task. He works with materials consisting of events that are at the same time unique and repetitive. Two events may be alike in certain respects; they will never be alike in all respects. He must ask himself how these differences affect the validity of a theoretical proposition derived from either one of them. Professor Morgenthau illustrates the problem in these terms:

> We might have learned from one situation that it is wrong to make concessions to an imperialistic nation or to intervene in a war between two other nations. Obviously, it cannot follow that one ought never to make concessions to an imperialistic nation nor intervene in a war

[10] Nitze, p. 2.
[11] Fox, pp. 1-2.

between two other nations. A theoretical proposition is correct only under the assumption that all the relevant elements in the situation which have given rise to it are present in another situation and that no new circumstances are intervening, modifying their relevance.[12]

Yet who can say with absolute certainty that all essential elements unaltered by circumstances are present in two situations? It was wrong, we say, to make concessions to German imperialism. Is it equally wrong to yield at any point to Russian imperialism or to Chinese imperialism? Is Churchill's plea for a conference "at the summit" no less mistaken than Chamberlain's "Peace in our Time"? The Nazi will to power was a form of the general will to power, yet it was also unique in its fanaticism. Wisdom develops with the awareness of the presence of both constants and unique events on the historical scene. Theory confronted by ambiguities which call it into question at every turn must guard against taking itself too seriously. Often the best the theorist, no less than the diplomat, can do is to play by ear and be satisfied with a series of hunches.

If this is the fate of theory, there is a point at which theory and practice join hands in a common task. That the judgment and wisdom of the practitioner are the fruits of a pragmatic conception of theory is sometimes overlooked. This in spite of the fact that a prominent policy planner can say in reviewing the formulation of foreign policy: "Facts must be ordered to bring out significant generalizations; assumptions have to be made as to the probable causal interrelations between diverse factors; judgments must be made as to the hierarchy of values and of objectives."[13] Yet the relationship between theorists and policy-makers in the past has not been too creative. Theorists sometimes imply that those engaged in practice are lacking in original and valid insights and exempt from broader intellectual influences. Practitioners in turn maintain that a wrong theory can be worse than no theory at all. They regret that academic scribblers often philosophize at a level of abstraction and generality that so frequently is irrelevant for their task.

However, the limitations of theory inherent in the ambiguity of its materials encourage wider contacts between theorists and practitioners. Theory must have some place for the intuitive understanding of contingent factors in concrete situations. No one deals more continuously than the policy-maker with these contingencies

[12] Morgenthau, p. 4.
[13] Nitze, p. 1.

in relation to the constants of international life. Theory attempts to deal with a broad continuum of thought, whereas the decision-maker faced with concrete problems must work at nodal points on the continuum. A theory is as good as the repeated evidence of its validity. On this theorists and practitioners appear to agree. A theorist can say: "Analytical propositions, whatever the theoretical framework in which they are placed, which purport to 'explain' have first to be subjected to empirical testing and then reformulated to take account of the difference between the theoretical model and the actual observation."[14] A practitioner believes that through insights derived from concentrated experience the validity of theory at important points on a continuum may be tested.[15] The deductive intuition of the practitioner coupled with the empirical context within which he operates will be recognized as an important tool of theory only when the nature and limitations of theory are more fully perceived. . . .

SELECTION 21

LONG-RANGE RESEARCH IN INTERNATIONAL RELATIONS*

HAROLD GUETZKOW

HAROLD GUETZKOW is Professor of Political Science and Psychology at Northwestern University. He was Professor of Psychology at the Carnegie Institute of Technology, 1950-55. Among his many books and articles are Men and Hunger (1946) and Multiple Loyalties (1955).

This article has no practical suggestions for the conduct of either the cold or hot war with Russia. Instead it asserts that man's search for relief from wars needs to be directed by an adequate, basic theory of international relations. In lieu of offering as theory only another opinion the writer will attempt to outline some of the characteristics which an adequate theory may have eventually.

Top foreign policy makers probably feel they live in too urgent a world to concern themselves with the theories of modern social science. They devote little, if any, of their organizations' resources

---

[14] Fox, p. 5.
[15] Nitze, p. 1.
* Reprinted from The American Perspective (Fall 1950), pp. 421-440.

to theoretical studies which have no immediate bearing on day-to-day decisions. Yet, in making decisions, statesmen use assumptions about social behavior which they learned early in life and which may be valid only with reference to one ethnic group or not at all. As a result, their actions and policies are often self-defeating and their solutions to problems are severely circumscribed. In most cases the policy-maker is no doubt unaware of his assumptions about group behavior. It may be this unawareness which makes him content with inadequate and unworkable theories of international relations.

This article contends that the surest and quickest way to world peace is an indirect one—the patient construction over the years of a basic theory of international relations. From this theory may come new and unthought-of solutions to end wars and to guide international relations on a peaceful course.

The value of the scientific approach was emphatically underlined in World War II. The superiority of the United States' operations stemmed in large measure from successful exploitation of the world's scientific resources as they existed in 1940. Many authorities were impressed with the way in which basic natural science theory made military developments possible. Unfortunately, the reservoir of social theory is small and poor in quality, and little effort is being made to build it into a scientific resource.

This article will first consider areas in which the methodological tools used by the present-day worker in international relations must be broadened and sharpened. Then, it will suggest a few ingredients of basic theory in international relations.

I. CONSIDERATIONS ON METHODS . . .

In the early phases of the development of science, there must be systematic classification and description of phenomena. At first this description tends to be verbal, and only gradually do the characteristics become measurable in dimensions which are distinct from each other. In international relations, current theory tends to be descriptive. Most contemporary works are anchored to particulars—for instance, chapters on the international relations of specific states. This approach permits detailed narration with much attention to the substance of foreign relations; but it then is very difficult to construct propositions useful in analyzing more than the single concrete situation under discussion.

The latter phases of the development of a science are marked by the construction of analytic theories. The science is no longer content with descriptive generalizations but attempts to analyze relations and to develop general dynamic theories of how underlying forces bring about the phenomena observed in the earlier phases of the science. In international relations there are few signs today of such analytic theory developments. Even the more advanced power theories, which analyze international relations as the influence of one nation upon another because of the operation of national power (resources, population, and technology), are usually offered by political scientists as descriptive accounts, not as dynamic analyses. Moreover, the most advanced exponent of power theory today limits his concepts to the Western European countries.

The development of an analytical theory gives the scientist a powerful tool for discovering the mainsprings of action within a system of international relations. For instance, understanding is needed of the way in which communication, cultural uniformity, and social solidarity interact and affect the relations between nations. An analytic theory including such factors would be a valuable addition to a more fully formulated power theory. Such theory often provides unexpected derivations and quite new approaches to international affairs. One modern theorist has constructed a mathematical model of relations between states from which he deduces that military preparedness *decreases* security within the inter-nation system—a quite unconventional conclusion! His theoretical constructions also indicate the way in which an armaments race might be slackened. . . .

Few theorists venture to make predictions about future international events. Instead, they prudently limit themselves to *post facto* explanations of events. This is a realistic recognition of the limitations of our present state of social science. Lack of prediction, however, makes it difficult to test the validity of theories. In the long run, the usefulness of a theory depends upon its reliability in prediction.

Lack of interest in prediction partially stems from the background and training of students of international relations in the fields of philosophy, history and law. Distaste of predictions undoubtedly also comes from the bitter, unsuccessful attempts which lie scattered alongside the development of international relations theory. Because of the urgent demand for practical application, interest and effort have been centered on predictions of the grand strategies—just as now attention of the social scientist is focused on the American-Russian struggle.

It would be fruitful to limit at first the predictions to minor international occurrences, rather than risking an attempt to forecast important global events. Confirmation and denial of parts of theories might gradually lead to a more firmly bulwarked system, eventually enabling the social scientist to predict more and more imposing events in international relations. As aide to the policy-maker, the worker in international relations must make predictions. Yet he has never consolidated his propositions into a predictive system, so that he might test the validity of his theorizing. Until this is done, how can substantial progress be made in the construction of a testable theory of international relations?

In conclusion, what is advocated is a more thorough application of scientific methods to research in international relations. Emphasis should be given to the construction of analytic theories which specify concretely the dynamic mechanisms underlying various types of international relations. The mere building of analogies as exemplified in the personification of nations should be avoided. New theories should be capable of yielding predictions so that their validity may eventually be tested.

II. ELEMENTS NEEDED FOR THEORY CONSTRUCTION

But is it possible to construct a theory of international relations with the extension of methods proposed? What form would such theorizing take? How would it be possible to construct small islands of theory, which eventually might be tied together into a more definitive theory-system? This article can not answer these questions but presents only some explorations.

The process of theory construction requires three stages. First, using the nation as the primary unit, propositions would be developed to explain how national behaviors in the international scene originate within the state. Then, a general theory of the relations between any two states might be erected. Later, as one becomes more sure of his footing, this artificially restricted, binary theory might be elaborated into a multi-nation theory. This latter development would undoubtedly be accompanied by research on the functioning of international agencies as dynamic, supra-nation organizations.

Even the simplest theory will probably need to include propositions about four types of factors which operate to determine the foreign policy and behavior of a state:

(1) Domestic forces which are the wellspring of the state's internation behavior.

(2) The nature of the nation's decision-apparatus which translate the basic forces into foreign policies.

(3) The personal dynamics of the nation's leaders which mold the operation of the decision-making apparatus.

(4) The state of the nation's technology.

Of course, these groupings overlap. And undoubtedly much predictive potential of a theory constructed with them will come eventually from the interrelations which exist among variables. . . .

III. COMPONENTS OF AN INTER-NATION THEORY

In theorizing about the intra-nation formulation of foreign policy, one necessarily illuminates certain aspects of an inter-nation theory. At the least it seems necessary to differentiate two types of inter-nation behaviors: the more formal behavior of the state's decision-apparatus, and the informal relationships which exist between peoples of different nationalities.

Some of the same factors involved in an intra-nation theory will also determine inter-nation relations. For instance, inter-personal relations (as determined by the personality characteristics of the statesmen) will influence the outcome of international conferences. The state of technology will make changes in the traditional methods of handling inter-national relations, as exemplified by the transformation of the ambassador from plenipotentiary to mouth-piece as a result of rapid communication between home government and delegates abroad. Finally, economic factors are known to determine power interrelations among nations, as has been so dramatically illustrated in the operation of the Marshall plan. . . .

Some advances already are being made in theoretical construction regarding the operation of informal channels in international relations. For instance, analysis of the flow of international communications—postal and telegraphic, news, exchange of persons—has demonstrated the feasibility of making empirical tests of hypotheses in this area. The cultural anthropologists who formerly studied culture-trait exchanges among primitive tribes, are just beginning to take an interest in the diffusion of cultural products from one nation to another. . . .

IV. THE ORGANIZATION OF RESEARCH ACTIVITIES TO CONSTRUCT BASIC THEORIES OF INTERNATIONAL RELATIONS

It has been contended that with an extended methodology, it should be quite possible to construct an integrated set of theories about international relations. The formulation and testing of such theories would not, however, be easy. The sponsors of the research would need the patience of a Job and the determination of a Horatio Alger. . . .

Skeptics often claim that the social sciences will never make fundamental tests of their hypotheses because they can not experiment. Undoubtedly such limitations will make it difficult to test theories of international relations—but not impossible. Although the social scientist cannot conduct experiments at the time and place he desires them and with all scientific controls, often the events of the world can yield tests of his theories. For instance, would it not have been possible to test the validity of theoretical work on the interplay of economic and power factors in international relations at the 1950 trade agreements meetings? One might make preliminary, orientational checks on his theory on the results of the Annecy trade conferences in 1948. Then, with a revised theory, the scientist might make predictions of the outcomes of the 1950 meetings. The adequacy of one's theories would be "experimentally" checked by the deviation of the predictions from the actual outcomes. . . .

I am as fearful as my readers of the utilization of the results of basic research in international relations for immoral purposes. Derivations from the basic postulates might give rise to astoundingly successful psychological warfare programs. Perhaps some safeguard will be obtained, if the results are available simultaneously to all nations and all peoples. But even such openness in the scientist's proceedings will hardly guarantee the prevention of Machiavellian acts. The basic assumptions and many of the derivations of Nazi policy were forthrightly explained to the world in Mein Kampf, and particular campaigns were spelled out in some detail in books published some ten years before the operations were undertaken. Yet,

statesmen remained blind and persisted in their stereotyped thinking about inter-nation relations until World War II was upon
them. . . .

V. CONCLUSION

In summary, a basic theory of international relations will need
to be supplemented with a theory on the operation of international
organizations. Because international relations are not confined to
relations among nations, the final formulations will include the
operation of forces deriving directly from individuals as persons. It
will even be necessary to construct propositions about the effects of
the operations of private economic and educational agencies on the
international scene.

Out of the process of developing, integrating, and testing these
bodies of theory, it is to be expected that ideas will spring which
probably would never be conceived without the frame of reference
provided by the theory. These ideas may concern practical applica-
tions of the theory which will aid nations in the day-to-day handling
of international problems; or they may lead to new devices and techniques for the conduct of international relations. There appears to
be no other approach which holds any promise of enabling men of
good will to understand and control the present system of international relations, whose breakdown now threatens the world with
utter devastation.

III

Expert or Layman?—Can Democracy Survive in the Twentieth Century?

Whatever one believes to be the nature of international relations, that it is an art or that it is a science, there is general agreement among the commentators that the subject is big, complex, and difficult to comprehend. It is because of this that we have seen the development of one of the great debates of this century: Can a democracy successfully compete in twentieth century international relations? If international relations is a science, is it a science which can be mastered by the "man in the street" during his ten or twelve years of formal education and his casual reading? If it is an art, is it art which can be acquired by the common man who has little opportunity to travel abroad, to gain first-hand experience in official international relationships, or to engage in extensive studies of diplomatic history?

In a phrase, should control of international relations be entrusted to laymen or to experts?

This question, which was touched on in earlier readings by Lord Bryce and George Kennan is the subject of the following exchange between Walter Lippmann and Archibald MacLeish. The first reading (selection 22), from Mr. Lippmann's book, The Public Philosophy, *argues that the western democracies are declining because foreign policy is controlled by public opinion. While Lipp-*

mann's analysis suggests the desirability of restricting the role of public opinion because of its slow, negative, and narrow nature, MacLeish (selection 23) eloquently defends the whole range of individual freedom as a source of strength to the community. The two men do not seem to be separated so much by differences in what they want the world to be like as by differences in what they think it is possible for men to do with their freedom. Mr. MacLeish emphasizes that his adversary believes it is necessary to choose between freedom and effective community and then chooses the latter. But Mr. Lippmann replies (selection 24) that his choice is, in fact, dictated by objective limits on the possibility of freedom. Here the issue is joined.

The concluding reading (selection 25) is taken from C. Wright Mills' book, The Power Elite. It does not take a normative stand in the debate but offers an objective description of the process by which decisions are in fact made in our society. Mills' concept of an informal, de facto power elite may stand as an additional possibility to the two (expert or layman) assumed by the Lippmann-MacLeish debate.

SELECTION 22

THE DECLINE OF
WESTERN DEMOCRACY*

WALTER LIPPMANN

WALTER LIPPMANN *is an editor and author whose regular commentary appears in the New York* Herald Tribune *and many other newspapers. He has won the Pulitzer Prize and many other awards for his several books. Among his more prominent works are* The Good Society *(1937),* U.S. Foreign Policy: Shield of the Republic *(1943), and* The Public Philosophy *(1955). The following selection is Chapter One of the latter book and was reprinted as an article in the* Atlantic Monthly *of February 1955.*

When the world wars came, the people of the liberal democracies could not be aroused to the exertions and the sacrifices of the struggle until they had been frightened by the opening disasters, had been incited to passionate hatred, and had become intoxicated

---

with unlimited hope. To overcome this inertia the enemy had to
be portrayed as evil incarnate, as absolute and congenital wicked-
ness. The people wanted to be told that when this particular
enemy had been forced to unconditional surrender, they would
re-enter the golden age. This unique war would end all wars. This
last war would make the world safe for democracy. This crusade
would make the whole world a democracy.

As a result of this impassioned nonsense public opinion became
so envenomed that the people would not countenance a workable
peace; in 1917 they were against any public man who showed "any
tenderness for the Hun," or was inclined to listen to the "Hun
food snivel." Yet as soon as the terms of the settlement were known,
it was evident that peace had not been made with Germany. It was
not for want of power but for want of statesmanship that the liberal democracies failed. They failed to restore order in that great
part of the world which—outside of revolutionary Russia—was still
within the orbit of their influence, still amenable to their leadership,
still subject to their decisions, still working within the same economy, still living in the same international community, still thinking in the same universe of discourse. In this failure to make peace
there was generated the cycle of wars in which the West has suffered so sudden and so spectacular a decline.

Public opinion, having vetoed reconciliation, had made the
settlement unworkable. And so when a new generation of Germans
grew up, they rebelled. But by that time the western democracies,
so recently too warlike to make peace with the unarmed German
Republic, had become too pacifist to take the risks which could
have prevented the war that Hitler was announcing that he would
wage against Europe. Having refused the risk of trying to prevent
war, they would not now prepare for the war. The European democracies chose to rely on the double negative of unarmed appeasement, and the American democracy chose to rely on unarmed
isolation.

When the unprevented war came, the fatal cycle was repeated.
Western Europe was defeated and occupied before the British
people began seriously to wage the war. And after the catastrophe
in Western Europe eighteen agonizing months of indecision elapsed
before the surprise and shock of Pearl Harbor did for the American
people what no amount of argument and evidence and reason had
been able to do.

The record shows that the people of the democracies, having become sovereign in this century, have made it increasingly difficult for their governments to prepare properly for war or to make peace. Their responsible officials have been like the ministers of an opinionated and willful despot. Between the critical junctures, when public opinion has been inattentive or not vehemently aroused, responsible officials have often been able to circumvent extremist popular opinions and to wheedle their way towards moderation and good sense. In the crises, however, democratic officials—over and above their own human propensity to err—have been compelled to make the big mistakes that public opinion has insisted upon. Even the greatest men have not been able to turn back the massive tides of opinion and of sentiment.

There is no mystery about why there is such a tendency for popular opinion to be wrong in judging war and peace. Strategic and diplomatic decisions call for a kind of knowledge—not to speak of an experience and a seasoned judgment—which cannot be had by glancing at newspapers, listening to snatches of radio comment, watching politicians perform on television, hearing occasional lectures, and reading a few books. It would not be enough to make a man competent to decide whether to amputate a leg, and it is not enough to qualify him to choose war or peace, to arm or not to arm, to intervene or to withdraw, to fight on or to negotiate.

Usually, moreover, when the decision is critical and urgent, the public will not be told the whole truth. What can be told to the great public, it will not hear in the complicated and qualified concreteness that is needed for a practical decision. When distant and unfamiliar and complex things are communicated to great masses of people, the truth suffers a considerable and often a radical distortion. The complex is made over into the simple, the hypothetical into the dogmatic, and the relative into an absolute. Even when there is no deliberate distortion by censorship and propaganda, which is unlikely in time of war, the public opinion of masses cannot be counted upon to apprehend regularly and promptly the reality of things. There is an inherent tendency in opinion to feed upon rumors excited by our own wishes and fears.

At the critical moments in this sad history, there have been men worth listening to who warned the people against their mistakes. Always, too, there have been inside the governments men who judged correctly because they were permitted to know in time the uncensored and unvarnished truth. But the climate of modern democracy does not usually inspire them to speak out. What Churchill did in the thirties before Munich was exceptional: but the general rule is that a democratic politician had better not be right too soon. Very often the penalty is political death. It is much safer to keep in step with the parade of opinion than to try to keep up with the swifter movement of events.

In government offices which are sensitive to the vehemence and passion of mass sentiment public men have no sure tenure. They are in effect perpetual office seekers, always on trial for their political lives, always required to court their restless constituents. They are deprived of their independence. Democratic politicians rarely feel they can afford the luxury of telling the whole truth to the people. And since not telling it, though prudent, is uncomfortable, they find it easier if they themselves do not have to hear too often too much of the sour truth. The men under them who report and collect the news come to realize in their turn that it is safer to be wrong before it has become fashionable to be right.

With exceptions so rare that they are regarded as miracles and freaks of nature, successful democratic politicians are insecure and intimidated men. They advance politically only as they placate, appease, bribe, seduce, bamboozle, or otherwise manage to manipulate the demanding and threatening elements in their constituencies. The decisive consideration is not whether the proposition is good but whether it is popular—not whether it will work well and prove itself but whether the active, talking constituents like it immediately. Politicians rationalize this servitude by saying that in a democracy public men are the servants of the people.

This devitalization of the governing power is the malady of democratic states. As the malady grows, the executives become highly susceptible to encroachment and usurpation by elected assemblies; they are pressed and harassed by the higgling of parties, by the agents of organized interests, and by the spokesmen of sectarians and ideologues. The malady can be fatal. It can be deadly to the very survival of the state as a free society if, when the great and hard issues of war and peace, of security and solvency, of revolution and order, are up for decision, the executive and judicial departments, with their civil servants and technicians, have lost their power to decide.

When I describe the malady of democratic states as a derange-

ment in the relation between the mass of the people and the government, I am, of course, implying that there is a sound relationship
and that we should be able to know what it is. We must now examine this assumption. We are looking into the relation between,
on the one hand, the governing or executive power and, on the
other hand, the elected assembly and the voters in the constituencies.
The best place to begin is in the simple beginnings of our constitutional development—in the medieval English Parliament—before
the essential functions and their relation had become complicated
by their later developments.

No relationship, sound or unsound, could exist until the functions of execution and representation had become differentiated.
In primitive societies they are not differentiated. Under the Norman
and Angevin rulers the differentiation had not yet occurred. These
rulers "judged and legislated as well as administered." But by the
thirteenth century the differentiation is already visible, and the
essential relation in which we are interested can be recognized.
There is a writ issued under Henry III in 1254, summoning Parliament. The sheriff of each county is ordered "to cause to come before the King's Council two good and discreet Knights of the Shire,
whom the men of the country shall have chosen for this purpose in
the stead of all and of each of them to consider along with Knights
of other shires what aid they will grant the king."

Let us note the dualism. There is the government, which means
the king and his council of prelates and peers. Then there are the
knights of the shires representing the men of the counties. They
are to meet, and the king will ask the knights what aid they will
grant to him. This is the basic relationship. The government can
act. Because it can act, it decides what action should be taken, and
it proposes the measures; it then asks the representatives of those
who must supply the money and the men for the means to carry out
its decisions. The governed, through their representatives, the two
knights of the shire from each county, give or withhold their consent.

From the tension and the balance of the two powers—that of
the ruler and that of the ruled—there evolved the written and the
unwritten contracts of the constitution. The grant of aid by the
ruled must be preceded by the ruler's redress of their grievances.
The government will be refused the means of governing if it does
not listen to the petitions, if it does not inform, if it does not

consult, if it cannot win the consent of, those who have been elected as the representatives of the governed.

The executive is the active power in the state, the asking and the proposing power. The representative assembly is the consenting power, the petitioning, the approving and the criticizing, the accepting and the refusing power. The two powers are necessary if there are to be order and freedom. But each must be true to its own nature, each limiting and complementing the other. The government must be able to govern and the citizens must be represented in order that they shall not be oppressed. The health of the system depends upon the relationship of the two powers. If either absorbs or destroys the functions of the other power, the constitution is deranged.

The western liberal democracies are a declining power in human affairs. I argue that this is due to a derangement of the functions of their governments which disables them in coping with the mounting disorder. I do not say, indeed I think it impossible to know, whether the malady can be cured or whether it must run its course. But I do say that if it cannot be cured, it will continue to erode the safeguards against despotism, and the failure of the West may be such that freedom will be lost and will not be restored again except by another revolution. But for either contingency, for cure now or for recovery after a catastrophe, our first necessity is to work towards an adequate knowledge of the two functions, their nature, and their derangement.

In order to do so it is necessary at the outset to reduce the ambiguity of the term "the people." For it has two different meanings, which it may be convenient to distinguish typographically. When we speak of popular sovereignty, we must know whether we are talking about The People, as voters, or about *The People,* as a community of the entire living population, with their predecessors and successors.

It is often assumed, but without warrant, that the opinions of The People as voters can be treated as the expression of the interests of *The People* as an historic community. The crucial problem of modern democracy arises from the fact that this assumption is false. The voters cannot be relied upon to represent *The People.* The opinions of voters in elections are not to be accepted unquestioningly as judgements of the vital interests of the community.

To whom, for example, did the Preamble of the Constitution

refer when it said that "We the People of the United States . . . ordain and establish this Constitution"? On September 17, 1787, about forty members signed the draft on which they had been working since May 25 for one hundred sixteen days. In Article VII of their text they stipulated that if and when conventions in nine states had ratified it, then for those nine states The People of the United States would have ordained and established the Constitution. In this context a majority of the delegates elected to nine state conventions were deemed to be entitled to act as The People of the United States.

The inhabitants of the United States who were qualified to vote for these delegates were not a large number. They included no slaves, no women, and (except in New York) only such adult males as could pass property and other highly restrictive tests. We do not have accurate figures. But according to the census of 1790 the population was 3,929,782. Of these, 3,200,000 were free persons, and the adult males among them who were entitled to vote are estimated to have been fewer than 500,000. Using the Massachusetts figures as a statistical sample, it may be assumed that fewer than 160,000 actually voted for delegates to all the ratifying conventions, and of those voting, perhaps 100,000 favored the adoption of the Constitution.

The exact figures do not matter. The point is that the voters were not—and we may add that they have never been and can never be—more than a fraction of the total population. They were less than 5 per cent when the Constitution was ordained. They were not yet 40 per cent in 1952 when, except under the special conditions in the South, we had universal adult suffrage. Manifestly, the voters can never be equal to the whole population, even to the whole living adult population.

Because of the discrepancy between The People as voters and *The People* as the corporate nation, the voters have no title to consider themselves the proprietors of the commonwealth and to claim that their interests are identical with the public interest. A prevailing plurality of the voters is not *The People*. The claim that it is is a bogus title invoked to justify the usurpation of the executive power by representative assemblies and the intimidation of public men by demagogic politicians. In fact demagoguery can be described as the sleight of hand by which a fraction of The People as voters is invested with the authority of *The People*. That is why so many crimes are committed in the people's name.

The fact is that *The People* is not, as Jeremy Bentham assumed, the simple aggregate of living persons in a community. *The People* is also the stream of individuals, the connected generations of changing persons, that Burke was talking about when he invoked the partnership "not only between those who are living" but also with "those who are dead, and those who are yet to be born." *The People* is a corporation—an entity, that is to say, which lives on while individuals come into it and go out of it.

For this reason Bentham cannot have been right when he said that the interests of the community are no more than the sum of the interests of the several members who happen to compose it at any particular instant of time. He cannot have been right when he said that "the happiness of the individuals, of whom a community is composed, that is their pleasures and their security, is the end and the sole end which the legislator ought to have in view."

For besides the happiness and the security of the individuals of whom a community is at any moment composed, there are also the happiness and the security of the individuals of whom generation after generation it will be composed. If we think of it in terms of individual persons, the corporate body of *The People* is for the most part invisible and inaudible. Indeed, as a whole it is nonexistent in that so many are dead and so many are not yet born. Yet this corporate being, though so insubstantial to our senses, binds, in Burke's words, a man to his country with "ties which though light as air, are as strong as links of iron." That is why young men die in battle for their country's sake and why old men plant trees they will never sit under.

In ordinary circumstances voters cannot be expected to transcend their particular, localized, and self-regarding opinions. As well expect men laboring in the valley to see the land as from a mountain-top. In their circumstances, which as private persons they cannot readily surmount, the voters are most likely to suppose that whatever seems obviously good to them must be good for the country, and good in the sight of God.

I am far from implying that the voters are not entitled to the representation of their particular opinions and interests. But their opinions and interests should be taken for what they are and for no more. They are not—as such—propositions in the public interest. Beyond their being, if they are genuine, a true report of what various groups of voters are thinking, they have no intrinsic authority.

The Gallup polls are reports of what people are thinking. But that a plurality of the people sampled in the poll think one way has no bearing upon whether it is sound public policy. For their opportunities of judging great issues are in the very nature of things limited, and the statistical sum of their opinions is not the final verdict on an issue. It is, rather, the beginning of the argument. In that argument their opinions need to be confronted by the views of the executive, defending and promoting the public interest. In the accommodation reached between the two views lies practical public policy.

Faced with choices between hard and soft courses of action, the normal propensity of democratic governments is to please the largest number of voters. The pressure of the electorate is normally for the less painful alternative. That is why governments are unable to cope with reality when elected assemblies and mass opinions become decisive in the state, when there are no statesmen to resist the inclination of the voters and there are only politicians to excite and to exploit them.

There is then a general tendency to be drawn downward, as by the force of gravity, towards insolvency, towards the insecurity of factionalism, towards the erosion of liberty, and towards hyperbolic wars.

In the effort to understand the malady of democratic government I have dwelt upon the underlying duality of functions: *governing*—that is, the administration of the laws and the initiative in legislating; and *representing*—the living persons who are governed, who must pay, who must work, who must fight and, it may be, die for the acts of the government. I attribute the democratic disaster of the twentieth century to a derangement of these primary functions.

The power of the executive has become enfeebled, often to the verge of impotence, by the pressures of the representative assembly and of mass opinions. This derangement of the governing power has forced the democratic states to commit disastrous and, it could be, fatal mistakes. It has also transformed the assemblies in most, perhaps not in all, democratic states from the defenders of local and personal rights into boss-ridden oligarchies, threatening the security, the solvency, and the liberties of the state.

In the traditions of western society, civilized government is founded on the assumption that the two powers exercising the two functions will be in balance—that they will check, restrain, compensate, complement, inform, and vitalize each one the other.

In this century, the balance of the two powers has been seriously upset. Two great streams of evolution have converged upon the modern democracies to devitalize, to enfeeble, and to eviscerate the executive power. One is the enormous expansion of public expenditure, chiefly for war and reconstruction; this has augmented the power of the assemblies which vote the appropriations on which the executive depends. The other development which has acted to enfeeble the executive power is the growing incapacity of the large majority of the democratic peoples to believe in intangible realities. This has stripped the government of that imponderable authority which is derived from tradition, immemorial usage, consecration, veneration, prescription, prestige, heredity, hierarchy.

Under the stress and the strain of the great wars of the twentieth century, the executive power has become elaborately dependent upon the assemblies for its enormous expenditures of men and of money. The executive has at the same time been deprived of very nearly all of his imponderable power: fearing the action of the representative assembly, he is under great temptation to outwit it or by-pass it, as did Franklin D. Roosevelt in the period of the Second World War. It is significant, I think—certainly it is at least suggestive—that while nearly all the western governments have been in deep trouble since the First World War, the constitutional monarchies of Scandinavia, the Low Countries, and the United Kingdom have shown greater capacity to endure, to preserve order with freedom, than the republics of France, Germany, Spain, and Italy. In some measure that may be because in a republic the governing power, being wholly secularized, loses much of its prestige; it is stripped, if one prefers, of all the illusions of intrinsic majesty.

The evaporation of the imponderable powers, a total dependence upon the assemblies and the mass electorates, has upset the balance of powers between the two functions of the state. The executive has lost both its material and its ethereal powers. The assemblies and the mass electorates have acquired the monopoly of effective powers.

This is the internal revolution which has deranged the constitutional system of the liberal democratic states.

SELECTION 23

THE ALTERNATIVE*

ARCHIBALD MacLEISH

ARCHIBALD MACLEISH *is a poet who has been Boylston Professor at Harvard since 1949. From 1939 to 1944 he was Librarian of Congress and concurrently held several other government positions during the Second World War. Among his best known works are* Songs For Eve *(1954) and* J. B. *for which he was awarded a Pulitzer Prize in 1958.*

. . . Mr. Walter Lippmann, who is certainly one of the most perceptive readers of the American mind, has just published a book which can only be described as a retreat from the idea of freedom as that idea has been understood in this Republic. The thesis of his "The Public Philosophy" is this:

The democratic powers, with the United States as principal example, have suffered a precipitate and catastrophic decline in power and prestige. This decline has been brought about by the failure of the democratic machinery of government—a failure which Mr. Lippmann dates from 1917. What happened in that year was that the strain of "hyperbolic" war became too great for the governments involved: they ran out of "imperium," lost control of the war (meaning that they lost the power to end it by diplomatic means) and were reduced to submitting the issue to their peoples—which, in turn, meant that the issue had to be framed in terms of such absolutes as the people are capable of understanding—"war to end war," "war to make the world safe for democracy," and, twenty years later, war for the "four freedoms."

The result of all this was that no real peace could be made either in 1918 or in 1945 and that public opinion (or at least the pressure groups which exploit public opinion) has, ever since, exercised too much direct influence on the democratic governments. The governments can no longer effectively govern and their power and influence have gone down in consequence. The trouble is, in brief, that the people have played too large and too immediate a part in the direction or the attempted direction of their own affairs. There has been too much democracy and therefore too little gov-

* Reprinted from *Yale Review*, Vol. XLIV, No. 4 (June 1955), pp. 486-496.

ernment and the consequences may be very serious. "A continuing practical failure to govern," writes Mr. Lippmann, "will lead . . . to counterrevolutionary measures for the establishment of strong government."

What is the alternative? "The alternative," Mr. Lippmann tells us, "is to withstand and to reverse the descent towards counter-revolution. It is a much harder way. It demands popular assent to radical measures which will restore government strong enough to govern, strong enough to resist the encroachment of the assemblies and of mass opinions and strong enough to guarantee private liberty against the pressure of the masses." And what are these radical measures? What is this much harder way? Mr. Lippmann states it eloquently in words which will be widely read and deeply pondered. What it comes down to is the substitution, for the idea of greatest possible individual freedom to which we have been committed in this country since the end of the eighteenth century, of the idea of Natural Law, or what Mr. Lippmann prefers to call, "the Public Philosophy" —"the postulate that there is a rational order of things in which it is possible, by sincere inquiry and rational debate, to distinguish the true and the false, the right and the wrong." If democratic societies would accept the universal values of Natural Law as binding on all, government would be freed from its subservience to mass opinion since it would then appeal from mass opinion to the eternal precepts, and would be in a position to act on its own best judgment.

Now, the proposition from which Mr. Lippmann departs—the proposition that the democratization of war in 1917 was a mistake —will undoubtedly excite some debate. In Wilson's time and in Roosevelt's it was generally believed that the participation of the people in the determination of the great issue of war or peace, far from precipitating the collapse of democratic governments, promised a stronger and more effective democracy. The management of the great questions of war and peace by the bureaucrats of the Foreign Office and the Quai d'Orsay and the State Department, however logical it may have been in the political and dynastic wars of earlier centuries, seemed to men of my generation inappropriate to a time of vast world conflicts in which not professional armies but the people themselves were participants. We repeated with relish Clemenceau's remark that war was too serious a business to be left to the generals, and we spent a great measure of our youthful passion berating the diplomats and the politicians who, after the First World War was won, fumbled the peace and betrayed the hopes of the men and women who had fought it. The formulations of intent, which Mr. Lippmann now dismisses as "absolutes" incapable of realization by the diplomats and the politicians, were valued by men in danger and women in despair precisely for that reason. Men will die for peace and freedom but not for the terms of a treaty, and it was the conviction of my generation in the war of its youth and the war of its middle age that the American government and the governments of the free world had made some progress toward a more effective democracy by their recognition of that fact.

But the importance of Mr. Lippmann's book lies not in its history but in its philosophy, and particularly in the relation of its philosophy to the contemporary concept of freedom in the United States. For the concept of freedom is the real subject of Mr. Lippmann's argument. His concern is with "modern men who find in freedom from the constraints of the ancestral order an intolerable loss of guidance and support," who find "that the burden of freedom is too great an anxiety": "men who rise up against freedom, unable to cope with its insoluble difficulties and unable to endure the denial of communion in pubic and common truths." These modern men, says Mr. Lippmann, "have found no answer to their need and no remedy for their anguish in the principles and practice of freedom as they have known them in the liberal democracies of this century."

Readers of Mr. Lippmann's book may question whether he or anyone else is in a position to make so vast a statement as this last, but, whatever its universal truth, the particular truth of the declaration for Mr. Lippmann himself is evident. True freedom, to Mr. Lippmann, is not the freedom of the liberal democracies. True freedom "was founded on the postulate that there was a universal order on which all reasonable men were agreed: *within that public agreement* on the fundamentals and on the ultimates, it was safe to permit, and it would be desirable to encourage, dissent and dispute." True freedom for Mr. Lippmann, in other words, is freedom to think as you please and say as you think provided what you say and think falls within the periphery of what all reasonable men agree to be fundamentally and ultimately true. The basic philosophy of liberalism—the belief in the liberation of the individual human spirit to find its own way to enlightenment and truth—is thus rejected, and not only rejected but denounced. It is, in Mr. Lippmann's opinion, mere "Jacobin ideology." Worse than that, it is comparable to the doctrine of the totalitarian states, Communist as well as Fascist. Like the doctrine of the totalitarian states, the popular doctrine of what Mr. Lippmann calls "the mass democracies" rests upon the proposition that men may shape their own destiny and are capable of realizing their dreams of the good life. But this proposition, says "The Pubic Philosophy," is arrogance, and the belief on which it rests is delusion. Men are not gods and cannot establish heaven on earth. The claim that they can leads to disaster. It leads from Rousseau and the Jacobins to Marx and on to Lenin and Hitler and Stalin—and, it would appear, to "the mass democracies." It leads from a political religion to a popular religion based on the rise of the masses to power and so to "an everlasting war with the human condition: war with the finitude of man." The true Way is not this Way. The true Way is by submission and acceptance: acceptance of our mortal lot, and submission, if not to an elite who can govern for us (Mr. Lippmann does not say so), at least to the rule of those eternal postulates which fix the limits of finite human action and establish order in our mortal lives.

Now what is significant here is not the plea for a return to Natural Law. That plea has been heard again and again from Catholic philosophers over the course of many years. What is significant here is the revulsion against "mass democracy" of a writer whose career has been closely associated with the development of democratic ideas in our generation, and whose views have generally been found to be expressive of the opinions of an influential section of the American people. Mr. Lippmann's gloomy account of the present state and future prospects of the Western democracies will not surprise his readers: many of them will have had similar thoughts. Some will even agree with his conclusion that "the people have acquired power which they are incapable of exercising." A few, though not, I think, many, will go along with Mr. Lippmann's judgment that "prevailing public opinion" in the Western democracies over the last thirty years or so has been persistently wrong: "wrong at the critical junctures." But no reader who feels deeply about the democratic tradition will be able to avoid a sense of shock when he perceives what is actually being said by this distinguished democratic writer about the heart of the democratic philosophy and the democratic life—about freedom itself.

We know—we can scarcely avoid knowing—that there are millions of modern men who fear freedom or are frightened of the loneliness it implies or prefer to have their lives lived for them. If it were not so Hitler could never have come to power nor could the Communist states have survived. We have commonly assumed, however, that those who felt this way about the responsibilities of freedom were men who had not long been free—men whose families had lived for centuries in Germany or Italy or the old Austrian Empire or the empire of the Czars. We have even made the same observation about the increasing numbers of our own fellow citizens who press for conformity of opinion and the censorship of ideas: many of them, we notice, are relatively recent arrivals from countries where church or state has long been accustomed to police the minds of the people. What is novel in Mr. Lippmann's account is the fact that it is one of the most habituated of democratic journalists who advances the contention that true freedom in America ended with the end of the recognition of Natural Law in the late eighteenth century, and that the whole conception of the boundless liberty of the individual human spirit to which our own Republic has since been committed is a wrong steer, a tragic error.

It is one thing for an American, thoroughly familiar with the American situation, to assert that our position is dangerous and our society far from perfect. Most of us are aware that mass vulgarity afflicts our culture and mass hysteria our politics and that the government of the Republic is increasingly difficult. It is another thing altogether for such a commentator to assert that the ideas which have made a nation of us—the ideas which have shaped our development since the beginning of the nineteenth century—are pernicious ideas which should now be renounced: that the modern democratic belief in the greatest possible individual freedom itself is false doctrine.

But for all the concern it will arouse among the believers in modern democracy, Mr. Lippmann's is nevertheless a book which should serve them well, for it reveals in the most dramatic and personal way the nature of the influences which draw even the best of free men back from freedom in our time. What motivates Mr. Lippmann is not distrust of freedom as such: he protests his attachment to it often and with obvious sincerity. What motivates Mr. Lippmann is the conviction that the idea of full individual freedom and the idea of effective community are irreconcilable ideas and that there is therefore an ineluctable choice between them: that in that choice community must be preferred. He is unwilling or unable to believe that no such painful choice may be necessary: that full individual freedom may conceivably lead to a community of its own, effective in a new and different way. The decision for him is a decision between individual freedom as we know it and the form of community with which we have present literary familiarity—the community of the Roman and the Mediaeval periods. And between those two alternatives he does not hesitate. He will willingly sacrifice a large measure of individual freedom, including the future hope for its further development, in order to return to a society of order and reason held together by the restraints of the eternal verities. The road to the happy townland, as he sees it, is the road not by way of individual freedom but by way of like-mindedness and mutual agreement on the fundamental things. If we can agree among ourselves as to the Good and the True—if we can shame or silence those who have a different True or another Good—we will be *together;* we will no longer feel alone; our house will stand.

The greatest importance of Mr. Lippmann's book, in other words, is thus its demonstration, whether intentional or not, of the nature of the real issue before our generation in the United States. The immediate and present danger to American freedom is not the danger from without; the danger that it will be overwhelmed by the Communist conspiracy in one form or another. The immediate and present danger is the danger that the dream of American freedom will be subordinated to some other dream by men within the country who consider that they are acting for freedom's good and for the good of the Republic. Communism has no standing in the United States and its adherents have no influence, but the adherents of the doctrine of the ineluctable choice between community and freedom are numerous and influential and the dream of community they promulgate is a seductive dream in a time like ours—a dream which drags powerfully at the hearts of those who have lost, or those who have not yet learned, the difficult hope of which human freedom is the ultimate expression.

In a time when the dangers are dark and threatening and terrible like dangers in a nightmare, when the decisions are indecisive, when action, like nightmare action, seems to have no consequences, seems to move without motion like a runner in the sand—in such a time, the temptation to give up the long labor of liberty is a powerful temptation, and the vision of community becomes a vision which enchants. For the vision of community, being a vision from the past, is inevitably a vision in which everything is sure, everything is certain. Actions in the past have consequences. The sun shines from behind. To go back—back into the twelfth century, back into the world of Rome—is to go back into the light. And the longing for that distant light can be very strong.

It is for this reason that the apparent deterioration of our attachment to the idea of freedom must so concern us all. Unless we are truly committed to the forward dream of freedom, that other dream—the dream of the awakening into the past—may entice us, and if it does our greatness as a people will be over. No one truly wakes into the past. All any nation can wake into is what the past was when it too had still to be lived—darkness and danger and difficulty and only so much light as those who live in it can find. We Americans cannot wake into the state of mind which produced the great postulates of the medieval world: we can only continue, wherever we are, in dream or in reality, to struggle for the postulates which pertain to us. And these we will not find unless we are ourselves. We will be most ourselves when we are freest to discover who we are.

What is wrong, that is to say, with the dream of past community is the fact that it is not a dream but a remembrance. Mr. Lippmann's book ends in the sand because he has mistaken the direction of history. The flow of human life is not backward toward closer and closer association but forward toward greater and greater individuality. Man's journey is a journey from the remote insensibility of the jelly of his biological beginnings toward the fulfilment of consciousness, and the fulfilment of consciousness is an individual, not a herd, achievement. As his biological destiny is emergence in and to himself, so too is man's spiritual destiny. Ever-increasing consciousness, which means ever-increasing individuality, is the law of human gravity and it cannot be reversed. Particular generations may dread their emergence into individuality and loneliness as our generation dreads it. They may attempt to stampede backward into the warmth and darkness and protection of conformity as millions in Europe and Asia have done in our time, and as an increasing number of our fellow citizens would do here if they could drag the rest of us with them. But the flow of life is in the other direction. The mind can no more return to its womb than can the body. It can only go on—on in increasing intelligence when it can but, whether in intelligence or not, still on.

What we are really witnessing in our time, despite the outcries and the polemics, is not a vast human protest against a wrong steer into a hundred and fifty years of mistaken individual freedom, but a small human boggling in the face of a series of startling and decisive steps toward individuality—steps imposed in part at least by new techniques which tend to free men from their direct dependence on family and clan and tribe. The modern city is a lonely place and the modern universe is lonelier: men who fear loneliness wrap conformity around their souls and attempt to wrap it around their neighbors' also. But the evidence of the contemporary arts—and there is no other dependable evidence of the condition of the human soul in any age—is convincing proof that the human journey has not, for that reason, ended or turned back. On the contrary, as the arts suggest, it has never before pressed on so urgently toward individuality and individual freedom. " 'The Discovery and Colonization of Inwardness,' " writes Erich Heller, "—this might be a fitting title for the story of poetry from the Renaissance to our day." It might indeed, and never since the Renaissance have the discoverers gone deeper into that wilderness of the individual self than in our own time. Rilke is writing of Ibsen when he says: "farther in than anyone has yet been; a door had sprung open before you, and now you were among the alembics in the firelight." Ibsen had passed through the world of action and appearance "as one crosses a vestibule" until he came to the place "where our becoming seethes and precipitates and changes color, inside." But Rilke himself had made the same far journey. And so too have the novelists—Joyce and Proust and Kafka and their successors—who seem to us most characteristic of our time. In all the modern arts of words, in modern painting, in modern music, a common impulse is at work: an impulse, almost a compulsion, to penetrate the undiscovered country of the individual human consciousness, the human self.

One may or may not like the characteristic art of our epoch. One may regard its characteristic quality as a kind of fad—a passing by-product of the investigations of Freud and Jung. There is perhaps some basis for such an opinion. Freud and Jung and their colleagues have powerfully influenced all our contemporaries, and the manner of some modern art is undoubtedly mannerism. But the fact remains that modern art did not begin with the modern psychologists: Baudelaire had written the "Fleurs du Mal" and Rimbaud had written the "Illuminations" before modern psychology was born. And the further fact is that the direction of modern art is not a direction which the modern artists have alone devised. It is not an invented or a perverse or a wayward direction. It is the direction of all conscious life, for the realization of consciousness is the end which all such life must seek. What modern art means is merely that mankind has crossed over, not secretly and surreptitiously but openly now, into that inward country. We no longer assume the superior reality of the public world of objective reason. We assume instead the deeper reality of the world within—which is to say, the world which each human individual uniquely is.

It requires very little knowledge of any modern art to understand how painful this labor of "discovery and colonization" is: how dangerous always, how disastrous frequently. The map of the arts in our time is scored with abandoned settlements and roads that lead to nowhere. But it is not by the choice of those who attempt these discoveries that the task is hard. The task is hard in its own nature and its nature is imposed by the situation of modern man. Artists can no more give up and turn back than the rest of us, and the rest of us have no more choice than the artists. Safety lies, security lies, for us as for them, not in an attempt to return to the continent from which we came: the winds blow all one way in human history and, besides, that continent is no longer there. Safety lies, security lies, where hope lies—on ahead. It is not by renouncing individual freedom but by achieving it in the achievement of individuality that we will complete this passage in our mysterious journey. The postulates which will give us peace are not the postulates which satisfied us on another coast. They are the postulates which will express our life beyond—our life as individual human beings set free to be ourselves.

SELECTION 24

A REJOINDER*

WALTER LIPPMANN

WALTER LIPPMANN'S *answer to Archibald MacLeish's criticism of* The Public Philosophy *appeared with MacLeish's "The Alternative" in the* Yale Review. *It should be noted that the two prominent scholars were discussing Mr. Lippmann's complete book and not just the articles reprinted in the* Atlantic, *one of which is included above as selection 22.*

. . . The crucial question, as between Mr. MacLeish's essay and my book, is why he and I, each believing he is on the side of the angels, appear to differ so much on what is the idea of freedom as it has been understood in this republic. The concluding chapters of my book are concerned with the very issue on which we differ, and with what I have learned to believe is the way that the wisest men in the Western tradition have dealt with that issue.

Before we can deal with that issue, we must define it, and in his essay Mr. MacLeish has not, I submit, made the indispensable preliminary effort of clarification. He has two profoundly different but unseparated and undistinguished ideas of freedom. In some passages he holds that since the eighteenth century the American conception of freedom has been that "of the boundless liberty of the *individual human spirit.*" But in at least one passage he speaks of "the modern democratic belief in the greatest *possible* individual freedom."

Mr. MacLeish writes as if he thought he was saying the same thing in different words. But in my view there are here—as there are in the nature of things—not one idea of freedom but two ideas. In the one liberty is "boundless." In the other it is only as great as "possible;" it has bounds though they are to be made as wide as is possible.

It is with the relation of these two ideas of freedom that much of my book is concerned. They can be related, and accommodated the one with the other in human affairs, only if we begin "by recognizing," as I put it in my book, "the difference between the realm of existence, where objects are materialized to our senses, and the realm of essence, where they are present to the mind."

* Reprinted from *The Yale Review,* Vol. XLIV, No. 4 (June 1955), pp. 498-500. Copyright Yale University Press.

With Mr. MacLeish I believe in the "boundless liberty of the *individual human spirit.*" But I do not believe, and neither can he, that boundless liberty is "possible" in the public actions of everyone. The realm where liberty is "boundless" is in the realm of essence, in what Mr. MacLeish in his peroration so aply calls "the inward country." But in the outward country, in the public country of the diverse inhabitants of our plural society, freedom cannot be *boundless.* It can only be as great as is *possible.*

In the outward and public country there are bounds upon the freedom of individuals, and it is the business of political philosophy to discern where in the conditions of the historical period the bounds have to be, and where they do not have to be—in order that there shall be as much freedom as is possible for all individuals. If free men do not keep their public actions within the bounds, they will make free government unworkable, and in the ensuing disasters and disorders freedom will be lost. The Greeks were the first to realize this. And this republic was founded by men who were deeply and earnestly aware of this truth.

The mortal disease of free societies is to confuse the two realms, and to practice in the public world not a constitutional liberty but that boundless liberty which belongs to the inward country of the individual human spirit. That inward country may be the consciousness of genius and of a benefactor of mankind. It may be also the inward country of a Hitler or a McCarthy.

It is my recognition of the deep difference between the inward and the outward country that has caused Mr. MacLeish to accuse me of retreating from the traditional American idea of freedom. For he is one of those who do not distinguish the two countries.

This is what makes him say that I have "rejected, and not only rejected but denounced" the "basic philosophy of liberalism." But how does he define that basic philosophy? He defines it as "the belief in the liberation of the individual human spirit to find its own way to enlightenment and truth."

That will do very well, I would say, of liberalism applied to that inward country where men are impelled to seek "the realization" of "the individual human consciousness." But what about the public country, where it is necessary to find enlightenment and truth not in solitude within the individual consciousness but in the complex relations of multitudes of persons?

What is the philosophy of liberalism when it is meant not for the contemplative life but for the active? It is, I believe, what I have sought in my book to define and to illustrate as the public philosophy.

SELECTION 25

THE HIGHER CIRCLES*

C. WRIGHT MILLS

C. WRIGHT MILLS, *author and educator, is Professor of Sociology at Columbia University. He has also taught at the University of Maryland and has been visiting professor at Brandeis University and the University of Chicago. He is the author of* The Causes of World War Three *and many other works. The selection below is Part 6 of Chapter I in his book* The Power Elite. *Footnotes are numbered as in the original.*

It is not my thesis that for all epochs of human history and in all nations, a creative minority, a ruling class, an omnipotent elite, shapes all historical events. Such statements, upon careful examination, usually turn out to be mere tautologies,[7] and even when they are not, they are so entirely general as to be useless in the attempt to understand the history of the present. The minimum definition of the power elite as those who decide whatever is decided of major consequence, does not imply that the members of this elite are always and necessarily the history-makers; neither does it imply that they never are. We must not confuse the conception of the elite, which we wish to define, with one theory about their role: that they are the history-makers of our time. To define the elite, for example, as "those who rule America" is less to define a conception than to state one hypothesis about the role and power of that elite. No matter how we might define the elite, the extent of its members' power is subject to historical variation. If, in a dogmatic way, we try to include that variation in our generic definition, we foolishly limit the use of a needed conception. If we insist that the elite be defined

---

* From *The Power Elite* by C. Wright Mills. Copyright 1956 by Oxford University Press, Inc. Reprinted by permission.

[7] As in the case, quite notably, of Gaetano Mosca, *The Ruling Class* (New York: McGraw-Hill, 1939). For a sharp analysis of Mosca, see Fritz Morstein Marx, "The Bureaucratic State," *Review of Politics*, vol. I, 1939, pp. 457 ff. Cf. also Mills, "On Intellectual Craftsmanship," April 1952, mimeographed, Columbia College, February 1955.

as a strictly coordinated class that continually and absolutely rules, we are closing off from our view much to which the term more modestly defined might open to our observation. In short, our definition of the power elite cannot properly contain dogma concerning the degree and kind of power that ruling groups everywhere have. Much less should it permit us to smuggle into our discussion a theory of history.

During most of human history, historical change has not been visible to the people who were involved in it, or even to those enacting it. Ancient Egypt and Mesopotamia, for example, endured for some four hundred generations with but slight changes in their basic structure. That is six and a half times as long as the entire Christian era, which has only prevailed some sixty generations; it is about eighty times as long as the five generations of the United States' existence. But now the tempo of change is so rapid, and the means of observation so accessible, that the interplay of event and decision seems often to be quite historically visible, if we will only look carefully and from an adequate vantage point.

When knowledgeable journalists tell us that "events, not men, shape the big decisions," they are echoing the theory of history as Fortune, Chance, Fate, or the work of The Unseen Hand. For "events" is merely a modern word for these older ideas, all of which separate men from history-making, because all of them lead us to believe that history goes on behind men's backs. History is drift with no mastery; within it there is action but no deed; history is mere happening and the event intended by no one.[8]

The course of events in our time depends more on a series of human decisions than on any inevitable fate. The sociological meaning of "fate" is simply this: that, when the decisions are innumerable and each one is of small consequence, all of them add up in a way no man intended—to history as fate. But not all epochs are equally fateful. As the circle of those who decide is narrowed, as the means of decision are centralized and the consequences of decisions become enormous, then the course of great events often rests upon the decisions of determinable circles. This does not necessarily mean that the same circle of men follow through from one event to another in such a way that all of history is merely their

[8] Cf. Karl Löwith, *Meaning in History* (Chicago: University of Chicago Press, 1949), pp. 125 ff. for concise and penetrating statements of several leading philosophies of history.

plot. The power of the elite does not necessarily mean that history is not also shaped by a series of small decisions, none of which are thought out. It does not mean that a hundred small arrangements and compromises and adaptations may not be built into the going policy and the living event. The idea of the power elite implies nothing about the process of decision-making as such: it is an attempt to delimit the social areas within which that process, whatever its character, goes on. It is a conception of who is involved in the process.

The degree of foresight and control of those who are involved in decisions that count may also vary. The idea of the power elite does not mean that the estimations and calculated risks upon which decisions are made are not often wrong and that the consequences are sometimes, indeed often, not those intended. Often those who make decisions are trapped by their own inadequacies and blinded by their own errors.

Yet in our time the pivotal moment does arise, and at that moment, small circles do decide or fail to decide. In either case, they are an elite of power. The dropping of the A-bombs over Japan was such a moment; the decision on Korea was such a moment; the confusion about Quemoy and Matsu, as well as before Dienbienphu were such moments; the sequence of maneuvers which involved the United States in World War II was such a "moment." Is it not true that much of the history of our times is composed of such moments? And is not that what is meant when it is said that we live in a time of big decisions, of decisively centralized power?

Most of us do not try to make sense of our age by believing in a Greek-like, eternal recurrency, nor by a Christian belief in a salvation to come, nor by any steady march of human progress. Even though we do not reflect upon such matters, the chances are we believe with Burckhardt that we live in a mere succession of events; that sheer continuity is the only principle of history. History is merely one thing after another; history is meaningless in that it is not the realization of any determinate plot. It is true, of course, that our sense of continuity, our feeling for the history of our time, is affected by crisis. But we seldom look beyond the immediate crisis or the crisis felt to be just ahead. We believe neither in fate nor providence; and we assume, without talking about it, that "we"—as a nation—can decisively shape the future but that "we" as individuals somehow cannot do so.

Any meaning history has, "we" shall have to give to it by our actions. Yet the fact is that although we are all of us within history we do not all possess equal powers to make history. To pretend that we do is sociological nonsense and political irresponsibility. It is nonsense because any group or any individual is limited, first of all, by the technical and institutional means of power at its command; we do not all have equal access to the means of power that now exist, nor equal influence over their use. To pretend that "we" are all history-makers is politically irresponsible because it obfuscates any attempt to locate responsibility for the consequential decisions of men who do have access to the means of power.

From even the most superficial examination of the history of the western society we learn that the power of decision-makers is first of all limited by the level of technique, by the *means* of power and violence and organization that prevail in a given society. In this connection we also learn that there is a fairly straight line running upward through the history of the West; that the means of oppression and exploitation, of violence and destruction, as well as the means of production and reconstruction, have been progressively enlarged and increasingly centralized.

As the institutional means of power and the means of communications that tie them together have become steadily more efficient, those now in command of them have come into command of instruments of rule quite unsurpassed in the history of mankind. And we are not yet at the climax of their development. We can no longer lean upon or take soft comfort from the historical ups and downs of ruling groups of previous epochs. In that sense, Hegel is correct: we learn from history that we cannot learn from it.

For every epoch and for every social structure, we must work out an answer to the question of the power of the elite. The ends of men are often merely hopes, but means are facts within some men's control. That is why all means of power tend to become ends to an elite that is in command of them. And that is why we may define the power elite in terms of the means of power—as those who occupy the command posts. The major questions about the American elite today—its composition, its unity, its power—must now be faced with due attention to the awesome means of power available to them. Caesar could do less with Rome than Napoleon with France; Napoleon less with France than Lenin with Russia; and Lenin less with Russia than Hitler with Germany. But what was

Caesar's power at its peak compared with the power of the changing inner circle of Soviet Russia or of America's temporary administrations? The men of either circle can cause great cities to be wiped out in a single night, and in a few weeks turn continents into thermonuclear wastelands. That the facilities of power are enormously enlarged and decisively centralized means that the decisions of small groups are now more consequential.

But to know that the top posts of modern social structures now permit more commanding decisions is not to know that the elite who occupy these posts are the history-makers. We might grant that the enlarged and integrated economic, military, and political structures are shaped to permit command decisions, yet still feel that, as it were, "they run themselves," that those who are on top, in short, are determined in their decisions by "necessity," which presumably means by the instituted roles that they play and the situation of these institutions in the total structure of society.

Do the elite determine the roles that they enact? Or do the roles that institutions make available to them determine the power of the elite? The general answer—and no general answer is sufficient—is that in different kinds of structures and epochs elites are quite differently related to the roles that they play: nothing in the nature of the elite or in the nature of history dictates an answer. It is also true that if most men and women take whatever roles are permitted to them and enact them as they are expected to by virtue of their position, this is precisely what the elite need *not* do, and often do not do. They may call into question the structure, their position within it, or the way in which they are to enact that position.

Nobody called for or permitted Napoleon to chase *Parlement* home on the 18 *Brumaire,* and later to transform his consulate into an emperorship.[9] Nobody called for or permitted Adolf Hitler to proclaim himself "Leader and Chancellor" the day President Hindenburg died, to abolish and usurp roles by merging the presidency and the chancellorship. Nobody called for or permitted Franklin D. Roosevelt to make the series of decisions that led to the entrance of the United States into World War II. It was no "historical necessity," but a man named Truman who, with a few other men, de-

[9] Some of these items are taken from Gerth and Mills, *Character and Social Structure* (New York: Harcourt Brace & Company), pp. 405 ff. On role-determined and role-determining men, see also Sidney Hook's discussion, *The Hero in History* (New York: John Day, 1943).

cided to drop a bomb on Hiroshima. It was no historical necessity, but an argument within a small circle of men that defeated Admiral Radford's proposal to bomb troops before Dienbienphu. Far from being dependent upon the structure of institutions, modern elites may smash one structure and set up another in which they then enact quite different roles. In fact, such destruction and creation of institutional structures, with all their means of power, when events seem to turn out well, is just what is involved in "great leadership," or, when they seem to turn out badly, great tyranny.

Some elite men *are,* of course, typically role-determined, but others are at times role-determining. They determine not only the role they play but today the roles of millions of other men. The creation of pivotal roles and their pivotal enactment occurs most readily when social structures are undergoing epochal transitions. It is clear that the international development of the United States to one of the two "great powers"—along with the new means of annihilation and administrative and psychic domination—have made of the United States in the middle years of the twentieth century precisely such an epochal pivot.

There is nothing about history that tells us that a power elite cannot make it. To be sure, the will of such men is always limited, but never before have the limits been so broad, for never before have the means of power been so enormous. It is this that makes our situation so precarious, and makes even more important an understanding of the powers and the limitations of the American elite. The problem of the nature and the power of this elite is now the only realistic and serious way to raise again the problem of responsible government.

Conclusion

International relations result from the attempts of individual human beings to achieve their objectives by the most effective means possible. Whether their objectives are conceived in idealistic terms as the pursuit of moral ends or in realistic terms as the pursuit of self-interest, the task of fitting means to ends in international relations is a mammoth and complex one.

Man's success in completing this task depends on his success in the study of international relations. But scholars who have made this subject their life work have not been able to agree whether the study of international relations is an art or a science. And whichever it may be, they cannot agree whether its pursuit is properly a task for the common man or for committees of experts acting on his behalf.

While the academic battle rages on, however, millions of individuals participate daily in myriads of millions of international relationships. Whether these relationships are effective in the individual pursuit of means to ends depends upon many things including, quite likely, a sizeable element of chance. But the systematic study of the international relations process by high school, college, and university students and by the general public remains the best hope of mankind that its common aspirations for security and prosperity will be fulfilled.

Suggested Readings

A. ON THE DETERMINATION OF NATIONAL OBJECTIVES

AMERICAN ASSEMBLY. *Goals for Americans.* Washington: Prentice-Hall, Inc., 1960.

BLOOMFIELD, LINCOLN. *The United Nations and United States Foreign Policy: A New Look at the National Interest.* Boston: Little Brown and Co., 1960.

COOK, THOMAS I., and MALCOLM MOOS. *Power through Purpose; the Realism of Idealism as a Basis for Foreign Policy.* Baltimore: The Johns Hopkins Press, 1954.

MORGENTHAU, HANS J. *In Defense of the National Interest: A Critical Examination of American Foreign Policy.* New York: Alfred A. Knopf, Inc., 1951.

B. ON THE STUDY OF INTERNATIONAL RELATIONS

HOFFMANN, STANLEY. *Contemporary Theory in International Relations.* Englewood Cliffs: Prentice-Hall, Inc., 1960.

ISAACS, HAROLD. *Scratches on Our Minds: American Images of China and India.* New York: The John Day Company, 1958.

McLELLAN, DAVID, FRED SONDERMANN, and WILLIAM C. OLSON. *The Theory and Practice of International Relations.* Englewood Cliffs: Prentice-Hall, Inc., 1960.

NORTHROP, F. S. C. *The Logic of the Sciences and Humanities.* New York: The Macmillan Company, 1959.

WRIGHT, QUINCY. *The Study of International Relations.* New York: Appleton-Century-Crofts, 1955.

C. ON DEMOCRACY AND FOREIGN POLICY

ALMOND, GABRIEL. *The American People and Foreign Policy*. New York: Frederick A. Praeger, Inc., 1960.

BAILEY, THOMAS A. *The Man in the Street: The Impact of American Public Opinion on Foreign Policy*. New York: The Macmillan Company, 1948.

LIPPMANN, WALTER. *Essays in the Public Philosophy*. Boston: Little, Brown and Co., 1955.

——— *Public Opinion and Foreign Policy in the United States*. London: Allen and Unwin, 1952.